Language and Literacy

Language and Literacy

Functional Approaches

Edited by Rachel Whittaker, Mick O'Donnell and Anne McCabe

continuum

Continuum
The Tower Building
11 York Road
London SE1 7NX

80 Maiden Lane
Suite 704
New York, NY 10010

British Library Cataloguing-in-Publication Data
A catalogue record for this book is available from the British Library.

ISBN: HB: 0-8264-8947-8

Library of Congress Cataloging-in-Publication Data

Published in paperback 2008
ISBN: 9781847065704

Typeset by BookEns Ltd, Royston, Herts.
Printed in the United Kingdom by the MPG Books Group

Contents

List of Contributors

Frances Christie
Emeritus Professor of Language and Literacy Education, University of
Melbourne and Honorary Professor of English, University of Sydney

Caroline Coffin
The Open University

Bronwyn Custance
ESL Consultant, South Australia

Brian Dare
Lexis Education, South Australia

Carlos A. M. Gouveia
University of Lisbon

Michael Halliday
Emeritus Professor, University of Sydney

Mike Hart
School of Education and Development, University of KwaZulu-Natal,
South Africa

Ruqaiya Hasan
Emeritus Professor, Macquarie University

Ann Hewings
The Open University, UK

Susan Marshall
Education and Manpower Bureau of Hong Kong

J. R. Martin
Department of Linguistics, University of Sydney

Anne McCabe
Saint Louis University, Madrid Campus

Lorraine McDonald
School of Education, Australian Catholic University

Sarah North
The Open University, UK

Mick O'Donnell
Universidad Autónoma de Madrid

John Polias
Lexis Education, South Australia

Carol Thomson
School of Education, Training and Development, University of KwaZulu-Natal, South Africa

Robert Veel
University of Sydney

Paddy Walsh
Secondary Strategy Consultant (Literacy), Waltham Forest Local Authority, London

Rachel Whittaker
Universidad Autónoma de Madrid

Preface

Mick O'Donnell

The chapters in this book explore one family of approaches to literacy education, what we might call functional approaches to literacy, in particular, those stemming from systemic functional linguistics (SFL). The contribution of SFL to literacy education is particularly strong given that this linguistic approach developed in the context of language education.

In the early 1960s in Britain, language education was dominated by two conflicting approaches. On the one hand, classrooms were still under the sway of the traditional 'authoritarian' approach, where 'imparting knowledge was the main teaching practice, and in which the teacher's authority and the pupils' discipline were explicit elements in the pedagogic relationship' (Chouliaraki 1996: 104). On the other hand, the progressivists favoured a classroom 'working on the principles of child-centred pedagogy, mainly employing experiential and interactive methods (task-based pair work), and in which the pupils are seen as the main agents of their learning, and the teacher as a facilitator and as a monitor of their naturally developing capabilities' (ibid.).

There were, however, some who were not happy with either approach. In the early 1960s, M. A. K. Halliday and other linguists believed that the teaching of reading and writing should be informed by an understanding of how language works. This small group of linguists thus set out to talk to teachers in schools, asking how linguistics could help in teaching. Directly driven by the needs of language education, Halliday and his group set to developing a grammar of English that would answer the kinds of questions which teachers in classrooms need answered (which the Chomskian grammar of that time could not). This work was eventually funded by the Labour government, where they firstly developed a linguistically informed approach to teaching language and subsequently developed the teaching materials based on these ideas (e.g. the *Breakthrough to Literacy*, *Language in Use* and *Language and Communication*). The work was strongly informed by the work of Basil Bernstein on education failure, and that of James Britton and his group.

The early 1970s, however, were a difficult time in Britain. Opposition from both traditionalists and progressivists was strong. Chomskians were in full sway, and the previously generous Labour government was replaced by a Conservative one. Halliday consequently moved to greener pastures, to Sydney, Australia, becoming the founding Chair of Linguistics in 1975. Here, Halliday devoted time to developing further his functional grammar of English, which was taught within undergraduate courses. More importantly for this book, he also continued his devotion to language education, setting up an MA Applied course in 1978, with the main intent of training school teachers in enough linguistics to change the way they taught language. The first course included two educationalists, Fran Christie and Joan Rothery, later important figures within language education.

In 1979, Jim Martin (trained in SFL under Michael Gregory in Canada) took up a post in Halliday's department, and was one of the teachers in the MA course. He and Joan Rothery received funding to research how writing was taught in New South Wales schools (the *Writing Research Project*), and out of this work stemmed the genre-based literacy approach which is at the core of SFL-based language education. Their notion of genre was influenced by that developed by Ruqaiya Hasan, as well as Labov's narrative structure. Genre theory advocates that a text should be situated 'within the context in which it has been created so that an examination of the language choices in the text reflects its context and purpose' (Drury 2002).

In 1991, Martin started a further project, the *Write It Right* project, the goal of which was to research the nature of literacy demands within and across industrial sectors and to relate these findings to literacy in the secondary school Key Learning Areas. One result of this project was extension of the work on genre-based literacy, particularly through descriptions of academic genres within the disciplines of history, geography, science and maths.

SFL-informed approaches to language education, particularly those involving genre-based pedagogy, have spread throughout the Australian curriculum, and have had major influence over education practices throughout the world. The chapters in this book have been commissioned to firstly chart the development of the approach, and secondly to highlight the ongoing evolution of the approach around the world and across disciplines.

References

Chouliaraki, L. (1996), 'Regulative Practices in a "Progressivist" Classroom: "Good Habits" as a Disciplinary Technology', *Language and Education*, 10 (2–3): 103–18.

Drury, H. (2002) 'Teaching genres in the disciplines: Can students learn the laboratory report genre on screen?', in *Changing Identities: Proceedings of the Language and Academic Skills Conference*, University of Wollongong, 29–30 November 2001, CD-ROM.

An introduction to language and literacy

Anne McCabe and Rachel Whittaker

1 Why another book on literacy

It is hard to imagine what would remain of society as we know it today without the written word. Indeed, as we read this, it is difficult to build for ourselves an idea of the exclusion felt by those who do not possess literacy, given the role of the written word in our lives. In developed societies, understandings of our world and of ourselves are to a great extent results of our ways of creating and interpreting written texts, as Olson (e.g. 1996) has argued. In this line, Walter Ong (1982: 78) explains: 'Without writing, the literate mind would not and could not think as it does, not only when engaged in writing but normally even when it is composing its thoughts in oral form. More than any other single invention, writing has transformed human consciousness'. The role of literacy in creating and transmitting knowledge has been recognized by UNESCO, naming 1990 'International Literacy Year' and, later, 2003–12 was declared the International Literacy Decade. We can understand, then, what a major, global challenge literacy represents.

Arguably, more than any other invention, literacy moves the world, not only in terms of communication and commerce, but also in politics. For literacy puts educational systems, and the governments behind them, in the spotlight, giving an opportunity for everyone – expert or not – to contribute their opinions. The viewpoints expressed tend to be polarized, as the debate on literacy – generally equated with reading – moves back and forth like a ping-pong ball, between those who favour a back-to-basics analytic approach focusing on phonemic letter-sound equivalences on the one hand, and on the other those who favour a holistic approach, with the focus on 'look and say', by recognition of the shape of the word. In the same way, debates on the teaching of writing have advocated at different periods either a focus on orthography and normative grammar or on the progressivist approach, what Halliday (this volume) calls 'benevolent inertia': advocating simply letting children write and express their individuality.

In this book, Halliday shows how his work in the UK developed against a background of the authoritarian vs. progressivist debate in the 1960s. Paddy Walsh traces his pathway in language education in the UK, moving from a background of traditional grammar, through progressivism, and on to an explicit, genre-based pedagogy. The debate still goes on today around the world, and is discussed in this volume by Fran Christie, Jim Martin and Robert Veel in Australia, Carlos Gouveia in Portugal and Carol Thomson and Mike Hart in South Africa.

Despite this ongoing debate, it is surprising how little attention is given in language teaching to the language of the texts as a system, or to the texts themselves as semiotic artefacts with social functions. Many studies of literacy take a psychological approach, looking at the processes involved in reading and what goes on in an individual's head when learning to read. What is often forgotten in the debate is an important stratum of what makes up a written text – the lexicogrammar – along with the structures, functions and users of texts. This book takes this perspective, complementing the psychological studies, by focusing on the external; on the language we read and write and the social situations in which the written language plays a crucial part.

The chapters in this book, then, report on discussions of literacy which take as their point of departure the language system and the social function of the text. All have as their theoretical framework a linguistic model, that of systemic functional linguistics (SFL), a model which is functional from two points of view: the external, that of the function of language in society, and the internal, that of the way a particular language is organized to fulfil the functions it has: to represent the world, to create relations between those communicating and to signal the structure of text (Halliday 1994). Many educators have discarded linguistics when addressing literacy issues (cf. this volume Gouveia for a negative image of linguists in the debate in Portugal, Walsh for the same in the UK and Christie for some background on linguistics and language education), despite Gee's (2001: 647) admonition that 'linguistics has had much less an impact on education, and teachers know much less about language and linguistics, than the current state of our knowledge about language in education ... would seem to merit'. This book takes up the challenge, showing what linguistics has to offer the teaching of literacy.

The writers of these chapters are not only committed to using SFL as a means for bettering language education, but also are, or have been, at the chalkface, often working precisely with those learners who are most at risk, either because of their ravished education systems (e.g. in South Africa, due to apartheid, as reported in Thomson and Hart), their non-English-as-a-first-language backgrounds (e.g. in Australia, as evidenced by the work reported on by John Polias and Brian Dare, Susan Marshall and Bronwyn Custance), or because of their socio-economic background, a factor brought into the picture by both Walsh and Gouveia, and also addressed by Robert Veel in his report on the Disadvantaged Schools Program in Australia. The book provides insights into ways in which literacy development can be worked on throughout learners' lives, since, in some senses, all of us experience moments of risk when moving through educational systems or at the fast-changing workplace, where we meet increasingly sophisticated demands on our literacy. The chapters illustrate literacy demands at different moments in the education system: while learning to write about history, as described by Caroline Coffin; moving from junior to senior school when responding to poetry, as reported on by Marshall or from the science or the arts in undergraduate writing, as explained by Ann Hewings and Sarah North.

This is why we are convinced of the need for this book on literacy in the framework of SFL. The writers of these chapters have taken their inspiration from SFL precisely because this theory was to a great extent developed to address the needs of language education, as can be seen in Chapter 1, where Michael Halliday and Ruqaiya Hasan present a retrospective on their early work in literacy since the 1950s. The chapter shows how their work in linguistics and language description has always been driven by a need to solve problems in language education. Here, and in the rest of the book, it is clear how this work has had a profound impact on literacy practices in different parts of the world. For example, Martin gives background on the influential SFL-inspired genre-based literacy approach, and reviews selected Australian initiatives in this area, also focusing on recent SFL-based work by David Rose on English literacy in a South African school. Before turning to the chapters, however, which all illustrate and provide evidence for the effectiveness of that impact, we look at issues in language, education and literacy in order to provide the context for the research reported in the book.

2 Different views of language, different views of literacy

Education cannot be separated from language, for education comes about through language. As Halliday (1993: 93) says: 'When children learn language, they are not simply engaging in one kind of learning among many: rather, they are learning the foundation of learning itself'. Language, then, is the medium for most of what we learn both inside and outside school settings and literacy is 'not only one of the principal goals of education but also one of the principal means by which it is carried out' (Hannon 2000: 8). A more constrained view of literacy limits it to a psychological notion of decoding conventional symbols and ascribing meaning to them, or reproducing those symbols. Indeed, this is what small children are involved in doing in the early years of school. However, obviously, literacy does not stop at that point. Indeed, the delight little children looking at a road sign experience as they sound out S-T-O-P, and shout 'STOP'! realizing their achievement, later becomes a cause of shame and exclusion if that decoding still remains the extent of their literacy. This view of literacy ignores all the learning which needs to take place *through* the language, once the code, in this narrow sense, has been cracked, as well as the need for continued study of language and texts.

In fact, a narrow view of literacy based mainly on psychological models, while still very much in existence and often clamoured for, has been criticized by a number of literacy researchers (summarized in Barton 2001). Those who critique this narrower view favour one which takes into account the wider social contexts in which literacy practices take place. An example of this kind of critique has been provided by Jay Robinson (1987: 329):

> It will no longer do ... to consider literacy as some abstract, absolute quality attainable through tutelage and the accumulation of knowledge and experience. It will no longer do to think of reading as a solitary act in which a mainly passive reader responds to cues in a text to find meaning. It will no longer do to think of writing as a mechanical manipulation of grammatical codes and formal structures leading to the production of perfect or perfectible texts. Reading and writing are not unitary skills nor are they reducible to sets of component skills falling neatly under discrete categories (linguistic, cognitive); rather, they are complex human activities taking place in complex human relationships.

Indeed, change came about during the 1980s, when an 'awareness of the social nature of language flooded into the mainstream of literacy education' (Christie and Mission 1998: 5). Perez (2004) summarizes the work of several researchers (e.g. Cazden 1988; Cook-Gumperz

1986; Gee 1992; Heath 1983; Street 1984) in defining literacy as 'a set of social activities involving written language in terms of its function and context'; in other words, literacy is something that people use in order 'to achieve their goals in a variety of sociocultural contexts' (Perez 2004: 27).

An example of a more socially based notion of literacy is provided by Ken Hyland (2000: 146): ' "Literacy" refers to different strategies for conceptualising, organising and producing texts; it implies variations in the contexts and communities in which they are written, and the roles of reader and writer that they invoke'. This view suggests, firstly, that literacy is not something we achieve once and for all. Rather literacy is, like both first and second language learning, 'a life-long process' (Foley and Thompson 2003). Secondly, it also takes into account social networks and relationships which make up part of an individual's literacy formation. In this sense, it may be helpful for educators to think of the limits in their own literacy (Mace 1992), in order to understand the limits of those they are educating. For instance, many of us might be hard pressed to understand an article written by medical researchers for colleagues. In a view of literacy such as that proposed by Hyland, these problems would stem from lack of the strategies needed for conceptualizing medical research, as outsiders, not participating in the contexts and communities in which they are written; that is, we are not the intended reader (see Lassen, forthcoming, for an example of texts written for a very specific, targeted reader within a scientific community). In other words, literacy involves social practices in which we are effective through our language use, social practices in which we can participate successfully. The notion is, thus, dynamic: as literacy demands change, we meet new opportunities and challenges, at any professional level (Veel, this volume).

This kind of socially situated definition of literacy can lead us to question the whole concept, as do Rigg and Kazemek (1985: 7, in Cope and Kalantzis 1993: 52):

> before we label people as 'illiterate' or 'functionally incompetent' let us look at how individuals operate in a wide variety of specific situations with a wide variety of specific purposes. We don't have 23 million 'functionally illiterate' adults ... We have an uncounted number of real people, each one using literacy in different ways.

Cope and Kalantzis (1993: 52) continue:

> So a person who gets a job through a network of oral contacts and who follows the signs in the street should be considered no less a person than

someone else who reads job advertisements and has a written curriculum vitae.

All then are literate in some way. What is argued in this book is the need to make available the means to break barriers of exclusion if people want to expand their effectiveness to more and more contexts.

In a sense, every new context involving written language, with its specific contextual conventions of register and genre, is a possible site of exclusion based on illiteracy. Obviously, the more explicit the teaching of successful written language in school contexts, the better our chances of being able to transfer this understanding to new contexts. This position is shown in practice in many of the chapters in this volume.

Another approach to literacy expands the application of the term in another way. Some educators and literacy researchers have questioned restricting 'literacy' to written language. Gee writes: 'Literacy is seen as a set of discourse practices, that is, as ways of using language and making sense both in speech and writing' (Gee 1986: 719). Halliday (1996) notes this perspective: 'In many instances the term *literacy* has come to be dissociated from reading and writing, and written language, altogether, and generalized so as to cover all forms of discourse, spoken as well as written. In this way it comes to refer to effective participation of any kind in social processes' (Halliday 1996: 340). We do also of course 'read images' (Kress and van Leeuwen 1996) as more and more of the texts we have to interpret and produce are multimodal (e.g. Kress and van Leeuwen 2001; O'Halloran 2004). However, as Halliday points out, extending the use of the term does not allow for an important distinction to be made: 'The problem is that if we call all of these things literacy, then we shall have to find another term for what we called literacy before; because it is still necessary to distinguish reading and writing practices from listening and speaking practices. Neither is superior to the other, but they are different' (Halliday 1996: 341). In this volume we follow this approach; the selected chapters all focus on literacy in writing.

3 The importance of understanding the nature of written language

It is hard not to make a connection between the ability to effectively control written language in a variety of contexts and positions of dominance and power. If it is the purpose of formal education to allow all individuals to be able to participate fully in society – which includes the choice as to what extent they wish to participate in, subvert, or avoid these positionings – then it is also the purpose of education to help students understand the role of language and how it functions in meaning-making activities. Teachers, then, have an obligation to bring students in on those 'secrets about the relation of form and purpose in language' that Cope and Kalantzis (1993: 60) suggest they possess. Gouveia's analysis of the literacy debate in Portugal shows resistance to the explicit teaching of genre and register based on rejection of the unknown, voiced in the cries of back to basics, and on fear of tradition losing its value, as focus on appreciation of literature gives way to introducing learners to different text types. Gouveia suggests this resistance to a change in the curriculum effectively defends privilege, leaving power in the hands of those who grow up knowing the rules – the conventions of written language – given their access to a range of text types in their homes. For those who do not have such a background, who 'are not already a participant in the culture of power, being told explicitly the rules of that culture makes acquiring power easier' (Delpit 1988: 282, in Cope and Kalantzis 1993: 57). We need, then, knowledge of the way genres of all kinds – educational genres (permitting access to higher studies) and workplace genres (allowing entry to the different professional and administrative levels) – are structured and constructed through language.

However, it is important to point out here that, while a focus on language is indeed necessary, not all ways of working with language and grammar can provide the kind of information needed for an understanding of literacy. Hasan (1996: 415) has stressed that: 'Learning about the nature and structure of language is not an expendable educational activity', though back to the basics is not the solution. Knowledge about language 'is important *if and only in as much as* it contributes to a conscious understanding of the resources of one's language for acting with it ... what we need to avoid is the danger of ending up by focusing only on formal structures of language without relating them to their social functions' (Hasan 1996: 417, emphasis in original). This focus on language from a functional perspective has to be carried right through the education system, as Rothery insists: 'If we want our students to develop high levels of literacy and a critical orientation, we must engage them, at all levels, in an explicit focus on language' (Rothery 1996: 120). Such a focus is the topic of the chapters in this volume, which give many examples of classroom use.

Work on language also benefits the learning process, since many educational problems stem from language problems. Awareness of language brings with it both deeper awareness of the concepts studied, and gives insights into difficulties learners experience in school subjects, as language becomes more abstract, and taxonomies more detailed. This can be seen in various chapters in the book. Working on the language of history texts, for example, Coffin shows the changing representations of time and ways to express temporal frameworks. Polias and Dare describe how young children learn about the complexity of a specific process. Several chapters describe work on nominalization, helping students both to produce better written texts and to gain understanding of the subject matter. Thus, during language learning, another type of development occurs. As Halliday writes, 'language is the essential condition of knowing, the process by which experience **becomes** knowledge' (1993: 94, original emphasis).

It would seem, then, that there is a need for an approach providing literacy development through transmitting an understanding of the ways in which texts come to mean and the ways in which they function in society. Already, the SFL-inspired genre-based approach to pedagogy has gone some way towards providing this understanding in classrooms. However, while the research and its applications – explicit teaching of grammar and text structure from a functional point of view – has had many positive results, it has not been without opponents, both those who thought it was too progressive (and advocated a return to traditional grammar) and those who found it too restrictive, and called for freedom for children to express themselves, as illustrated in Walsh's experience (this volume). Indeed, an unfortunate and dramatic example of governmental rejection of the approach can be found in the history of the LINC project (Carter 1990, 1996). Yet, this resistance has not stopped those intent on raising learners' awareness of how language works, and the chapters in this book show the sort of work which can be carried out in classrooms, providing students with the kind of knowledge about language (KAL) that is proving to be effective in literacy development. In fact, in his chapter, Martin highlights one of the distinctive features of Australia's genre-based literacy programmes: the role played by KAL in the curriculum. According to Martin, this raises questions about which levels of language are brought to consciousness, what kind of terminology should be used and how and when this metadiscourse should be managed in a teaching/learning cycle.

Here a further objection has been raised against explicit focus on language: learners could be overwhelmed or bored by theoretical labels and analysis of functions. However, Williams (1988: 38) has provided evidence from observation of children interacting with teachers in classrooms to say that 'functionally oriented grammatical description is accessible to young children, and that studying language in this way is enjoyable' and, according to the teachers involved, 'the children's knowledge of functional grammar was associated with greater reading fluency than that of their peers'. Indeed, several of the writers in this volume bring up the challenge of using terminology in classrooms, and all dismiss it as a problem, whether they use more established terms and labels, or whether they come up with labels and terms which they feel are closer to the students' experience. Polias and Dare provide examples from primary schooling, where students learn about participants, processes and circumstances, and secondary contexts, where students focus on nominalization as a key resource in learning how to produce more academic texts. Their findings, and those of Custance, point to the potential for developing metalinguistic understandings in even the youngest students. McDonald also highlights a range of grammatical features, including a novel's selection for mood in narration and dialogue, and patterns of tense and transitivity, to demonstrate how discussion about language in a classroom of 11-year-olds makes critical appraisal possible, and argues for an explicit pedagogy and use of metalanguage to enhance student understanding. Equally, in Marshall's case study she argues for using more metalanguage in the classroom, although she chose not to use SFL terms in helping a learner to meet the school leaving performance standards in the critical discussion of literary texts in English. At the same time, she and her learner had to come up with names for the grammatical resources – complex nominal groups, nominalization, Theme and Rheme patterns, modality – needed for transforming the learner's initial essay into an effective final one, resources which the learner readily grasped, and found delight in manipulating.

In all, what emerges from reading the chapters is the satisfaction and enjoyment that the researchers and teachers transmit in writing about their language-focused work in the classroom, as the type of discussion which a functionally oriented approach enables is one which is meaningful, creating 'a milieu that is child-centred but in which the teacher functions as a guide, creating structure with the help of the students themselves' (Halliday 1978: 210).

This volume brings together a group of researchers committed to the application of their work in linguistics to education, and we feel a strong commitment to making this work known. However, many of the collaborators we do not know: those teachers whose work in the classroom has been studied here, and who are the ones who have the hardest job and get the least recognition. We would like to thank all of those who have contributed. We have had many and fruitful contacts with the authors during the writing of the chapters. At the same time, we cannot forget all those other voices which have made these texts possible with their enthusiasm and response in their classes, and the student writers of the texts which have been analysed. We hope this book will contribute to work in literacy and to realizing the potential of those for whom these skills do not 'come naturally', of whom there are many in every country.

References

Barton, D. (2001), 'Directions for literacy research: Analysing language and social practices in a textually mediated world', *Language and Education*, 15 (2–3), 92–104. Available: www.multilingual-matters.net/le/015/0092/le0150092.pdf

Carter, R. (1990), 'Introduction', in R. Carter (ed.), *Knowledge about Language and the Curriculum. The LINC Reader*. London: Hodder and Stoughton, pp. 1–20.

— (1996), 'Politics and knowledge about language: the LINC project', in R. Hasan and G. Williams (eds), pp. 1–28.

Cazden, C. B. (1988), *Classroom Discourse: The Language of Teaching and Learning*. Portsmouth, NH: Heinemann.

Cook-Gumperz, J. (1986), 'Literacy and schooling: An unchanging equation?', in J. Cook-Gumperz (ed.), *The Social Construction of Literacy*. Cambridge, UK: Cambridge University Press, pp. 16–44.

Cope, W. and Kalantzis, M. (eds) (1993), *The Powers of Literacy: A Genre Approach to Teaching Literacy*. London, Falmer and Pittsburgh: University of Pittsburgh Press.

Delpit, L. (1988), 'The silenced dialogue: power and pedagogy in educating other people's children', *Harvard Educational Review*, 58, (3), 280–98.

Foley, J. and Thompson, L. (2003), *Language Learning: A Lifelong Process*. London: Arnold.

Gee, J. (1986), 'Orality and literacy: from *The Savage Mind to Ways With Words*', Review Article in *TESOL Quarterly* 20, (4), 719–46.

— (1992), 'Socio-cultural approaches to literacy (literacies)', *Annual Review of Applied Linguistics*, 12, 31–48.

— (2001), 'Educational linguistics', in M. Aronoff and J. Rees-Miller (eds), *Handbook of Linguistics*. Oxford: Basil Blackwell, pp. 647–63.

Halliday, M. A. K. (1978), *Language as Social Semiotic: The Social Interpretation of Language and Meaning*. London: Arnold.

— (1993), 'Towards a language-based theory of learning', *Linguistics and Education*, 5, 93–116.

— (1994), *An Introduction To Functional Grammar*, Second Edition. London: Edward Arnold.

— (1996), 'Literacy and linguistics: a functional perspective', in R. Hasan and G. Williams (eds), pp. 339–76.

Hannon, P. (2000), *Reflecting on Literacy in Education*. Independence, KY, USA: Taylor and Francis.

Hasan, R. (1996) 'Literacy, everyday talk and society', in R. Hasan and G. Williams (eds), pp. 377–424.

Hasan, R. and Williams, G. (eds) (1996), *Literacy in Society*. London: Longman.

Heath, S. (1983), *Ways with Words*. New York: Cambridge University Press.

Hyland, K. (2000), *Disciplinary Discourses: Social Interactions in Academic Writing*. Harlow, UK: Pearson Education.

Kress, G. and van Leeuwen, T. (1996), *Reading Images. The Grammar of Visual Design*. London: Routledge.

— (2001), *Multimodal Discourse. The Modes and Media of Contemporary Communication*. London: Arnold.

Lankshear, C. (1987), *Literacy, Schooling and Revolution*. Lewes: Falmer Press.

Lassen, I. (forthcoming), 'A discourse analytical study of de-contextualization and literacy', in A. McCabe, M. O'Donnell and R. Whittaker (eds), *Advances in Language and Education*. London: Continuum.

Mace, J. (1992), *Talking about Literacy*. London and New York: Routledge.

O'Halloran, K. (ed.) (2004), *Multimodal Discourse Analysis*. London: Continuum.

Olson, D. (1996), *The World on Paper*. Cambridge: Cambridge University Press.

Ong, W. (1982), *Orality and Literacy: The Technologizing of the Word*. London and New York: Routledge.

Perez, B. (2004), 'Language, Literacy and Biliteracy', in B. Perez (ed.), *Sociocultural Contexts of Language and Literacy*. Mahwah, NJ, USA: Lawrence Erlbaum, pp. 25–56.

Rigg, P. and Kazemek, F. E. (1985), '23 million illiterates? By whose definition?', *Journal of Reading*, 28 (1), pp. 1–18.

Robinson, J. L. (1987), 'Literacy in society: Readers and writers in the worlds of discourse', in D. Bloome (ed.), *Literacy and Schooling*. Norwood, NJ: Ablex, pp. 327–53.

Rothery, J. (1996), 'Making changes: developing an educational linguistics', in R. Hasan and G. Williams (eds), pp. 86–123.

Street, B. (1984), *Literacy in Theory and Practice*. New York: Cambridge University Press.

Williams, G. (1998), 'Children entering literate worlds: perspectives from the study of textual practices', in F. Christie and R. Mission (eds), *Literacy and Schooling*. London and New York: Routledge, pp. 18–46.

Part One

Development of the SFL Literacy Approach

1 Language and Literacy

Michael Halliday and Ruqaiya Hasan

Part 1: Michael Halliday

1 Early experience

It is often thought, especially in Asian countries, that I have spent some of my career as a teacher of English. So let me say right from the beginning that I have not. I have been a language teacher; but not, except for part-time classes in 1947–8, a teacher of English. Mostly I have been a teacher of Chinese, and that is where I began to ask questions about the place of the understanding of language in language education, in the broader sense, and also in the more specific, narrower sense of language teaching.

During the Second World War, the British government decided that it would be a good idea if they trained people in a number of languages for the various Asian-Pacific theatres of war. These programmes got going at the end of 1941, when the War Office sent around to the schools for volunteers to be trained in a number of languages. The initial set of languages concerned were Chinese, Japanese, Turkish and Persian (Farsi). Those of us who happened to fall into the right cohort (a birthdate period of 12 months) were invited to apply, and I thought this might be a good idea. I was always interested in learning languages, spoken languages in particular, which I had been prevented from doing in my school career. So I applied and was accepted for the Chinese course, which was being taught at the School of Oriental and African Studies of the University of London, but on behalf of the War Office. Just about my seventeenth birthday I embarked on what was to be 20 months of very intensive study of Chinese. Looking back on this in later life, I realize how very well the courses were organized and implemented. It really was a very efficient language teaching exercise. It was of course privileged in the sense that here we were, a group of young men, with nothing else to do except be taught Chinese, or Japanese, or whichever we were assigned to. And that's the sort of thing that doesn't happen in life. So we were very privileged in that sense, and we were given this very intensive training for 20 months, and then scattered around the various theatres of war to do whatever duties were assigned to us.

These courses, which were found to be very successful, were expanded just towards the end of the war, when it was assumed that the Far East War, the war in East Asia, would continue still for quite a long time. And so, in 1945, four of us who had been in the first course were summoned back to London to act as instructors in the greatly expanded courses, particularly in Chinese and Japanese, that were taking place from early 1945 onwards. So my experiences as a language teacher began just after my twentieth birthday, and I was assigned to teach Chinese to these services courses. For most of the next 12 or 13 years, that was my career; not in the army of course, but after I came out, I continued to be a teacher of Chinese as a foreign language (that is, of Chinese to Anglophones) until the end of the 1950s. And it was initially that experience which forced me into trying to explore seriously how language works, because, already as a student, from a position of considerable ignorance about language, I raised all kinds of questions. Some of them got answered, some of them didn't. But as a teacher I was a lot more conscious of the need to provide explanations of problems faced by the learners, to try to develop some kind of coherent notion of a language, how it works, how it was learned, and so forth, in order simply to improve the quality of the language teaching. I think we all felt this. We became aware, I think at that time, that there was such a thing as linguistics. I remember that was when I first heard of J. R. Firth, the first Professor of General Linguistics in London, who later on became my teacher, although I don't think I had any contact with him at that time. But the notion that I began to build up at that time about the structure and the organization of language was very much problem-based: it was driven by the need to solve particular problems in teaching the language and to explain features of the language to the learners. And that could mean everything from, say, the Chinese tone system, the nature of Chinese writing and therefore of writing systems in general, to the relations between grammar and vocabulary (one became aware that the old notion of the textbook of having a grammar in one place and the vocabulary in another really wasn't much use – you had to see the whole thing as a single continuum), and the basic concept of grammatical units – there was no sense of a clause in those days;

there was a simple sentence and a complex sentence, but there was no sense that there was some really critical unit where all the work was done of turning meaning into form. It just didn't exist. So this was where I started asking questions.

2 Edinburgh

There came a moment at the end of the 1950s when my career changed. I moved out of Chinese studies and Chinese teaching into linguistics. So, instead of teaching a language, I was teaching linguistics. Conceptually, this sounds harder; but actually, it's not: it's much easier to teach about language than to teach language. At that time, then, I was appointed to the University of Edinburgh as their first teacher in General Linguistics, in what was a Department of English Language and General Linguistics. So this meant that my linguistics had to be tied closely to English.

This was a Scottish university in which a much higher proportion of the students went out into school teaching than was typically the case at that time in England, where there was a much sharper distinction between teacher education and university studies. Our department, headed by Angus McIntosh, frequently had visits from former students who had gone out into school teaching, and Angus would invite them back to talk about their experiences: what they felt they had gained from their English degree, and what they hadn't gained, what they felt they needed when they got up to teach in front of the class which they simply hadn't had in their courses. So we learned an awful lot in a very short time (at least I did!) from finding out what the teacher needed to know. And it was at that point that the suggestion came up that our little group of linguists, who were by now assembled in Edinburgh, should work together with some of the teachers in Scottish schools on bringing together ideas from modern linguistics and from language teaching – or rather, not just language teaching practice, but language education practice – in the schools. And in addition to our Department of English Language, there was also in Edinburgh the School of Applied Linguistics, which was founded at about the same time on the initiative of the British Council, who wanted somewhere that they could send their scholarship-holders from overseas to be trained as teachers of English in their own countries, and that was headed by Ian Catford. We had a small group: John Sinclair, who at that time was a recent graduate in the department just going into his Ph.D. studies; Ian Catford, head of the School of Applied Linguistics; Ken Albrow, from the Department of Phonetics headed by David Abercrombie and myself. Edinburgh was a real centre of language studies in the UK at that time.

We organized ourselves so that we met with different groups of teachers in Edinburgh at that time. We used to meet each group once a fortnight – they gave up their Saturday mornings for this. There came a request then from Jordanhill College in Glasgow – would someone go over there? Now, I come from Leeds, which is a big industrial city, and I really liked Glasgow better than Edinburgh, because it reminded me of Leeds, so I said all right, I'll go and meet with the Glasgow group. So I used to go over to Glasgow, and worked there with Bill Currie and one or two other language educators at Jordanhill. It was a very bright group there. They brought together on Saturday mornings a group of Glasgow teachers, and we worked together on issues like linguistics and language education (although at that time the term 'language education' didn't exist, so it was either linguistics and English teaching, or more generally linguistics and language teaching). This gave me my first real contact with teachers, so that I was a learner in the sense of actually finding out what went on in the classroom, or what kind of demands they felt they needed to make on linguists and on linguistics.

3 London

In 1963, I moved to University College London, at the invitation of Randolph Quirk. Hugh Smith and Quirk had instituted a Communication Research Centre (CRC) at University College, and I was brought to the CRC with the specific task of developing work in language education along with teachers in the London area. So I had to formulate a proposal to the Nuffield Foundation, which was the main source of funding in England for educational research at that time.

3.1   Nuffield Programme in Linguistics and English Teaching

I wrote a document in which I tried to summarize the aims. I have no copies of it; it must have been extremely naive, but what it was saying was something like this: it seemed that the time had come to take up some of the achievements of modern linguistics and bring these together with the experience of teachers and see to what extent this could be incorporated in some way or other into classroom practice, in the context not of English as a foreign language, but of English as the mother tongue. And the question arose: at what level would we seek to make contact with the educational process?

I started off by saying that I wanted first of all a small group of linguists, to work on the grammar of English from the point of view of its relevance to English teaching, to language teaching. The Nuffield Foundation did what they always do: they passed the application up to the Inspectorate of Schools in the Department of Education in London, and they summoned me to a meeting, the Inspectors and the Nuffield representatives, and they said 'Look, we're interested in your project, but why don't you want the teachers there at the start?' And I just said 'Well, we're not ready for them. We don't know how to talk to them yet – we need to do two years' work first'. So they said 'If you take the teachers in right from the start, we will double your money'. That was the 1960s, these sorts of things really happened. I had applied for a certain sum of money, and they more or less doubled it on the condition that we had the teachers in right from the start. So I kind of gulped. You don't turn that sort of thing down. Of course they were right, absolutely right.

The next question that was raised by the Inspectorate was: 'If this is going to be a curriculum development project, where are you going to move into the curriculum?' Now, I had been talking to people about that, and I said it seemed to me that there were three points where we might have something to contribute: either in the initial literacy teaching, so right in the beginning of the primary school, teaching reading and writing; or secondly, the middle school point, the transition from the primary to the secondary, which is always a weak spot, particularly in language education; or thirdly, higher up in the secondary school, where the impact would be via the teaching of literature. I said I think we should think of one or other of these three. And they said: right, you take all three.

In the 1960s, the typical model for curriculum development projects was that you produced materials, you tried them out, went back and forth for two or three years and then they went into the schools. So that was our brief. We started the project in 1965, with a little group of teachers and linguists working together. And I think this was a first, certainly in anything to do with language: we had tertiary, secondary and primary teachers in the same basement (you always got basements for these research projects), all working together on a joint project. So, on the teaching side, we had David Mackay, principal of a London primary school and a wonderful teacher; Stephen Lushington, as the middle school representative, together with Andrew Philp from the Scottish system, and Peter Doughty, who was a secondary school teacher specializing at the upper level. On the linguists' side we had Eirian Davies, and then Ruqaiya came and Ken Albrow and myself.

Ruqaiya and I weren't married then; that came after, and then she had to leave of course.

We had a lot of very interesting discussions, especially on the grammar, though it was a learning exercise on both sides. We had to learn about what went on in the classroom, and what was needed; they had to learn what we had to say about language; and both had to work towards a grammar that would be relevant to educational processes, educational tasks and problems. Already at Edinburgh we had done quite a lot of work in what we might now call proto-systemic grammar.

The brief then was that we would be given a trial period of three years in which we had to come up not with the finished product, but with a very clear blueprint of what we planned to do. If they approved of this, and they regarded the provisional achievements as adequate, they would then give us extra funding to increase the size of the team so that we could actually produce curriculum materials at these three levels.

We worked of course at University College London; but we had as our immediate context and contacts some very important colleagues in and around. One was a group at the Institute of Education, led by Jimmy Britton, a marvellous man: Britton, Nancy Martin and Harold Rosen carried out a writing research project, and we came together with them. At one point in the programme we ran a joint course along with them, part of a Masters course.

Our other very important colleague was Basil Bernstein. After a brief and somewhat sketchy career in the RAF during the war, Bernstein had become a teacher in a working class district in a London school, and he had become very much concerned with problems of educational failure. This was during the 1950s, which was a period of immense optimism. For the first time in Britain (and I think anywhere), there were entire school populations where no one was being dragged back by poverty. They all had enough to eat and they all had enough clothes to wear. But many children still weren't succeeding in school. For Basil the initial question that started him off in life was 'Why not? What essentially lies behind this educational failure?'

I met him first in 1960 or 1961, when, having heard about his work in London, we invited him to give a talk to one of our linguistics seminars in Edinburgh. He came up and he talked about the work that he had been doing at the time: he had been recording discussions among teenagers of different social classes, around a particular motif that he had given them; the topic was capital punishment – a very important issue in Britain at the time. He was trying to find out what were the systematic differences in the forms of discourse that they used, but he had no linguistic background with which to do it. So I remember that, after his talk, which we all found very interesting, we pinned him down in the bar at the staff club, for the whole evening until it closed, and we just hammered at this together and we said, 'Look, you've got to get together with some linguists to look at this from the point of view of what you are actually investigating: the grammar'. He said afterwards that he was absolutely worn out by this encounter. But he did in fact try very hard then to find some kind of linguistic underpinning for his own work.

Frankly we weren't ready for him: we had something of a grammar, but we had no semantics. We had hardly a clear concept even of semantics as a coherent stratum within the organization of language; that came partly through the demands Bernstein was making on our own work and our own abilities.

Ruqaiya had joined our own project at the beginning, in 1965, just after the first few months, but it then became clear that it was not appropriate for her to be in a project in which I was director. Bernstein was by that time keen to grab her for his project, and so, in 1968, Ruqaiya moved over to the Sociological Research Unit at the Institute of Education, where Bernstein was director.

3.2   Schools Council Programme in Linguistics and English Teaching

About this time (1968), the first phase of the project was coming to an end. I had gone back to the Education Department and made a proposal for the second stage of the project. This was approved; the project was expanded and was then taken over so that, from being a Nuffield Foundation project, for the second stage of its history it became a Schools Council project. The Schools Council at that time was a very effective national body, which funded and oversaw a number of important projects; they took over the Nuffield Science project, the Nuffield Maths project, and so on. These all came under the umbrella of the Schools Council. So our project changed its title at this point, from NPLET (Nuffield Programme in Linguistics and English Teaching), to SCPLET (Schools Council Programme in Linguistics and English Teaching). It was agreed the project would be funded for a further three years, and the brief now was to use the experience that we had to produce curriculum materials for the three levels that I mentioned above: initial literacy, the middle school, and what we came to refer to as 16 plus.

From the beginning, when we started working together, we found that the teachers at the primary and tertiary (i.e. university) levels very quickly got on the same wavelength – they knew exactly what each other was on about. The secondary teachers, however, were out on their own. Why did this happen? The primary teachers knew what they had to do: they had to teach children to read and write, and there was a clear criterion of success: did they learn to read or did they not? There was no difficulty in seeing this as a linguistic task, which could be furthered through a deeper awareness of language. Just towards the end of the first phase, a young Australian teacher, Brian Thompson, had come into the project, joining the primary group. By the time we moved into phase two of the project, he and David Mackay together had worked out an outline of the programme that they would develop, which became *Breakthrough to Literacy*.

The thinking at the secondary level was further behind. The problem was that there was no operational concept of 'language' then; there was English and there was Literature. It seemed obvious to us, as naive linguists, that literature was made of language, and therefore there was something to say about it from a linguistic point of view. But it turned out not to be obvious to teachers of English, who thought there was nothing to say about language except what they could say from their vantage point as teachers of literature. The 16 + group had to define their goals from the start.

Breakthrough to Literacy

So the primary group, David Mackay, Brian Thompson and Pamela Schaub, got down to work and produced the materials that came to be known as *Breakthrough to Literacy*, the idea being that you were as it were breaking through from the spoken language to the written language.

The motivation for the project was essentially that the children should be freed as soon as possible to control their own reading and writing. So there were no primers in the set of 'Breakthrough' materials. There was a sentence maker, in which there were stands constructed which had words on them; the children would work together with the teacher, initially deciding which sentences *they* wanted to make, and the teachers would help them to construct them. Gradually the children took over the task of constructing the sentences, and they got their own words added. The next task was to deconstruct the words into letters, so that after the sentence maker, they had a word maker; and then the sentences that they produced would be put together, again initially written out by the teacher, into a book; and then gradually the children took over the task of making their own words and sentences, turning them into their own reading folder, and so on.

It was a very interactive programme: they all worked in small groups, about 5 or 6 around a table, and they would constantly interfere with each other, saying 'no, you got that wrong, you put that *there* ... that's the right word, *there*.' It was really fascinating to go into those classrooms and see it used.

This continued to be used for quite some time, David Mackay took it up to Stornoway, and developed a *Breakthrough* in Scots Gaelic. He then went down to the Caribbean and developed a *Breakthrough* for the Netherlands Antilles. A number of Australian teachers also took it over: it was quite widely used throughout New South Wales, and also in Western Australia with Aboriginal learners.

But most successful of all was its uptake in South Africa, with the *Molteno* project, which is still going on. I recently received a letter from Vic Rodseth, which said:

> Breakthrough is going from strength to strength. At the latest count, we have courses in 36 different African languages, the latest surge the result of Ghana taking it on for every grade 1 class in the country ... An important aspect of Breakthrough in African languages is that it is better than Breakthrough in English ... Kids on Breakthrough for African languages really take off.

That was a follow-up from a visit that Ruqaiya made to South Africa two years ago to work with some of their linguists.

So *Breakthrough* was developed very quickly; it was tried out first in just a few schools, then again and then a third time, with expanding populations each time and with a lot of workshopping and discussion in between. The project was particularly tried in inner city schools where there was a high risk of educational failure, and with large migrant populations, so they were conceived neither as 'mother tongue' nor as EFL (English as a foreign language) materials, but rather were located in a context that is now familiar in so many of our big cities today, where a given class might consist of any range of learners from those who are totally monolingual in English to those who haven't heard a word of English until they get into the classroom. It was in that kind of context that these materials were first tried out. Finally, *Breakthrough to Literacy* was put out by Longman as a project in the open market (Mackay *et al* 1970).

Language in Use

The 16+ group (upper secondary) took much longer to get going. Partly this was because we had to be very cautious: we daren't mention the word 'grammar'. Grammar was a dirty word in schools in those days, in the sixties.

There were two or three important bits of background here. One was current ideological thinking, current ideologies in education itself. This was set up as a confrontation between the traditional so-called 'authoritarian' classroom, and the new 'progressivist' classroom. What would come to be labelled progressivism, I called 'benevolent inertia', because it was a view of education in which teachers simply had to sit back, put their feet up on the table and keep quiet, and learning would take place by itself, by magic.

It has been a feature of systemic linguistics in all its applications along the line that we get trapped in these artificial confrontations between two positions, neither of which we hold, and each one labels us as the other. We had to say no, we do not believe in the old style authoritarian classroom; but nor do we believe in benevolent inertia. We think the teacher has to provide structure. The teacher is the guide, the materials are there as an aid, and it is for the teacher to use them in whatever way is appropriate. But in order to use them properly, the teacher does have to have basic insights into the nature of language, and the processes whereby language is learnt, both spoken and written. The 16+ team then had to say 'well, whatever we do, we mustn't mention grammar'. Peter Doughty, Geoffrey Thornton and John Pearce – that was another three person team – came up with a very original project named *Language in Use*. The notion of language variation was of central importance in this project.

We wanted to say: yes, there is an awful lot of work to be done on language at this level. But you can do it without mentioning grammar. What you are looking at is the way in which language varies, in terms of register variation – variation according to function. For example, what are the differences among different levels of formality, between spoken and written language, between technical and less technical language, and so on. Within this framework they were able to produce around 110 units for working on language. These were designed such that a unit could be the work for anything between a single afternoon and a whole term, depending on whether the teacher and the students could pick it up and run with it.

Peter Doughty said that we shouldn't spell the examples out too much because, if we do, the teachers won't think of them for themselves; so we are not going to give them any models. And I said this won't work, they have got to have models. This argument went on for quite a long time, and finally the publishers came in and said that we had to have some models, so there were some *Language in Use* workbooks, called simply *Workbooks of Language in Use*, which set out examples of how these different units on varieties of English could be implemented in a classroom context. An important aspect was that the project contextualized the teaching of literature within the framework of language as a whole. And of course, we hoped that grammar would come in by the back door, as long as we didn't mention it.

Language and Communication
The middle school group had one unfortunate appointment in the team, and that held up the project for quite a long time; but finally Ian Forsyth and Kathleen Wood produced an excellent middle school programme called *Language and Communication* (Forsyth and Wood 1977).

Summary
The three eventual outputs from this project were *Breakthrough to Literacy*, *Language in Use* (Doughty *et al* 1971) and *Language and Communication*. The Breakthrough team also produced some beautiful little reading books and the *Language in Use* team persuaded Arnold to undertake an important series of books on language education. It was really at that point that the term 'language education' gradually came to be a concept, in the sense that a very important aspect of the whole project was to bring into focus the notion that language was a fundamental aspect in the educational process.

It was in this same decade (the 1960s) that we first started to hear about 'language across the curriculum'. Maths and science teachers started to look at the linguistic problems in the learning of maths and the sciences. So, during the 60s, things changed quite substantially in terms of the recognition of the place of language and the place of understanding about language within the educational process – though not of course without a lot of resistance.

Changing funding environment
Meanwhile, however, the political situation had changed. The Schools Council did not follow up their project. This has always been a problem, with educational research in general, at least in Britain. You get it funded. You produce something. And then they say, 'OK, now we will give the money to someone else'. The view that we held was this: if you are taking this project seriously, then follow it up. You have

got to finance the training of teachers to use these resources, you have got to support the production and distribution of the resources, you have got to allow for in-service activities of one kind or another; otherwise, how will they be promulgated? But they preferred to devote funds to something else. So you had to reckon with the fact that once you produced the stuff, that was it as far as they were concerned. As far as we were concerned, that was just the beginning.

In any case, the government then disbanded the Schools Council. It became a very different background in the 1970s, with much less commitment to innovative research.

3.3   OSTI Programme in the linguistic properties of scientific English

We had one other project going on which was not directly related to education, but was related in the sense that it was designed to develop the grammar as a resource for text analysis; this was the programme into the linguistic properties of scientific English. Rodney Huddleston was in charge of that team, which included himself, Dick Hudson, Eugene Winter and a computer programmer, Alec Henrici – because we then started getting the computer into the picture in order to test our grammars and pursue quantitative studies. They produced a long report *Sentence and Clause in Scientific English*, which was the result of their analysis of a very large body of data in nine different 'cells' (varieties of scientific English: three levels, or 'brows', in each of three scientific subjects).

3.4   Development of SFL

It was particularly during this 1960s period that what we now know as SFL came into being. My own background had been as a student of linguistics: first in China, with a brilliant Chinese teacher called Wang Li and then in London with an equally brilliant teacher, J. R. Firth. Firth had developed a kind of post-Saussurean system-structure theory. I say 'post-Saussurean' because, unlike almost all other followers of Saussure, Firth took seriously the Saussurean project of language as having both a syntagmatic and a paradigmatic organization. I inherited that notion from Firth. Gradually, through having to write descriptive grammars and apply them to texts, first in the analysis of Chinese, then in work on English, I changed the framework to a certain extent and developed the notion of system networks; particularly during this period of interacting on the one hand with the teachers and on the other hand with the group working on scientific English, I was able to come towards something a little closer to what you would understand as a systemic-functional analysis today. And from the end of that period there were other linguists, beginning with Robin Fawcett and Margaret Berry, who became part of the whole project.

The important point for language education as a whole was to try and develop a comprehensive overview of language, one which was rich in different perspectives, or dimensions if you like: language as a variable system; that of realization and linguistic strata, coming of course from the tradition of European linguistics via Firth, Hjelmslev, the Prague School and others; and our own concept of metafunction, which wasn't present elsewhere, except in terms of functional theories that had been imported from outside language, from people such as Karl Bühler and Malinowski, which were functional theories of the utterance, but not recognized as a dimension of the grammar.

So a lot of these fundamental developments initially took place in this 1960s period, and this whole experience of interaction between language specialists and teachers played a critical part.

3.5   On theoretical and applied linguistics

I have never made a distinction between theoretical and applied linguistics. To me, the theory and the application are constantly reinforcing each other: if you want to apply, you have to have a theory to apply, but the theory in turn is developed through the feedback from the application, through being extended into new areas, and so on.

This has always been a point of contrast with the mainstream formal traditions within linguistics. We are quite happy to cohabit with them, but they typically make a very sharp distinction between theoretical and applied linguistics, something we are still living with, particularly in the United States, where the mainstream tradition was highly formal, and anything which looked like application was simply thrown out; it wasn't part of the linguistic scene at all. This was true for a very long time, before an independent concept of applied linguistic theory came to have a place in the field. This explains why, in SFL gatherings, you will find a regrettably small proportion of American participants, because there has been such a domination of what is a formal rather than a functional approach to language. Now these are not contradictory approaches: we all have to deal with linguistic form. Rather, they are differences of emphasis. But we have always found that in educational contexts, it is essentially the functional orientation which is more relevant.

3.6   Language development

I wanted to add that we used to have the primary school teachers coming for workshops to the department, and they used to raise this problem: we get to know these kids at 5 or 6 years old, but how much language have they learnt before that? I read a lot of the literature available at the time on early language development, and there really wasn't very much, apart from one or two works, for instance a lovely book by Ruth Weir (1962) called *Language in the Crib*. Others simply counted vocabulary, which doesn't tell you very much. At that time, we had a baby of our own, and it happened that I had accepted a position at the University of British Columbia, in Vancouver, but the Canadian government refused us admission. They wouldn't let us in to work in Canada, which meant that I had a lovely period of about a year and a half when I was unemployed, and consequently, I was able to study our child's developing language in very great detail. I always regretted that I didn't write in the introduction to *Learning How to Mean* (Halliday 1975), 'with thanks to the government of Canada for making this possible'.

4 Sydney

At the beginning of 1976, we moved to Sydney and I started up the Department of Linguistics at Sydney University. Sydney had a Dip.TEFL., run by Charles Taylor; but there were no postgraduate courses in applied linguistics anywhere in Australia, so I talked with Bill Connell, Professor of Education, and we worked out a proposal for a joint MA/M.Ed. in Applied Linguistics (Language in Education), which was launched in 1978 – the first intake included both Joan Rothery and Frances Christie, who quickly became leaders in the field.

   Jim Martin joined the teaching staff in 1979, and in 1980 together with Joan Rothery set up the Writing Research Project to study practices in the teaching of writing in New South Wales primary schools. Jim then followed this up with a major project with the Disadvantaged Schools Program in Sydney, and it was at that time, working with teachers in geography, history, maths, and science, that he developed the 'genre-based' approach to teaching and learning, analysing the forms of written discourse that the learner had to control in order to succeed in a subject-based curriculum.

   Meanwhile, the MA/M.Ed. programme was attracting a large number of students from Australia and overseas: within a few years we had over a hundred enrolled. They had varied interests and specializations, not all of them in education; but the single most usual occupation was the teaching of English as a second or foreign language, either overseas or in Australia – many of the Australian participants worked in the Migrant Education Service, Child or Adult. The courses were given in the late afternoon and evening, because the majority of the students were working during the day: they then had to face up to four hours of coursework before they had finished the day's chores.

To me these enterprises seemed like a resumption of what we had been doing in London in the sixties. There had been a hiatus, partly because Ruqaiya and I had moved around, but also because I felt that the sort of functional approach I had been working with was not going to be followed up – I had taken refuge in sociolinguistics and child language studies. This was short-sighted of course, because others, particularly Robin Fawcett and Margaret Berry in the UK, and Michael Gregory in Canada, were actively pursuing and extending the work; but I had got rather cut off – I had spent too much of this time in the United States. So it was a real pleasure to get involved once again with people in language education, in a new context of time and place; and a nice lead up to ending my (official) career.

Part 2: Ruqaiya Hasan

1 Pakistan and Edinburgh

I could tell you some very funny stories. Some of them border on 'dark humour' – for example, imagine teaching *Alice In Wonderland* to people who don't know the difference between 'go' and 'went'. So, as you teach, you must remember not to laugh at jokes, because the rest of the class is not going to laugh; and by laughing, you would be telling them that you understand something they could not.

Other stories have to be given a background. Like many, I first encountered grammar in the context of being taught language, both Urdu, my mother tongue, and English, a second language. Now, the Urdu grammar did not bother me, and thinking back on it I can now guess why: its terminology was functional. So if it said that a *jumla* (roughly, a *clause*) was *khabriya* (literally 'news-giver') then I knew that in the clause there will be some sort of 'news' about something or someone: usually the 'news' consisted of classifying or identifying information; so in terms of SFL *jumla khabriya* was a relational clause, with some entity (called *ism-e-zaat*, literally 'noun/name of individual or class') classified or identified by reference to something (called *ism-e-sifat*, literally 'noun/name of quality'). Examples offered by Misbah-ul-Qawaed are *white is my favourite colour* and *Zaid is a human being*. But the grammar of English was considerably different: the language of description was entirely formal and the terms were neither semanticized nor put in the context of the use of that language. There was English language and there was English grammar, and they seemed to have nothing to do with each other. So I ignored all the inconsequentialities the teachers brought into their discourse by way of teaching grammar such as gerund, infinitive, adjectival complement, past participle and so on. It's not surprising I came to linguistics completely convinced that grammar was a profitless pastime.

So why did I choose to turn to linguistics in the first place? Well, there were two reasons: first, I was teaching English language to the first year at the university by introducing them to bits of English literature such as *Alice in Wonderland, Julius Caesar*, Johnson's *Letter to Lord Chesterfield*, Russell's *On the Nature of Truth* and other such 'valued' texts. The majority of these students had come up to the university from a vernacular medium school; a minority were from an English medium, which meant their spoken English was pretty good. The first group worked hard on English, but from a position of grave disadvantage. They knew they would get nowhere unless their command of English improved, because it was now the medium of instruction. I could see how it destroyed my students' self-confidence to work so hard and to gain so little. So this was a big challenge. Something had to be done to help them, and I didn't know what. I tried everything, even stooped to using Nesfield's Grammar, which used to be a standard grammar text for students of English where I come from, and as a student I myself had avoided it strenuously – I thought it might help as a teacher. However, it failed me every time. So I was on the lookout for something that would teach me to teach English more effectively. At the same time, I developed a feeling of great resentment about ESL (English as a second language) in our educational context, seeing it as a means of 'intellectual colonization' – a perspective that remained with me until Kachru's notion of 'world Englishes' (e.g. Kachru 1986) and his theory of re-semanticization became known.

What really led me to Edinburgh was my postgraduate teaching. I was supposed to be teaching students English literature. And very soon I realized that all I was doing by way of teaching literature was to tell them what I or some critic had thought about a literature text, and it was effectively these same opinions they had to reproduce in their term papers and in exams. Of course, this is how *I* was taught literature, but now I found it truly appalling – what kind of teaching was this where all you were being required to learn was to repeat someone else's opinions without understanding why they said what they did? Now this mattered to me a lot, because, you know, at that time I believed that I was going to save my corner of the world by teaching people literature. Literature in those days seemed to me not only to offer an understanding of human life, but also to cultivate in the reader a sense of better things humanity could achieve. I felt if my students could read literature with understanding, they would probably understand how things work in this world, what is wrong with it and how it can be put right; they wouldn't have to depend on me or anyone else. Yes, the idea that teaching is about enabling independent understanding has always been a passion with me. So now I had two challenges: how to facilitate the learning of English language for my disadvantaged students and how to help my literature students to form their own independent judgements about the uplifting messages of literature.

Help came in the end from the British Council, who offered me a generous scholarship. The scholarship was to do a postgraduate diploma in Applied Linguistics at the University of Edinburgh. I came to Edinburgh in the hope of not only learning something about effective ESL teaching but also, and even primarily, to explore what one could do about teaching literature more effectively. The sum total of my knowledge of linguistics was certain chapters of Bloomfield's (1933) *Language*. So when I had my first meeting with Michael, I told him about my interest in the teaching of literature, and went on to add, 'I doubt if linguistics will be much use, but I will give it a try; what I would really like to be able to do is to understand the philosophy of language.' He didn't look too happy, but all he said was 'Uuh!'

That first year in Edinburgh was great. We were taught by Ian Catford, Ronald Mackin, David Abercrombie, Lindsay Criper, Beth Ingram and Michael Halliday. Occasionally we also encountered Peter Strevens, Peter Ladefoged and Betsy Uldall. Our group was truly international, with students from South America, Africa, India, Pakistan and Japan. I learned a good deal – that of course was not difficult from a zero level knowledge of linguistics! Beginning the year as a sceptic about the usefulness of grammar, I ended it with a linguistic analysis of Angus Wilson's short story 'Necessity's Child' for my special topic dissertation. I realized that English grammar does not have to be meaningless – the patterns of language, systematically related to meaning, could form a firm basis for a viable analysis of meaning in literature texts.

I didn't get an extension of the British Council scholarship: they favoured work on ESL/EFL, and my research was on the application of linguistics to the study of literature. So it was lucky that I was appointed as a part time Assistant Lecturer in English for Foreign Students, a section of the department directed by John Sinclair. This is great, I said, I now know some grammar that can be used for teaching EFL. So I tried out both the early TG and the scale and category version of SF grammar, and I came to an interesting finding: it was really easy, for example, to teach students how to transform the 'active' clause into 'passive', but when it came to teaching where and why you use the passive construction rather than the active, well, you couldn't say much using the TG framework. About this time, the early 1960s, Michael had been working on the significance of the clause initial position, which was later called 'Theme'. Interestingly, this was useful in explaining some of the semantic work that the passive construction did. A lot of ESL/EFL teaching was using TG inspired grammar at that time, but with several experiences of this kind I concluded that in the end TG does not have the answer to the problem of effective language teaching; language learning is not about manipulating structures – the main issue is cultivating the ability to mean appropriately, which requires relating grammar to meaning, not ignoring it.

Meanwhile, I was also working on my Ph.D. under the supervision of Angus McIntosh and Michael Halliday, who was replaced by John Sinclair in the final year as that's when he moved down to University College London. But he generously read and commented on all of my chapters, anyway. I had chosen to work on a grammatical study of contrasting features of style in two contemporary novels – one by Angus Wilson and the other by William Golding. This was based on an exhaustive grammatical analysis at the clause and group rank of a little over a 10,000 clause sample derived randomly from the two novels. I guess it was the first large-scale corpus based grammatical analysis in terms of scale and category grammar as developed up to 1963. Since there was no written account of these categories in any one place, the dissertation contained an account of the grammatical categories as well. Also, I examined the relevance of the categories of context and register to the language variety of literature – this I found fascinating. So the research was satisfying as a starting point, but it also showed up what was missing. It was obvious that simply doing grammatical analysis and presenting an account of that analysis in the form of umpteen tables just didn't get to the heart of literature: there is no direct connection between the percentages of structure types and reader's evaluation. What one needed was to somehow show the significance of all this grammatical patterning. Further, the discussion of context and register pointed to hidden depths that my dissertation had scarcely managed to probe in any true sense of the word.

So the experience of the research emphasized the importance of social context, its relation to text, and the role of society in the creation of conventions as well as the need to find some way of representing the relations between grammar and meaning. In a way, this is what prepared the ground for my interest in Bernstein's work, though up to this time Bernstein was just a name to me, I didn't really know his work.

2 Leeds

In January 1964 I joined a research project directed by Sam Spicer at Leeds University; it was called Nuffield Foreign Languages Teaching Materials Project. I actually completed the last stages of the writing of my doctoral dissertation in Leeds while starting my first full-time job: I was in charge of the section dealing with the description of children's natural use of language.

The aim of the project was to produce materials for teaching French at the primary and secondary schools – materials that were based on how children talked in everyday life in the target language, and it employed teachers of French to help with this. For children's language data, it collaborated with a similar research project set up in France – well known as CREDIF. The CREDIF researchers were to collect French data, we, the English, and the data sets as well as aspects of their analysis would be exchanged. The idea was to collect spontaneous talk by children at various stages of schooling, not in the schoolroom context, but rather as ordinary casual interaction. My job was to collect the English data and to devise a descriptive framework for its analysis. The first challenge was to try and create some kind of environment in which the children might, despite my physical presence, begin to ignore me, and talk to each other as if I wasn't there. I began with the primary schools, and one of the most important things I learned from this project was respect for children's own understanding of the world. Every time I listened to the recordings, I was amazed at how 'grown up' the children were, and how silly it was to teach them 'run, Spot, run' and other banalities of the kind that appeared in the textbooks presumably as examples of language that represented their maturational stage! The children I was recording from ordinary primary schools were discussing all sorts of serious subjects. A part of one of those discussions has found its way into Halliday (1985); this was about the meaning of 'the', and the difference between 'the' and 'it'. The children were wondering whether it was better to call a newborn baby 'it', or just 'he/she' which could be factually wrong if one didn't know the baby's sex. And one of them said: *Why don't we call it 'the' – 'hello the!'?* I enjoyed doing these recordings and in fact if one ignored the initial 'warm-up' stage the 'conversations' were pretty natural.

I worked on this project for one year and during that time we finished the primary school recordings. For the grammatical description of this language data, we used the scale and category grammar already written up in my doctoral dissertation – with updates that were coming thick and fast from UCL – but the processing of this analysis was a separate matter. Unlike the analysis of my doctoral research materials, it could not be processed manually. So we sought help from our computational colleagues, and they said the number of descriptive variables was so large no computer would be able to do anything about it. They suggested modifications to the analysis to suit the computer, and a balancing act began – where one had to decide what aspect of analysis should be 'distorted/simplified' to suit the computer's capacity for handling data. These negotiations were both tedious and discouraging. About this time I got an appointment on the Nuffield project at UCL, which is where all the action was, anyway. Sam Spicer then appointed Richard Handscombe as my successor. Richard overlapped with me for about three months or so, during which time he was initiated into the work of the project. But I rather think at that stage Richard was not very interested in grammatical analysis; so after I left, the negotiations with the computer department were shelved (as I recall) and most of the data was analysed on the basis of other criteria, e.g. establishing the sort of topics that interested children. Richard continued with the recording into the secondary school stage. So at least the research produced a rich resource in terms of data of children's casual conversation.

3 University College London

I transferred to Michael's NPLET project in early 1965. This project had teachers and linguists working together. The linguists were supposed to take up the linguistic description of some part of English language, which would become a resource in language teaching; it was the teachers' job to decide what to take and how to integrate it in their teaching materials. Given my interests, I chose the area of connectivity

in text. The early part of this research was published in the first series
of project publications; it was called 'Grammatical Cohesion, Part I'.
This, together with the work on ellipsis and substitution, is what later
became the basis of our *Cohesion in English* (Halliday and Hasan 1976).
The teachers and linguists on this project worked in the same location;
there was constant interaction, both social and academic. It was very
interesting to hear teachers' views on education, their assessment of
what was needed to improve language education. But at the same
time, one experienced a certain amount of inability to decide how to
present what one knew as linguistics in a way that would be useful for
language teachers. I don't know how far we succeeded in this, but
certainly we worked together closely. One of the pieces in the first
series was written in collaboration between Stephen Lushington and
myself (later published by Longman) called *The Subject Matter of
English* (Hasan and Lushington 1968), where we problematized some
popular language teaching strategies, e.g. drills and substitution
tables, which were the rage at that time. The article questioned the
efficacy of teaching isolated structures, and suggested that it was
important to teach about continuity, using text as part of the teaching
material.

   During this time on the UCL project, the most striking thing from
my point of view was the collaboration with the Sociological Research
Unit (SRU) under the direction of Basil Bernstein. We held joint
seminars with them, and those discourses opened new horizons. The
seminars were fantastic but even more fantastic were the post-seminar
pub sessions, because that was really where you engaged someone,
discussing a problem in reasonable detail. I myself had read one or two
pieces of Bernstein's work by this time. And now I must admit that I
had been quite sceptical about the notion of codes. Until that time, I
hadn't heard Bernstein speak. I think he was very much more effective
in face-to-face discourse than in writing – at least for me – and it
became quite clear to me that along with connectivity of discourse, it is
very important to think of language in terms of its different sorts of
varieties and to figure out what underlies variation of different kinds.

   Meanwhile, Michael had been working quite closely with Geoffrey
Turner and Bernie Mohan, who were both researchers in Bernstein's
SRU. It was also becoming clear that Bernstein's linguistic criteria for
the identification of codes would not stand up in their early
formulation, but that the problem was really with linguistics itself:
we, as linguists, did not have what was needed to state the criteria. The
problem had to be tackled from more than one direction. On the one
hand, you had to focus on grammar as a resource for meaning, and on

the other you had to relate that knowledge in a systematic way to
Bernstein's 'real' conception of code, not code as interpreted by many,
including even some of those working with him. The expression
'grammar as the resource for meaning' had not yet come into use, but
the systematicity of the wording-meaning relation was drawing our
conscious attention to itself as a result of the work for example on
transitivity and on cohesion. The seminar discussions pushed us into
greater awareness of this aspect of language. Then the other part of the
story, namely relating meanings to codes, called for an understanding
of why it is possible for meanings to be shared, and how this sharing
occurs. Unless the social is taken seriously, this problem would not be
resolved successfully, because each of us can mean anything that we
want – at least in theory – but we can only mean 'together/
interactively' if we have something in common. Meaning as a resource
for action, reflection and relation is in itself without constraint – it is
open and available, but an individual's own habitual orientation to
meaning is not so free. Between meaning as a semiotic resource and
meaning as practice lies our social history. This I understood to be the
basic claim of Bernstein's code theory. I don't suppose I articulated
these ideas clearly but even a sort of dim perception of these relations
became a very powerful impetus, at least for me, though the fact is that
all of us on the project were deeply interested in Basil's code theory and
considered it relevant to educational practices and outcomes.

It was around this same time that many of Michael's ideas,
eventually published as *Explorations in the Functions of Language*
(Halliday 1973), appeared on the scene as lectures, seminar offerings
and so on, for instance, the work Michael did on context-based
semantic networks, particularly taking one of Bernstein's scenarios,
where a child walks into the house with a dirty piece of broken glass
and the problem is: what are the meaning options available to the
mother? Michael did a paradigmatic representation of the options of
meaning available to the mother, and provided indicators of the
(range of) patterns relevant to their realization; he used Roget's
Thesaurus to identify the process types that would be relevant for the
realization of semantic systemic options. One had to go to Roget's for
help because, while the transitivity networks were being made more
and more specific, they were nowhere as advanced as they are today.
That was the first real semantic network, because it represented
meaning paradigmatically, as a resource, and showed how the
meaning option was realizationally related to options in wording. I
have often thought that when you ask about a research project: what
has it produced?, there could be two rather different approaches. One

is to answer by looking at the tangible things – concepts, empirical findings – it has produced here and now; and the other is by assessing *where* the research has taken us – what potential it offers for development. To me, this latter approach has seemed more important in the 'scheme of things' and, from that point of view, the semantic network was a very important development.

While at the UCL project, I also had the privilege of giving a course on the application of linguistics to the study of literature. This was when I began to tie up some of the loose ends that had remained in my doctoral research. I elaborated on the elements of a stratal theory which would have the power to furnish the resources for the analysis of a literature text, as well as to link the text to the social context so as to show the part cultural history plays in the creation and reception of verbal art. Everything I did by way of linguistics pushed me more and more to the recognition of the centrality of meaning and social context – it has seemed to me that language is important to us only because it is a resource for meaning. If Michael's focus – if I may put it this way – has always been *look at grammar, think grammatically*, my impulse has been to ask *what is the meaning and how did this meaning manifest itself to me?*. So, to me, the entry into any situation is by attending to its meaning. To my mind, this does not exclude wording: it is just a different way of getting to the semiotic power of language. There is no competition between meaning and wording, no reason to privilege one or the other: they are two sides of the same coin; you simply do not have to treat both sides as if in every respect they were identical.

4 Sociological Research Unit

I joined Basil Bernstein's SRU in 1968. By that time, I had become more consciously aware of some of these ideas, although I don't suppose I could have sat down and written it all up or given a lecture on it in any coherent kind of way, but I knew I had to move in that direction. This is what would allow me to explore the role of meaning in human life.

My research task at Basil Bernstein's unit was to do an analysis of children's stories. These stories were told by children in response to a particular instruction. The children were shown four toys: a sailor, a boy, a girl and a dog and also a teddy bear. They were told: *this teddy bear wants to go to sleep. Tell him a story, about this sailor, this boy, this girl and their dog*. The children were differentiated by social class and gender. What the children said in response to the instruction represented a whole range of different text types including even a nursery rhyme or two or a quasi-travelogue but they were all being referred to as 'story'. This did not seem quite right to me: if you say to someone 'tell me a story', but they say something quite different instead, would you still take it as a story? What exactly is a story? How do I know that something is a children's bedtime story? And this is where my interest in the linguistic identity of nursery tales began. So at this initial stage, I was beginning to formulate my ideas about the structure of children's stories. The data had to be analysed from two perspectives, firstly from the perspective of structure: what is the structure of the story, and secondly from the perspective of connectivities in the text – what was soon to be called *texture*. The categories of the latter were already clearer to me because of the earlier work on cohesion which had explored the entire range of grammatical cohesion except the cohesive conjunctive, and lexical ties. So the actual analysis began there, and at that point something very interesting happened: as I analysed the text for connectivity in terms of cohesive ties, I found that two of the stories might have exactly the same number of cohesive ties, but the degree of coherence might not be the same. So then, the question arose: how far does cohesion go towards the creation of coherence in a text? My investigation revolved around two problems: how to recognize a bedtime story and how to account for variation in coherence. The analysis of cohesion formed the basis for the latter; the analysis of nursery tales' generic structure potential (GSP) answered the former question.

I did complete all of the assigned work on children's stories, but regretfully I never published it as a research report in book form for two reasons. First, at this stage, around 1971, we became peripatetic. I had a small child (the 'Nigel' of *Learning How to Mean*) and, moving from country to country with him, it became very difficult to continue academic work, especially when it came to writing up the research on coherence and on the nature of children's stories. I was unwilling to give our child to just anybody to look after, so most of the time I looked after him. My contact with the academic community was pretty close to absent, and I found it difficult to write without such contact. Still I did persist, and I wrote at least three reasonable length chapters, but as I wrote, it became obvious to me that what I was writing could not be just one book, it would need to be at least two volumes. The main reason was that a lot of the criticism of Bernstein's work had been that no data was provided, and no samples of actual analysis. So I was insisting that *all* of the data that I was analysing must be included, all of the analyses must be there to see, and then my discussion of that analysis as well as the theory that lies behind that discussion must be produced. It stood to reason that all this could not be done in one volume. Routledge, with whom I had signed the contract, said they would either do one, or none. So I said: OK, we will do none.

Of the three chapters that I had written, one was called 'On measuring a text'. At that point, (early 1970s) corpora were just beginning to be compiled. It was quite fashionable to talk about a 10 million word corpus, or a 20 million word corpus, and I had problems with that. I thought if one is trying to measure the extent of a corpus, or the length of a text such as a story, then words would not provide any sort of significant measure. Discourse is not a collection of words; what you need as its measure is some kind of meaningful unit such as, for instance, *message*, that makes sense to people as a unit of interaction, and, thinking about how a message is construed, you would take a ranking clause as a measuring unit. So I set about to show clause recognition criteria, which is what I used for measuring children's stories. The second chapter was called 'cohesive categories' and the third, 'The structure of children's stories', although this last one was less developed than the first two – it was mostly a set of notes on each of the elements and the possibilities of their ordering, etc. I was describing a range of structural configurations all relatable to what I was calling 'structure potential' or 'general structure'; any configuration derived from this general/potential structure acted as a recognition criterion for the register known as 'bedtime story'.

These chapters, particularly the first two, were circulated in mimeographed forms among colleagues and students. Whether they influenced any readers or not, their content was in the air, with ideas about cohesive harmony, overt-covert conjunction, text structure as an indicator of text type. And later, they became part of such publications as 'Coherence and cohesive harmony' (Hasan 1984a), 'The nursery tale as a genre' (Hasan 1984b) and 'Text in the systemic-functional model' (Hasan 1978). For me, this last was more like taking up where I had left off with the stories, but connecting the notion of generic structure potential to context, because the problem that the stories gave rise to was: OK, here are the elements of the structure of a story, but none of the elements has any very direct relation with the context in which the stories are produced or received. So what is the difference between a story and a text produced by way of a buying-selling interaction or a job interview, and so on? These were some of the spin-offs from my job at the SRU, and they linked up with aspects of my doctoral research.

5 Australia

I had left Bernstein's Unit in early 1971. Let me skip the period (though it was academically varied and stimulating first at Northwestern in Illinois and then at the University of Essex) up to the end of 1975, when I came to Australia. Almost immediately, Arthur Delbridge, Head of Linguistics at Macquarie University, appointed me as lecturer. It was the most stable period of my academic life and I loved it. My teaching covered not only what some might call 'pure' linguistics but also 'applied linguistics'. And in all these years of teaching I was always grateful to have had the terrific formative years in Edinburgh and in London. For lack of space I will just draw attention to some areas which turned out to be very productive in terms of new connections for SFL-based study of language. The first of these was the course I taught on Text Linguistics/Discourse Analysis. I was already working on my theory of generic structure potential, and its relation to context of situation. 'Text in the systemic-functional model' was written that year. A contribution to this aspect of discourse analysis was made by Eija Ventola, who did her MA dissertation on the structure of casual conversation. Two years later she enrolled for a Ph.D. with me; she was planning to work on what she called service encounters. Unfortunately, Macquarie did not have a postgraduate scholarship scheme then; so we lost her to Sydney University where she worked on the structure of text with Jim Martin. So there was some cross-fertilization of ideas there between my approach and Martin's work on genre. Certainly, there are some important differences between the two approaches; nonetheless, there is also a good deal in common. Anyway, from this point on, the genre analysis took off under Jim's guidance, and everyone is familiar with its great contribution to educational linguistics first in Australia and then internationally. The second important development arising directly from that course was the application of cohesion and my cohesive harmony concept to the analysis of acquired language disorders. Here the work of Elizabeth Armstrong, Lynn Mortensen, Alison Ferguson and a group of young speech pathologists has made remarkable use of SFL; their work is internationally recognized in the field, even though the language disorder scene is dominated by a psycholinguistic approach with a sixties flavour.

One of the 'service courses', i.e. tailored to the needs of a specific group, was 'Language and the child', which formed part of teacher education programme. Its inspiration came from *Learning How to Mean* and from the work of the project at UCL, including the Bernsteinian angle on education and daily life. It always irked me that Bernstein kept being misread even by respected scholars such as Labov. Teaching sociolinguistics further strengthened this impression. So I geared up to do empirical research in the linguistic aspects of coding orientation. With Macquarie University research funding I began a pilot project in 1981 on 'The role of everyday talk between mothers and children in establishing ways of learning'. Helen Fraser, one of our Honours students, worked on it. Four case studies were conducted on the basis of naturally occurring talk between mothers and children – two mother-child dyads were from the working class and two from the middle class. The idea was to do a semantic analysis of the talk to examine whether there existed any indication of coding orientation. Now, I had also been teaching semantics (with Yon Maley) and Yon used to teach the speech act theory. I read Austin with great interest, Searle with a little less, and began to wonder how one might approach the description of messages in terms of SFL. In 'Language and the child', students often conducted a mini-research, collecting some data of children's natural interaction and attempting its analysis. Halliday (1984) gave a little lead into how one might go about the paradigmatic description of messages at the semantic level. I developed this a little more for the analysis that Helen Fraser was about to begin. The difficulties Helen had in using that network to analyse the data were the starting point for further work for the description.

I got federally funded to begin a research project in 1983 in the area of my pilot project; in fact the two had more or less the same descriptive name. The early semantic network used by Helen became the basis for a much more developed semantic network. The context of discourse for my data was predetermined in two respects: the interactants were to be mothers and their preschool children (3;6–4;0 yrs old) and the mode was spoken, dialogic; however, the field was not predetermined (for further details Hasan and Cloran 1990; Hasan 1989; Hasan in press; Cloran 1994; Williams 1995). I therefore could not use a context-specific semantic network; besides the research on semantic networks I had been doing for my semantics lectures had already made me think that we need to follow the lead of lexicogrammar. In doing SFG, we do not make context-specific system networks of transitivity, tense, mood or whatever; our aim is to describe the language's entire potential, not just the potential specific to a particular text type. I saw no reason why systemic analysis should not follow the same principle at the semantic level. With the experience of the pilot data, and keeping in mind the meta-functional nature of language, I set out to represent my view of the systemic options in meaning available to an English speaker at the message rank (realized typically as a ranking clause) up to a certain degree of delicacy. Thus, the semantic systems in the network are not context-specific but metafunctionally responsible (Hasan 1996; Hasan *et al* in press). For each option in the system network, I went on to specify the range of grammatical patterns which are capable of realizing it. The network implicates three strata: the contextual, the semantic and the lexicogrammatical: the three are related by the dialectic of realization. The system network is thus capable of analysing both the contextual activation of meaning selection and the semantic activation of lexicogrammatical selections; just as it is capable of analysing how semantic options are construed lexicogrammatically and how contextual phenomena are construed semantically. There is no claim that this semantic network is either complete or infallible, but then linguistic descriptions never can be. I see my semantic network as a development (not a replication) of Halliday's early 1970s' work; it is simply a contribution to Halliday's theory for the description of discourse at a level above the level of grammar.

From 1983 to 1987 this group of related projects was funded federally. I had an excellent helper in Carmel Cloran, whom I believe I first met in my 'Language and the child' course. She stayed with the project throughout its duration, and made a substantial contribution to its success. The first project of the group made a comparison of habitual ways of meaning in correlation with social class and gender provenance of the speakers; statistically robust evidence was found for postulating semantic variation as one kind of variation in language, which correlated with the social positioning of speakers. For the first time, the analysis of large-scale natural language data foregrounded the linguistic criteria for Bernstein's coding orientation.

In the second phase, we followed the children into their first year at school and compared the semantic style of mothers and teachers: again the results supported Bernstein's claim that pedagogic discourse and middle class discourse of socialization share a good deal in their coding orientation. A small number of the subject children were also recorded in peer group interaction and in simulated pedagogic contexts. The final research in this group was called 'The formation of person impression on the basis of everyday talk'. The results of this project, though highly suggestive, have so far not been published, though I have presented them at international conferences.

Carmel then embarked on a Ph.D. with me and she luckily chose to work at the level of semantic description. So far I had imagined only three ranks at the semantic level: text, message and message component. Carmel postulated the concept of 'rhetorical unit' intermediate between text and message: a text consists of one or more rhetorical units, and each of the latter consists of one or more messages. She offered semantic classification of rhetorical units and provided their lexicogrammatical criteria: using this classification, a text may be analysed in terms of its constituent parts, such as generalization, explanation, commentary, and so on. She made use of this unit to show substantial variation across social classes in the framing of discourse: middle class mothers maintained weaker boundaries between semiotic activities as opposed to the working class mothers who kept 'things apart' – another marker of coding orientation (see Cloran 1994).

Almost concurrently, Geoff Williams worked for his doctoral dissertation (Williams 1995). He extended that part of my semantic network which concerned 'question-response' systems so as to meet the needs of his specific context, and conducted analysis of substantial data. The results of his investigation also strongly supported Bernstein's code theory. Are these findings relevant to education experts? Yes, without doubt. Have they made any substantial impact on educational practices? Speaking honestly, no! The reasons are interestingly thought-provoking but too complex to be discussed on this occasion (for some detail, see Hasan, in press).

My interest in the relationship of linguistics and literature was kept alive by David Butt who was the first Ph.D. candidate I supervised at Macquarie University. Thanks to his efforts, there is now a flourishing course on Linguistic Stylistics for the postgraduate level.

References

Bloomfield, L. (1933), *Language*. New York: Holt, Rinehart and Winston.

Cloran, C. (1994), *Rhetorical Units and Decontextualisation: an Enquiry into some Relations of Context, Meaning and Grammar* (Monographs in Systemic Linguistics 6). Nottingham: Nottingham University.

Doughty, P., Pearce, J. and Thornton, G. (1971), *Language in Use*. London: Edward Arnold.

Forsyth, I. and Wood, K. (1977), *Language and Communication* (books 1 and 2). London: Longman.

Halliday, M. A. K. (1973), *Explorations in the Functions of Language*. London: Edward Arnold.

— (1975), *Learning How to Mean: Explorations in the Development of Language*. London: Edward Arnold.

— (1984), 'Language as code and language as behaviour: A systemic-functional interpretation of the nature and ontogenesis of dialogue', in R. P. Fawcett, M. A. K. Halliday, S. M. Lamb, and A. Makkai (eds), *The semiotics of culture and language, Vol. 1: Language as social semiotic*. London: Pinter, pp. 3–35.

— (1985), *An Introduction to Functional Grammar*, London: Edward Arnold.

Halliday, M. A. K. and Hasan, R. (1976), *Cohesion in English*. London: Longman.

Hasan, R. (1978), 'Text in the systemic-functional model', in W. Dressler (ed.), *Current Trends in Textlinguistics*. Berlin/ New York: Walter de Gruyter, pp. 228–46.

— (1984a), 'Coherence and cohesive harmony', in J. Flood (ed.), *Understanding Reading Comprehension*. Newark: IRA, pp. 181–219.

— (1984b), 'The nursery tale as a genre'. *Nottingham Linguistics Circular*, 13, 71–102.

— (1989), 'Semantic variation and sociolinguistics', *Australian Journal of Linguistics*, 9, (2), 221–276.

— (1996), 'Semantic networks: A tool for analysing meaning', in C. Cloran, D. Butt and G. Williams (eds), *Ways of Saying: Ways of Meaning: Selected Papers of Ruqaiya Hasan*. London: Cassell.

— (in press), *The Collected Works of Ruqaiya Hasan, Volume 2: Semantic Variation: Meaning in Society*, (ed. J. Webster). London: Equinox.

Hasan, R. and Cloran, C. (1990), 'A sociolinguistic study of everyday talk between mothers and children', in M. A. K. Halliday, J. Gibbons and H. Nicholas (eds), *Learning, Keeping, and Using Language, Vol.1*. Amsterdam and Philadelphia: Benjamins, pp. 67–100.

Hasan, R. and Lushington, S. (1968), *The Subject Matter of English*. London: Longman.

Hasan, R., Cloran, C., Williams, G. and Lukin, A. (in press), 'Semantic networks: The description of meaning in SFL', in R. Hasan, C. Matthiessen and J. Webster (eds), *Continuing Discourse in Language*, Volume 2. London: Equinox.

Kachru, B. (1986), *The Alchemy of English: The Spread, Functions and Models of Non-Native Englishes*. Oxford: Pergamon.

MacKay, D., Thompson, B. and Schaub, P. (1970), *Breakthrough to Literacy*. London: Longman.

Nesfield, J. R. (1961), *English Grammar, Past and Present*. London: Macmillan.

Weir, R. (1962), *Language in the Crib*. The Hague: Mouton.

Williams, G. (1995), *Joint Book Reading and Literacy Pedagogy: a Socio-semantic Examination*. Ph.D. thesis, Macquarie University, Sydney, Australia.

2 Literacy teaching and current debates over reading

Frances Christie

1 Introduction[1]

Never a week passes without the word 'literacy' being visibly displayed in the community, or being discussed on radio or television. 'Literacy' features regularly in the daily press, often in association with editorials about declining standards, particularly of reading. In educational directorates throughout the English-speaking world literacy now looms prominently in statements of curricula, while governments devote significant resources to various testing regimes intended to monitor and report on students' progress in control of literacy. A veritable flood of books and scholarly journals devoted to literacy appeared over the last 20 years of the twentieth century. Furthermore, over the same period of time, many university schools of education created chairs and/or departments with titles such as 'Language and Literacy Education' or 'English and Literacies Education'. Overall, by the end of last century, literacy education had emerged as a significant theme in educational theory, research and debate. It remains significant in the early twenty-first century.

The concern for literacy and its teaching – to which systemic functional linguistic (SFL) theory has made a major contribution – is a significant development. However, I shall suggest that it is best understood against a background knowledge of the emergence of the wider notion of language education and its purposes. Where the programme in language education is adequately conceived, it embraces teaching and learning *language*, and teaching and learning *about* language, spoken and written. Its concerns will be both for the meanings constructed and negotiated in language, and for the language structures in which such meanings are expressed. This dual concern involves holding a robust theory of the nature of the language system and its purposes, and an equally robust commitment to a pedagogy that makes a knowledge of this system explicitly available to learners. When the language programme fails to have at its heart such theories of language and of language pedagogy, it is often accompanied by a loss of knowledge of the language system, its purpose and its structures. As a case in point, in the contemporary world, literacy is often foregrounded at the expense of a wider view of language and the language programme. The result is that teachers often lack a comprehensive sense of language, its meanings and its structures and they tend to fall back on some rather tired formulas for teaching a range of 'language skills', such as 'phonics'.

Nowhere is this tendency more marked than in much contemporary discussion about the teaching of reading. Indeed, at the time of writing this chapter, the interested reader could be forgiven for feeling a strong sense of déjà vu when examining the debates about reading and its teaching that had resurfaced in the UK and Australia, as well as other parts of the English-speaking world. Inquiries into the teaching of literacy – but essentially of reading – had been instituted in both the UK (e.g. Johnston and Watson 2005) and Australia (Rowe *et al* 2005). Once again, the battle lines have been drawn as proponents of 'whole language' and of 'phonics' take to the fray, heedless of the fact that there is nothing particularly new about the issues as they characterize them. Indeed, the arguments have all been heard before, though frequently in different guises. Despite some real gains over the last half century, language education is still often beset by debates over 'form and function', 'process and product', 'phonics and whole language' and, more recently, over 'autonomous' and 'ideological' models of literacy (e.g. Street 1997). Such dichotomies create false distinctions, unhelpful to pedagogic practices, but also misguided in their understanding of the language system. They are, in fact, part of the same general problem that has been addressed by Halliday (for a recent discussion see Hasan 2005) in considering *process* and *system* in language. The two are manifestations of the same phenomenon of language, though viewed from different perspectives: they are not to be understood as different phenomena, as Saussure's famous distinction between *langue* and *parole* implied. Similarly, for the purposes of language pedagogy, we necessarily teach both 'form and function', or 'process and product'. Hence, in teaching reading, we also necessarily teach both the spelling system involved in creating written texts (an aspect of which is the 'phonics' approach) and the meanings constructed in the texts (an aspect of the 'whole language' approach).

It is a matter of some urgency to affirm the values of a functionally based theory of language to inform and underpin the language education programme, including the teaching of literacy. Much promising work was done in the latter half of the twentieth century in building a useful model of language education. It is time to reaffirm its values as we move on into the twenty-first century, and to clarify, among other matters, what constitutes an adequate functionally based programme for teaching reading.

As a point of departure for undertaking such an enterprise, I shall begin by outlining something of the major developments that led to a theory of language education, while also pointing to some of the problems that emerged in at least some formulations of this theory. The term 'language education' is in fact a relatively recent one, dating from the second half of the twentieth century. It is a very useful one, breaking away from older models of talking about teaching which focused on various 'language skills', normally conceived and taught as relatively discrete activities. Language education has the merit that, in principle at least, it focuses on the nature of language itself as a major resource in living and in learning.

2 The emergence of 'language education' as a theme in curriculum theory and research

Language education had its origins in the 1960s, though the term itself came into use a little later. That was the period in which linguists as various as Chomsky (e.g. 1957) and Halliday (e.g. Halliday *et al* 1964) were achieving recognition for their work, though developing very different models both of language and of linguistics as a study. The decades of the 1960s and 1970s saw a great deal of research into language development in young children (sometimes termed 'language acquisition'), much of it building on the model of Chomsky (e.g. Braine 1971; Menyuk 1971), though he claimed no educational relevance for his work (Chomsky 1981). The dominant paradigms from the USA in the tradition of Chomsky assumed a model of language and its learning in 'innatist', rather than 'environmentalist' terms, and their tendency was to examine control of syntactic structures at the expense of interest in meanings and functions. Halliday (1975) was one of those who early challenged such innatist views, developing a model that stressed the learning of language as a social phenomenon, undertaken very much in interaction. This was a theme that both Painter (1999) and Torr (1997) were to develop and explore more fully later on. Other researchers from the USA such as Bloom (1970), who was a doctoral student of Labov, developed models of language development that paid greater attention to functions as well as structure in learning language. Yet other American researchers in the tradition of Hymes (e.g. Hymes 1972) adopted more socially

motivated models of language than did Chomsky, asserting an interest
in what Hymes called 'communicative competence', a term that
suggested the importance of learning more than the 'rules' of language
structure.

While all the linguists briefly alluded to contributed to the
emergence of a theory of language education, there were others –
many of them very suspicious of what linguists had to offer – who also
contributed. These included a cluster of English specialists interested
in the study of the role of language in personal development and
learning, some of whom gathered at the Institute of Education at the
University of London in the 1970s. They included, for example,
Britton (1970) Barnes (e.g. Barnes *et al* 1969), Rosen and Rosen
(1973), and Dixon (1967). The title of Dixon's book, *Growth through
English*, captured something of the preoccupations with language and
learning that emerged in the late 1960s and well into the 1970s. Those
who adopted what were sometimes referred to as 'growth models of
language' were, on the whole, more concerned with notions of personal
growth and learning *through* language than they were with the nature
of the language system itself, or with notions of learning *about*
language. Some indeed (e.g. Barnes 1978) seriously questioned the
relevance of linguistics to the study of language in children's learning.
In fact, while Barnes often had interesting things to say of children
learning *through* language, especially in small groups (e.g. Barnes 1976;
Barnes and Todd 1977) he had little to say of learning *about* language.
In this he was like many other language education theorists who
emerged in the 1970s and early 1980s.

Other language education theorists, including those who worked
with Halliday in the *Nuffield/Schools Council Programme in Linguistics and
English Teaching* (1964–71), clearly did work with a different model of
language and learning (see Chapter 1 this volume and discussions in
Hasan and Martin 1989 and Christie and Unsworth 2005). Indeed,
the model of language development proposed by Halliday was one
that stated that language development involved learning language,
learning through language and learning about language. Learning
language and learning *through* language involved learning the
language system and learning through that about aspects of one's
world. Learning *about* language involved learning about the resource of
language itself, its spelling and handwriting systems, its phonology, its
grammar and its registers. The various curriculum materials that
emerged from the project were very influential in the UK and in other
parts of the English-speaking world, and some, such as *Breakthrough to
Literacy*, are still in use in some parts of the world today.

Nonetheless, among many English teachers and theorists about language education there always was a strong resistance to talk of teaching knowledge about language (see discussions with respect to Australia in Christie 2003 and 2004a). A model of language education had emerged which foregrounded matters to do with growth through language and, for the purposes of pedagogy, its effect was to marginalize considerations of teaching knowledge *about* language ('KAL', to use the term later introduced by Carter 1990). Such a model of language education was matched, and indeed partly stimulated by, various progressivist and/or constructivist trends in curriculum and educational theory that became influential from the 1970s on (Christie 2004b, 2004c; Muller 2001), and that were often destructive because of their failure to address issues of the knowledge that should be taught in schools, including KAL.

So general and pervasive would the progressivist or growth model of language education become by the 1980s, that it led to a concern to establish appropriate pedagogic models of English language, in order to redress what was seen as a significant decline in understandings of the KAL that should be taught. In England, this caused the government to set up the Kingman Committee ('The Kingman Report' 1988), charged with developing a model of the English language for teaching purposes. Its work led in turn to that of the Cox Working Group ('Cox National Curriculum English Working Group' 1989), and finally, out of the often heated debates provoked by the work of the Kingman and Cox groups, there emerged the 'National English Curriculum' (1995). (See Chapter 7 for more on this topic.) A similar concern to establish a stronger statement about the nature of the English language programme would lead in Australia to the adoption of *English: A Statement for Australian Schools* (1994).

By the 1970s and early 1980s, the commitment to policies of language education led to curriculum statements about the values of teaching 'listening, speaking, reading and writing', where these were variously described as 'language skills' or 'language modes'. A review of all the English language curriculum documents throughout Australia in 1977 (Christie and Rothery 1979), for example, revealed that all states identified listening, speaking, reading and writing as important skills, development of facility in each of which was held central to the language education programme. Processes in learning language were thus clearly deemed important, though what constituted the KAL to be taught was not very visibly displayed. In fact, talk of the need to structure and sequence programmes devoted to teaching and learning such knowledge was often resisted. Where KAL was taught, it was often suggested, this should be as part of some other activity, such as discussing some issue, examining a piece of literature, exploring ideas or themes, and so on. Of course, it is possible – and indeed desirable – to look for opportunity to develop the teaching of KAL as a consequence of engagement with other activities. However, such a policy constitutes an insufficient basis for the development of a full language programme. That is because, for the purposes of school learning, the nature of the language system itself cannot be understood without an overt and principled focus on language itself. What aspects of the language system – its spelling, its grammar, its vocabulary, for example – are the focus will necessarily change, depending on the pedagogic purposes involved. These matters are discussed at some length in Christie (2004a), with special reference to the teaching of grammar. Such matters are also relevant for the teaching of reading, and for the claims that have been made from time to time for learning to read by means of approaches which focus on the meanings constructed in texts at the expense of much interest in the structures in which they are expressed. This is typical of many 'whole language' approaches to literacy and its teaching.

3 'Literacy' as a theme in language education

The word 'literacy' is relatively recent, though the word 'literate' is considerably older. A literate person was originally one of letters, and according to the Oxford Dictionary the word 'literate' dates from the fifteenth century. However, the Oxford also states that the noun 'literacy' dates from the late nineteenth century and, while it clearly was in use in the twentieth century, it does not seem to have been widely used in much educational discussion and curriculum design. Barton (1994: 22–3) who investigated the matter in the early 1990s, estimated that 'prior to 1980 hardly any books had literacy in the title' and he went on to say that the number rapidly increased after that. The decision of Halliday and his colleagues to name one of the more successful of their programmes *Breakthrough to Literacy* was in these circumstances the more interesting. Originally named the 'Initial Literacy Project', set up in 1965, the new title was adopted to capture the sense of young children 'breaking through' into the world of written language (Mackay *et al* 1989: 333–48). As for the use of the word 'literacy', Halliday has advised (personal communication) that he had in mind problems talked of during the war regarding the often limited literacy capacities of members of the armed forces and the consequent concern to improve literacy levels. Certainly, it is clear that in the aftermath of the war the international community was interested to improve literacy in both developed and developing countries. In the 1960s the newly formed UNESCO organized regional meetings of ministers of education, all of them concerned among other matters to address problems of widespread 'illiteracy' in many parts of the world (Tanguiane 1990: 9). Such deliberations would lead eventually to the adoption in 1985 of a plan to hold an International Literacy Year, an event that occurred in 1990. Overall, though the word 'literacy' thus featured widely in many contexts after the 1960s, it seems not to have been in wide use in English language curriculum statements until the late 1980s and early 1990s, nor did it feature as a term in most language education research. From the early 1990s on, 'literacy' became increasingly widely used. Australia adopted a Government White Paper, *Australia's Language. The Australian Language and Literacy Policy* (1991), which was later superseded by *Literacy for all, the Challenge for Australian Schools* (1998). *The National Languages Institute of Australia*, originally set up in 1990, became known in 1992 as the *National Languages and Literacy Institute* (which was closed down in 2004). Henceforth literacy was referred to more frequently in all state English curriculum documents (Christie 2003). In England, the 1990s saw the introduction of the *National Literacy Strategy: Framework for Teaching Objectives*, though this and the associated Numeracy Strategy have in more recent years been combined into the one strategy, referred to as the *Primary National Strategy*.

There are at least two benefits in use of the word 'literacy', rather than simply 'reading and writing', as Halliday and his colleagues no doubt acknowledged. One of these is that the term recognizes the essentially related nature of the two activities of reading and writing, and it carries the important pedagogic implication that the two should be taught as intimately related, breaking what had been some time-honoured practices of teaching the two as separate activities. The other, related benefit was that the term 'literacy' drew attention to the fact that the written language is different from that of speech; what is at issue in learning to be literate, then, is learning to master the written code. Mackay *et al* (1989: 337) wrote of their endeavours in developing *Breakthrough to Literacy*, 'Our most immediate task was to invent materials that would place learners in continuous control of the written language they were producing in becoming readers and writers'. A programme with very similar aims was to be developed in Australia under the title the *Mt Gravatt Developmental Language Reading Program*, led by Hart and Walker (see Hart *et al* 1977, Walker *et al* 1985). Both programmes sought to engage young readers in working with meanings and with the language structures in which these were expressed. Both programmes sought to have children move frequently from reading to writing and vice versa, so that they built a strong sense of the interrelatedness of the two modes. Neither programme espoused the time-honoured earlier models of teaching and learning reading by means of teaching discrete 'language skills'. Instead, both programmes were functionally based, working with a strong sense of purpose and context in using language, creating opportunity for children to learn through language and to learn about it.

The two programmes were successful and, as already noted, *Breakthrough to Literacy* is still in use in some parts of the world, while the work of the *Mt Gravatt Reading Program* has had a significant impact in a number of ways. Gray (e.g. 1980, 1985), who was a member of the original Mt Gravatt team, went on to develop early literacy programmes with young Aboriginal children in Alice Springs, using some of the principles he had learned in the earlier reading programme. He adopted a term he took from Cazden (1977): a *Concentrated Language Encounter* (CLE). A CLE approach offers a carefully planned sequence of language learning activities which provide children with opportunities to learn language, learn through it and learn about it in meaningful and structured ways. Such structured ways involve deliberate and overt instruction in patterns of spelling, as well as systematic building of knowledge about the overall structure and unity of the text, be that read or written. The activity involves a steady building of a shared experience, so that shared understandings of the text and of the reading process are created.

Walker, also one of the original Mt Gravatt team, used the notion of a CLE with colleagues to develop literacy programmes, initially for Thailand and later for other developing countries (Walker *et al* 1992; Rattanavich and Christie 1993; Rattanavich and Walker 1996). They acknowledged a significant intellectual debt to Gray (Walker *et al* 1992: vii).[2]

Gray (e.g. 1990, in prep.; Gray and Cowey 1997; Rose *et al* 1999) has continued to develop and expand his programmes for Indigenous education in Australia, and he can claim significant success in improved reading performances using standardized tests (Gray *et al* 2003a, 2003b). Rose (e.g. Martin and Rose 2005, also Martin, this volume) is also pursuing similar pedagogic principles in programmes for teaching reading and writing for academic purposes to Indigenous students, particularly at secondary and tertiary levels, where the need to handle grammatical metaphor, among other matters, becomes an issue. Despite the undoubted gains made in development of reading programmes of the kind briefly discussed, arguments continue about the most desirable pedagogies to use in teaching reading.

4 Rival models of teaching reading

Arguments about alternative models of teaching reading are at their liveliest in programme development for the earliest years, for these are the years in which the initial 'breakthrough' into the written code should ideally occur. It is in these years, as a necessary part of learning to read, that an understanding of aspects of the English spelling system needs to be established. Much of the argument is in fact about how best to facilitate a mastery of English orthography, a matter to which I shall return below. It needs to be noted, however, that it does somewhat oversimplify matters to see development of control of reading as uniquely a responsibility of the first years of schooling. This is because, for reasons now well researched in the SFL tradition, we can say with some confidence that control of the grammar of writing is a development of late childhood to adolescence, with the emergence of control of grammatical metaphor (Halliday 1993; Derewianka 2003; Painter *et al* 2005; Aidman 1999; Christie 2002a). Hence, though for the purposes of teaching reading a great deal of important work must go in the early years to mastering the spelling and writing systems, it is also clear that children are embarked on a considerable developmental journey in learning the grammar of written language; this journey will last well beyond the primary years and into secondary schooling. It is very easy to slip into the habit of seeing learning to read as about some essential skills in recognition and use of the spelling and writing systems, so that these skills, once mastered, are then recycled for the rest of the child's life in a reasonably unproblematic way. This does not do justice to the considerable demands of processing and using written language as students grow older and need to handle the written texts both of secondary education and of adult life.

A really adequate model of teaching reading will recognize that reading is about more than spelling, for it involves a comprehensive sense of the language system and its teaching. Unsworth (2001: 14–16) for example, reviews several models of literacy (Macken-Horarik 1996; Hasan 1996; Freebody and Luke 1990; Green 1988), all of them acknowledging what he terms *recognition literacy*, *reproduction literacy* and *reflection literacy*. The first of these refers to ability to recognize the resources in which meaning is constructed in written texts: the spelling and writing systems, as well as sentence and text organization. *Reproduction literacy* refers to ability to deploy and reproduce these resources in socially relevant ways. *Reflection literacy* refers to ability to reflect upon the practices by which written texts are produced, and ability to critique these where necessary. Capacity in the latter 'presupposes reproduction literacy, which presupposes recognition literacy' (Unsworth 2001: 15). Models of teaching reading for the most part have not been cast in the latter terms, because most have been preoccupied with some aspects only of what we have termed *recognition literacy*.

Historically, there have been at least three models for the teaching of reading.[3] The alphabetic is the oldest, dating from the Greeks, and it involved learning to recognize and name the various letters. The 'look and say' method involved showing children written words – often, though not always in a simple phrase – and asking the children to recognize them, after which they were later encouraged to identify the letters that constituted the words. The 'phonic' method involved learning the letters primarily by identifying the sounds or the phonemes with which they were associated, and such programmes tended to group letters by sounds. All these methods evolved very early and arguments in favour of them were variously proposed (Davies 1973). However, the arguments assumed a particular significance from the nineteenth century on, for this was the period in which teacher training was formally instituted, originally in systems such as the early monitorial schools in England, and later in the first teacher training institutions. Joshua Fitch, one of Her Majesty's Inspectors of Training Colleges, gave a series of lectures (1880) on teaching, in which he identified the three models of reading, and suggested that none of the three was adequate. The most satisfactory way to teach reading he suggested, involved a blending of all them. Into the twentieth century, long after the disappearance of figures such as Fitch, these arguments still appeared, though they have been expressed differently. The 'look and say' method evolved over time as an aspect of the 'whole language' approach, while the 'phonic' method came to involve some amalgam of what were originally the alphabetic and 'phonic' methods. Among contemporary discussions there is some argument over 'analytic' and 'synthetic' phonic methods, discussed by Brooks (2003).

Above I noted that many of the arguments over approaches to the teaching of reading are really about approaches to the teaching of English orthography. The English spelling system is quite complex for at least two reasons (Mountford 1998; Seymour *et al* 2003 cited by Brooks 2003: 7). The first is that English syllable structures are complex. The second reason is that the orthographic system is not as regular as many 'phonic' approaches would suggest: that is to say, the sounds associated with letter patterns vary, depending on their disposition in the spelling of different words (e.g. compare 'cough' and 'through', and also 'threw' and 'blue'). The phonological structure of English is such that when we speak, we create a melodic unit or 'line', which may in turn be understood to create a regular beat or 'foot'; each foot in turn is made up of a number of syllables. Each syllable consists of an onset and a rhyme (sometimes also written as a 'rime', Treiman 1994), and these create the consonant and vowel phonemes which our spelling system is intended to represent (Halliday and Matthiessen 2004: 5). In addition, rhythm creates a problem for English spellers, in that the unstressed vowels often found in English feet tend to collapse into a neutral central position (called phonetically the 'schwa'), so that it is hard to hear the 'full' phoneme as it would be realized under stress. One example would be the 'uh' sound in 'the'. This is why shifting the stress around from one form of a word to another may help with learning to spell (e.g. 'supplement/supplementation', 'explanation/explain' or 'derivation/derive').

When we teach spelling, we teach capacity to deploy letters in varying combinations – often 'blends' – to represent the phonemes. There is a significant developmental task for children in learning to spell, and at least one authority (Snowling 1994: 111) has estimated that learning to control what she called the 'basics' of English orthography takes four to five years, while the learning of 'exceptional' spelling is a lifelong task. A comparative study examining children learning to read in 12 European languages (Seymour *et al* 2003 cited in Brooks 2003: 7) has suggested that English-speaking children take considerably longer to learn to read than do speakers of other languages, such as Finnish.

Learning to read, however, as already noted, is about more than learning to spell, crucially important though spelling is. One reason we know this is that we all learn to spell successfully many more words than we are ever formally taught to spell. We learn some important principles for identifying and interpreting features of written language, including its spelling system, with which we become successfully independent readers and writers. Such principles, with respect to spelling, involve achieving control of at least three things: a sense of the phonemes, referred to by reading theorists as 'phonemic awareness'; a sense of the graphemes, referred to by the same theorists as 'graphemic awareness' and some sense of the shape and pattern of lexical items on the page, such that similarities between words such as 'beak' and 'speak' are observed (and of course also heard). The latter is sometimes referred to by reading theorists as 'lexical analogy' (Brown and Ellis

1994). Both auditory and visual memory are called upon, and well planned repetition and practice can bring out and reinforce the patterns involved.

But apart from a knowledge of the spelling system, in learning to read we learn to anticipate and predict the emerging meanings in a written text, interpreting what is said while also shaping what is to come. Thus, in order to develop a sense of this, children need to develop capacity to segment or 'chunk' sequences of written texts into meaningful units as they read, and hence to process information as they go (Perera 1984: 280–306). Capacity to 'chunk' or segment texts is certainly assisted by the production of clear, well presented texts set out on the page, and the display, in early picture books, is significantly assisted by well chosen illustrations that guide the reading process (Williams 1998). Sometimes, of course, such early books involve only pictures. Children and their mentors – be they parents or teachers – can become accustomed to following the sequence of pictures on the page from left to right, developing a sense of given and new information (Kress and van Leeuwen 1996; Unsworth 2001), and engaging in talk around the pictures and any associated verbal text. Capacity to 'chunk' texts into meaningful units will also be fundamentally assisted by the sounds of the teacher's voice, bringing to the act of reading all the benefits of intonation, stress, rhythm and pause, which will establish reading behaviour (Perera 1984: 273) in either young beginning readers, or in those older students and adults who experience difficulties. These prosodic features of the text will help establish familiarity with the field at issue and with its meanings and, at the same time, build a growing sense of the grammatical organization of the written language in which the meanings are made. Development of a sense of the prosodic features of texts as well as of their grammatical organization goes on well beyond the initial years, as the writers of the Bullock Report, *A Language for Life* (1975: 92) recognized when they argued that teachers should go on teaching reading beyond the first years of schooling.

Both Gray and Rose, to whose work I alluded earlier, make considerable use of joint reading, allowing time and opportunity for exploration of the sounds and meanings of words as they are deployed in a text. This facilitates comprehension and it builds confidence to move on into further reading, working with texts that constitute a greater challenge. It is also of course essential to the building of *reproduction* and *reflection literacy*. Joint reading and writing provide opportunity for discussion and critique and for building pleasure in texts and their meanings.

5 A functional model for teaching literacy, including teaching reading

Learning to read, then, like all other aspects of learning language, is a matter of learning *in use* and *in context*. It will involve both *learning language* and *learning through it*. But it must also involve some *learning about language*. This will embrace matters as various as developing a metalanguage for dealing with 'words', 'letters', 'punctuation' and the spelling and writing systems; it will also embrace developing a knowledge of the grammatical organization of written language and the kinds of texts that writing produces. A knowledge of all these matters starts early (Torr and Simpson 2003), though an understanding of the grammatical organization of writing, especially with respect to grammatical metaphor, is relatively slow in developing, lasting into the secondary years of schooling at least (Christie 2002a).

Thus, the concern in a successful literacy programme must be to teach for an understanding of both the patterned systematic ways in which written language is constructed and the meanings that are expressed in the language. The successful programmes referred to earlier – *Breakthrough to Literacy*, the *Mt Gravatt Reading Program* and the *CLE Program* – all have sought to pursue pedagogies that teach reading – including spelling – in use, and with understanding. Gray's most recent work with Indigenous students involves a programme for *Accelerated Literacy Pedagogy* (2005; in prep). Rose's methodology, referred to as *Learning to Read: Reading to Learn*, described at some length by Martin and Rose (2005), has similar aims and strategies. An introductory account, for pre-service education, of a functionally based approach to the teaching of reading is provided in Christie (2005: 86– 107).

All the teaching programmes alluded to are functionally based, and all employ similar fundamental principles. Thus, in Gray's case (1999) in working with young Aboriginal children some years ago, some initial steps involved the teacher in building a shared knowledge of, and interest in, the field for reading. This might be by engaging in some shared activity of the kind that Gray and his colleagues pursued with their students, such as making visits to the local post office, or perhaps cooking in the classroom. A text for reading would be developed around that activity (often written by the teacher in consultation with the children); the teacher would display and read this with the children, stopping for frequent discussion and allowing for frequent repetition in later lessons, each time drawing the students more and more fully into talk of the words and their spelling, as well as their meanings. In similar fashion, Mackay *et al* (1989: 340–1) in developing *Breakthrough to Literacy*, reported a teacher involving young children in writing and reading about the experience of being 'new children' at school; again, there was a frequent movement between reading and writing the words needed for this, so that an understanding of both the spelling and writing systems was established, as well as an understanding of the meanings established in deploying those words. Movements through activities of the kind outlined allow for a great deal of systematic attention being paid to structures and meanings.

While Gray still uses the methods described above initially, he also involves young children in reading with their teachers carefully selected children's texts, chosen for their imaginative and lively use of language (Gray in prep). Australian writers selected for young children include Emily Rodda, while for older Aboriginal students, many of whom have poor literacy even at the secondary level, he selects writers such as Paul Jennings or John Marsden. He absolutely rejects use of conventional sets of readers for early or remedial readers, on the grounds that their language is impoverished and that they offer no pleasure or challenge to children. Extensive reading of well selected reading texts leads into writing of texts by the children on similar fields of experience.

Rose (Rose 2004; Rose *et al* 2004; Martin and Rose 2005) has developed a similar strategy, mainly working with Aboriginal students at secondary and tertiary levels, and developing reading and writing skills for academic work. He draws on reading pedagogy in the style of Gray and his colleagues, and also on genre-based pedagogy as proposed by Rothery and others (e.g. Martin 1999). Using carefully selected reading materials, he develops a detailed *Reading Interaction Cycle*, scaffolding students through several stages as they move with growing confidence in their reading, note-making, revising, joint writing and thence towards independent writing and reading. Among other matters, such a process serves to 'unpack' examples of grammatical metaphor which often create the dense and complex features of academic writing.

What is central to all the reading programmes outlined is a commitment to working with students' well established understandings of the language system, and moving through a series of pedagogically structured phases to the building of increased knowledge about *what is written and how it is written*. Hence, the teacher and students start with the field involved and with establishing some shared understanding of the language used to build that field. Depending upon the background of the students and their prior experience, this phase may last for some time and be revisited more than once to build confidence and understanding. Reading of the text commences only when some shared sense of what is to be read and what it is about has been established, and the teacher's guidance, as well as the use of his or her voice in facilitating this step, will be crucially important. The reading will stop at selected points for talk about the meanings and the words in which they are expressed, including discussing their spelling and the features of the punctuation that facilitate the reading, assisting the 'chunking' of the text. The teacher will invite the students to participate in joint reading, guiding the students over time towards enhanced capacity to read individually. All these activities constitute aspects of *learning language* and *learning through language*, and they lead into a further phase, involving *learning about language*. Here, detailed work is done on matters as various as the spelling system, the grammatical organization, the clause and sentence structures, as well as the text types involved. The teaching of such KAL will be planned, deliberate and explicit, and such KAL will be revisited where necessary. Both reading and writing skills are invoked and developed at different stages in the resulting curriculum cycle, so that while it is literacy capacity that is at issue overall, reading or writing (and indeed speaking and listening too) will be the focus of the activity at different points in the cycle. Cycling through language learning in this way will lead to a process of logogenesis (Halliday and Matthiessen 2004) – one we can term *curriculum logogenesis* (Christie 2002b). Evidence for such logogenesis will be apparent in the enhanced *recognition* and *reflection literacy* in the students.

To return then, to the issues with which I started this chapter, 'language education' as a term emerged in the latter years of the twentieth century, ushering in a new stage in language teaching curriculum theory, and bringing with it the benefits of a commitment to the education of language capacities as a necessary aspect of the processes of schooling. 'Literacy' as a theme emerged from the concerns for language education, and this too was a desirable development, bringing with it an important recognition of the essential interrelatedness of reading and writing. The teaching of reading is indeed a very important aspect of the overall language programme, and it will be taught most effectively where its relationship to other aspects of the programme is foregrounded. Debates over the rival claims of alternative models of the teaching of reading can, and should, be finally put to rest.

Notes

1. I am grateful to Dick Walker, Mary Macken-Horarik and Maree Stenglin who all made helpful suggestions on the first draft of this chapter.
2. The CLE-based programmes with which Walker was associated received financial support from Rotary International. Extensive information about the CLE programmes is available at a website maintained by Rotary International (www.cleliteracy.org, Access: 9 September 2005).
3. Snow and Juel (2005) have offered a recent review of the history of debates about reading pedagogy in the USA.

References

Aidman, M. (1999), 'Biliteracy Development through Early and Mid-Primary Years: a Longitudinal Case Study of Bilingual Writing'. Ph.D. thesis, University of Melbourne.

Barnes, D. (1976), *From Communication to Curriculum*. London: Penguin Education.

— (1978), 'The study of classroom communication in teacher education', in M. Gill and W.J. Crocker (eds), *English in Teacher Education*. Armidale, NSW: University of New England, pp. 85–94.

Barnes, D., Britton, J. and Rosen, H. (1969), *Language the Learner and the School*. Middlesex, England: Penguin Books.

Barnes, D. and Todd, F. (1977), *Communication and Learning in Small Groups*. London: Routledge and Kegan Paul.

Barton, D. (1994), *Literacy. An Introduction to the Ecology of Written Language*. Oxford, UK and Cambridge, USA: Blackwell.

Bloom, L. (1970), *Language Development: Form and Function in Emerging Grammars*. Cambridge, MA: MIT Press.

Braine, M. D. S., (1971), 'The acquisition of language in infant and child', in C. Reed (ed.), *The Learning of Language*. NY: Appleton-Century-Crofts, pp. 7–95.

Carter, R. (ed.) (1990), *Knowledge about Language and the Curriculum*. London: Hodder and Stoughton.

Britton, J. (1970), *Language and Learning*. London: Penguin Books.

Brooks, G. (2003), *Sound Sense: The Phonics Element of the National Literacy Strategy. A Report to the Department for Education and Skills*. www.literacy-trust.org.uk/Research/phonicsreviews.html, Access: 10 September 2005.

Brown, G. D. A. and Ellis, N. (eds) (1994), *The Handbook of Spelling Theory: Theory, Process and Intervention*. NY, Brisbane, Toronto and Singapore: John Wiley and Sons.

'Bullock Report, The' (1975), *A Language for Life. Report of the Committee of Inquiry appointed by the Secretary of State for Education and Science under the Chairmanship of Sir Alan Bullock*. London: HMSO.

Cazden, C. (1977), 'Concentrated versus contrived encounters: suggestions for language assessment in early childhood education', in A. Davies (ed.), *Language Learning in Early Childhood*. London: Heinemann, pp. 40–59.

Chomsky, N. (1957), *Syntactic Structures*. The Hague: Mouton.

— (1981), 'Mark these linguists. Interviews with Noam Chomsky, Dell Hymes and Michael Halliday, *The English Magazine*, 7, 4–11.

Christie, F. (2002a), 'The development of abstraction in adolescence in subject English', in M. Schleppegrell and C. Colombi (eds), *Developing Advanced Literacy in First and Second Languages. Meaning with Power*. NJ: Erlbaum, pp. 45–66.

— (2002b), *Classroom Discourse Analysis. A Functional Perspective*. London and NY: Continuum.

— (2003), 'English in Australia', *RELC Journal*, 34, (1), 100–19.

— (2004a), 'Revisiting some old themes: the role of grammar in the teaching of English', in J. A. Foley (ed.), *Language, Education and Discourse: Functional Approaches*. London and NY: Continuum, pp. 145–73.

— (2004b), 'Authority and its role in the pedagogic relationship of schooling', in L. Young and C. Harrison (eds), *Systemic Functional Linguistics and Critical Discourse Analysis. Studies in Social Change*. London and NY: Continuum, pp. 173–201.

— (2004c), 'The study of language and subject English', *Australian Review of Applied Linguistics*, 27, 1, 15–29.

—(2005), *Language Education in the Primary Years*. Sydney: University of New South Wales Press.

Christie, F. and Rothery, J. (1979), 'English in Australia: an interpretation of role in the curriculum', in J. Maling-Keepes and B. D. Keepes (eds), *Language in Education. The Language Development Project Phase 1*. Canberra: Curriculum Development Centre, pp. 197–242.

Christie, F. and Unsworth, L. (2005), 'Developing dimensions of an educational linguistics', in Hasan, Matthiessen and Webster (eds), *Vol. 1*, pp. 217–50.

'Cox National Curriculum English Working Group, The' (1989), *English for Ages 5 to 16: Proposals of the Secretary of State for Education and Science and the Secretary of State for Wales*. London: Department of Education and Science and the Welsh Office.

Davies, F. (1973), *Teaching Reading in Early England*. London: Pitman Publishing.

Department of Education, Employment and Science (1998), *Literacy for All, the Challenge for Australian Schools. Commonwealth Literacy Policies for Australian Schools*. Canberra: Commonwealth Department of Education, Employment and Science.

Derewianka, B. (2003), 'Grammatical metaphor in the transition to adolescence', in Simon-Vandenbergen *et al* (eds), pp. 185–220.

Dixon, J. (1967), *Growth through English*. London: National Association for the Teaching of English and Oxford University Press.

'*English. A Statement for Australian Schools*'. *A Joint Project of the States, Territories and the Commonwealth of Australia initiated by the Australian Education Council* (1994), Carlton, Victoria: Curriculum Corporation.

Fitch, J. (1880), *Lectures on Teaching*. Cambridge: University Press.

Freebody, P. and Luke, A. (1990), '"Literacies" programmes: debates and demands in cultural context', *Prospect*, 5, 7–16.

Gray, B. (1980), '"Concentrated encounters" as a component of functional language/literacy teaching', in T. L. Lee and M. McCausland (eds), *Proceedings of the Conference, Child Language Development: Theory into Practice.* Launceston, Tasmania: Launceston Teachers Centre, pp. 223–35.

— (1985), 'Helping children become language learners in the classroom', in M. Christie, *Aboriginal Perspectives on Experience and Learning: the Role of Language in Aboriginal Education.* Geelong, Victoria: Deakin University Press, pp. 87–107.

— (1990), 'Natural language in the Aboriginal classroom: reflections on teaching and learning style,' in C. Walton and W. Eggington (eds), *Language: Maintenance, Power and Education.* Darwin, NT: Northern Territory University Press, pp. 23–60.

—(1999), *Accessing the Discourses of Schooling. English Language and Literacy Development with Aboriginal Children in Mainstream Schools.* Ph.D. thesis, University of Melbourne.

— (2005), 'Changing the institutional reality of Indigenous education'. A plenary paper given at the *Symposium on Imagining Childhood: Children, Culture and Community*, organized by the School for Social and Policy Research, Charles Darwin University, and held at Alice Springs, 20–22 September 2005.

— (in prep), *Accelerated Literacy Programs for Aboriginal Children.*

Gray, B. and Cowey, W. (1997), *High Order Book Orientation: The Lion and the Mouse.* Canberra: Schools and Community Centre, University of Canberra.

Gray, B., Cowey, W. and Axford, B. (2003a), *Scaffolding Literacy with Indigenous Children in School.* Canberra: Schools and Community Centre, University of Canberra.

— (2003b), *The Northern Territory Accelerated Literacy Project. Fourth Report.* Canberra: Schools and Community Centre, University of Canberra.

Green, B. (1988), 'Subject-specific literacy and school learning: a focus on writing', *Australian Journal of Education*, 32, (2), 156–79.

Halliday, M. A. K. (1975), *Learning How to Mean. Explorations in the Development of Language.* London: Arnold.

— (1993), 'Towards a language-based theory of learning', *Linguistics and Education*, 5, (2), 93–116.

Halliday, M. A. K., McIntosh, A. and Strevens, P. (1964), *The Linguistic Sciences and Language Teaching.* London: Longman.

Halliday, M. A. K. and Matthiessen, C. M. I. M. (2004), *An Introduction to Functional Grammar* (third edition). London and NY: Arnold.

Hart, N. W., Walker, R. F., Gray, B. N., Walker, G., Kock, L. and Gartshore, A. (1977), *The Mount Gravatt Developmental Language Reading Program.* Sydney: Addison-Wesley and Mt Gravatt College of Advanced Education.

Hasan, R. (1996), 'Literacy, everyday and society', in R. Hasan and G. Williams (eds), *Literacy in Society.* London and NY: Addison Longman, pp. 377–424.

— (2005), 'Introduction: a working model of language', in R. Hasan, C. M. I. M. Matthiessen and J. Webster (eds), *Vol. 1*, pp. 37–54.

Hasan, R. and Martin J. R. (eds) (1989), *Language Development: Learning*

Language, Learning Culture. Meaning and Choice in Language. Studies for Michael Halliday. Norwood, NJ: Ablex.

Hasan, R., Matthiessen C., and Webster, J. (eds) (2005), *Continuing Discourse on Language. A Functional Perspective, Vols. 1 and 2*. London and Oakville: Equinox.

Hymes, D. (1972), 'Introduction', in C. Cazden, V. P John and D. Hymes (eds), *The Functions of Language in the Classroom*. NY: Teachers College Press, pp. xi–lvii.

Johnston, R. and Watson, J. (2005), *The Effects of Synthetic Phonics Teaching on Reading and Spelling Attainment*. Edinburgh: Scottish Executive Education Department.

'Kingman Report, The' (1988), *Report of the Committee of Inquiry into the Teaching of English Language*. Committee chaired by Sir John Kingman. London: HMSO.

Kress, G. and van Leeuwen, T. (1996) *Reading Images: The Grammar of Visual Design*. London and NY: Routledge.

Mackay, D., Schaub, P. and Thompson, B. (1989), 'The Breakthrough connection: "Breaking through the sound barrier into the written word" '. In R. Hasan and J. Martin (eds), pp. 333–48.

Macken-Horarik, M. (1996), 'Literacy and learning across the curriculum: towards a model of register for secondary school teachers', in R. Hasan and G. Williams (eds), *Literacy in Society*. London and NY: Addison Longman, pp. 232–78.

Martin, J. R. (1999), 'Mentoring semogenesis: "genre-based" literacy pedagogy', in F. Christie (ed.), *Pedagogy and the Shaping of Consciousness. Linguistic and Social Processes*. London and NY: Cassell, pp.123–55.

Martin, J. R. and Rose, D. (2005), 'Designing literacy pedagogy: scaffolding democracy in the classroom', in R. Hasan, C. M. I. M. Matthiessen and J. Webster (eds), *Vol. 1*, pp. 251–80.

Menyuk, P. (1971), 'Syntactic structures in the language of children', in A. Bar-Adon and W. F. Leopold (eds), *Child Language. A Book of Readings*. NJ: Prentice-Hall, pp. 290–9.

Mountford, J. (1998), *An Insight into English Spelling*. London: Hodder and Stoughton.

Muller, J. (2001), *Reclaiming Knowledge*. London and NY: Routledge.

'National English Curriculum, The' (1995), London: Department for Education and Science and HMSO.

Painter, C. (1999), *Learning through Language in Early Childhood*. London and NY: Cassell.

Painter, C., Derewianka, B. and Torr, J. (2005), 'From microfunction to metaphor: learning language and learning through language', in R. Hasan, C. M. I. M. Matthiessen and J. Webster (eds), Vol. 2.

Perera, K. (1984), *Children's Writing and Reading. Analysing Classroom Language*. Oxford and NY: Blackwell and Deutsch.

Rattanavich, S. and Christie, F. (1993), 'Developing text-based approaches to the teaching of literacy in Thailand', in G. Gagné and A. C. Purves (eds), *Papers in Mother Tongue Education 1* (Mother Tongue Education Research Series). NY: Waxmann Münster, pp. 97–110.

Rattanavich, S. and Walker, R. F. (1996), 'Literacy for the developing world', in F. Christie and J. Foley (eds), *Some Contemporary Themes in Literacy Research*. NY and Berlin: Waxmann Münster, pp. 17–45.

Rose, D. (2004), 'Sequencing and pacing of the hidden curriculum: how Indigenous children are left out of the chain', in J. Muller, B. Davies and A. Morais (eds), *Reading Bernstein, Researching Bernstein*. London: Routledge Falmer.

Rose, D., Gray, B. and Cowey, W. (1999), 'Scaffolding reading and writing for Indigenous children in school', in P. Wignell (ed.), *Double Power: English Literacy and Indigenous Education*. Melbourne: National Languages and Literacy Institute of Australia, pp. 23–60.

Rose, D., Lui-Chivizhe, L., McKnight, A. and Smith, A. (2004), 'Scaffolding academic writing and writing at the Koori Centre', *Australian Journal of Indigenous Education, 30th Anniversary Edition*, www.atsis.uq.edu.au/ajie

Rosen, H. and Rosen, C. (1973), *The Language of Primary School Children*. London: Penguin Education and the Schools Council.

Rowe, K., Purdie, N. and Ellis, L. (2005), *A Review of the Evidence-Based Research Literature on Effective Teaching and Learning Strategies for Students with Learning Difficulties. A Draft Discussion Paper Prepared for the Committee and Reference Group for the National Inquiry into the Teaching of Literacy*. Melbourne: Australian Department of Education and Science and ACER.

Simon-Vandenbergen, A. M., Taverniers, M. and Ravelli, L. (eds) (2003), *Grammatical Metaphor*. Amsterdam and Philadelphia: Benjamins.

Snow, C. and Juel, C. (2005), 'Teaching children to read: what do we know about how to do it?', in M. Snowling (ed.), *The Science of Reading: A Handbook. Part VII Teaching Reading*. London and NY: Blackwell, pp. 5–24.

Snowling, M. (1994), 'Towards a model of spelling acquisition: the development of component skills', in G. D. Brown and N. C. Ellis (eds), *The Handbook of Spelling. Theory, Process and Intervention*. Chichester, NY, Brisbane, Toronto and Singapore: John Wiley and Sons, pp. 111–28.

Street, B. (1997), 'The implications of the "New Literacy Studies" for literacy education', *English in Education*, 31, (3), 45–59.

Tanguiane, S. (1990), *Literacy and Illiteracy in the World: Situation, Trends and Prospects. International Year book of Education*, Vol. XLII. Paris: UNESCO.

Torr, J. (1997), *From Child Tongue to Mother Tongue: A Case study of Language Development in the First Two and a Half Years* (Monographs in Systemic Linguistics 9). University of Nottingham: Department of English Studies.

Torr, J. and Simpson, A. (2003), 'The emergence of grammatical metaphor: literacy-oriented expressions in the everyday speech of young children', in Simon-Vandenbergen *et al* (eds), pp. 169–84.

Treiman, R. (1994), 'Sources of information used by beginning spellers', in G. D. Brown and N. C. Ellis (eds), *The Handbook of Spelling. Theory, Process and Intervention*. Chichester, NY, Brisbane, Toronto and Singapore: John Wiley and Sons, pp. 72–92.

Unsworth, L. (2001), *Teaching Multiliteracies across the Curriculum*. Buckingham and Philadelphia: Open University Press.

Walker, R., Smith, J. A., Parkes, B., Keen, E. and Gartshore, A. (1985), *The

Mount Gravatt Developmental Language Reading Program (second edition). Melbourne: Longman Cheshire.

Walker, R., Rattanavich, S. and Oller, Jnr., J. W. (1992), *Teaching all the Children to Read*. Buckingham and Bristol, USA: Open University Press.

Williams, G. (1998), 'Children entering literate worlds: perspectives from the study of textual practices', in F. Christie and R. Misson (eds), *Literacy and Schooling*. London and NY: Routledge, pp. 18–46.

3   The *Write it Right* project – Linguistic modelling of secondary school and the workplace

Robert Veel

1 Introduction

This chapter provides an account of the *Write it Right* project (WIR), a school and industry based language education project which took place in New South Wales, Australia, between 1991 and 1995. The comparatively large scale and duration of the project meant that it had a significant and enduring impact both on school language education practice in most states of Australia and on the research and teaching of the 'Sydney School'[1] of language education. I provide a synopsis and general introduction to the project for researchers and practitioners, and, with the benefit of hindsight, assess the contribution it made. In presenting examples of our work, I have tried to draw from as wide a range of WIR's research and publications as possible, without attempting to provide a complete or coherent account of any one area of research. The publication list at the end of this chapter will guide readers wishing to find out more about a particular school subject or industry.

The 1990s was an active and stimulating time in language education in Australia. Both society and the political elite still took seriously the idea that school education could contribute to society by providing opportunities for students from all backgrounds to participate fully in a rapidly changing economy and society. The systemic functional (SF) model, with its emphasis on language as a social practice and its well established tradition of dialogue with educational sociology and literacy teaching,[2] was in a good position to contribute rigorous and practical models for researchers and practitioners. The strong interest in our work at the time meant that academic investigation and educational trialling of our ideas was diverse and widespread – going well beyond the geographical limits suggested by the term 'Sydney School'. In writing a retrospective piece more than 10 years after the project began, it is sometimes difficult to clearly define where WIR began and ended and where the work of other groups and individuals permeated the project. Although making its own distinctive and considerable contribution, the project was also characterized by its openness to collaboration and critique by other individuals and groups, and the contribution made through this kind of dialogue on the published materials should not be underestimated. This chapter will therefore also seek to identify and describe the broader context and influences/inspirations for the WIR team. It is assumed that the reader has a basic familiarity with genre-based approaches to literacy and with the SF model of language, although there is no technical discussion of texts in the chapter.

2 Background to the project

WIR was funded by the Education and Training Foundation, a body responsible for conducting workplace-based research and training. The Education and Training Foundation itself was funded by industry as part of legislated training guarantee requirements. $1.4 million of funds was obtained for WIR by the Disadvantaged Schools Program in the Metropolitan East Region of the New South Wales Department of Education (as it was then known). The Disadvantaged Schools Program was an initiative of the Labour Whitlam government (1972–75), rather reluctantly administered in the early 1990s by a New Right Liberal state government. The objectives of the project were 'to research the nature of literacy demands within and across industrial sectors and to relate these findings to literacy in the secondary school Key Learning Areas'.[3] Key products of the project were to be a series of reports on industry sectors and materials for newly created secondary school 'Key Learning Areas'. A project team was formed and housed at the Disadvantaged Schools Program's Sydney regional headquarters. It consisted of an industry research team of three, a school research and training team of up to six, and an academic consultant.

It is important to note from the outset that the objectives of the project were understood in different ways by the different industry, school and academic parties involved in the project. From the point of view of industry, WIR was to contribute to a broader agenda of making school education more 'relevant' to industry needs. The assumption, still widely held in Australia and elsewhere, was that schooling lacked clear relevance to industry and accountability. As a result schooling failed to meet the needs of contemporary workplaces, and Australia was less economically competitive as a consequence. In response to these perceptions, various government policy and funding shifts during the 1990s pushed education systems towards a more 'instrumental' approach to learning, based on the central tenet that any skill taught needed to be immediately measurable. Higher order skills were seen as the accumulation of lower order skills, learned and assessed at previous points in the education system. The push was strongest in vocational education, but also clearly evident in school education. The most obvious example of the new direction was the insistence that school syllabuses and classroom teaching be based on clear outcomes assessed by measurable behaviours. Education authorities and classroom teachers throughout Australia spent a great deal of time reconstructing existing programmes in order to meet the new requirements. In the field of vocational education, the Australian Qualifications Framework (AQF) became a powerful instrument for implementing the outcomes-based approach, and was eventually extended to all post-compulsory education (although its influence on the university system remains weak). Uncertainty, transcendence and ineffability, components of both romantic and progressive education models, were given little space in such an environment. Similarly, any discussion of the role of education in addressing systemic social inequalities was beyond the understanding of a mechanistic approach. In terms of language education, it was hoped that WIR would yield a set of clearly stated literacy requirements for a range of industries, so that schools could set about teaching these requirements, safe in the knowledge that they were relevant to the needs of Australia.

In this environment, it is at least curious that the Disadvantaged Schools Program (DSP), established by a socially progressive federal government to address issues of social inequality in education, was able to convince the Education and Training Foundation to fund WIR. Indeed, the vast majority of DSP initiatives would have been viewed as outmoded or irrelevant by funding bodies such as the Education and Training Foundation, being either too interested in social equity for its own sake to address issues of international competitiveness, or too loosely framed for the emerging outcomes-driven approach. A notable exception was the work of the Language and Social Power Project, a primary level language education project which had been underway at the Metropolitan East Region (New South Wales) of the DSP since the mid-1980s. Aimed directly at addressing issues of social inequality through equal access to powerful linguistic resources, the Language and Social Power Project drew on an explicit approach to describing text and a carefully developed pedagogy, the former derived from systemic functional linguistics (SFL) and the latter from Bernstein's sociology of education (then very unfashionable among progressive educators). The striking mix of classroom teachers, consultants and academic researchers over a number of years also meant the Language and Social Power Project had developed techniques for articulating complex sociological and linguistic models in educational practice, and for effectively arguing the case for them. The Metropolitan East Region DSP was therefore able to legitimately claim that it had the experience and resources to provide explicit and measurable descriptions of the language requirements of a range of contexts, including both school and industry. These descriptions could then be used to create benchmarks and visible outcomes for school language education, without necessarily subscribing to the New Right's mechanistic approach to school and vocational education.

How could a programme play into the hands of an outcome-driven model and still claim to be motivated by social equity? Anyone with a familiarity with Bernstein's sociology and the SF model of language would not be surprised by the claim that genre-based approaches to language education seek to address issues of systemic social inequity through detailed descriptions of text and context developed from broader sociolinguistic theories. Nevertheless, many critics saw a latent conservatism in the approach of WIR, claiming that through explicit description and teaching, the Sydney School's approach did nothing more than perpetuate the hegemonic textual practices of school and industry (e.g. Luke 1996). Martin has written extensively on this, arguing that it is the pedagogy which developed around the linguistic descriptions of text that allowed the Disadvantaged Schools Program's approach to be simultaneously visible and interventionist but also socially ('inter-group') motivated. Martin developed a model based on Bernstein (1990: 213) to explain the positioning of the DSP's pedagogy in relation to other theories and pedagogies (see Chapter 4 this volume). The DSP's approach was a visible pedagogy, like the outcomes-driven model, but unlike liberal and radical approaches. However it was an inter-group model based on the premise that language is a socially construed and socially located phenomenon, and that this would be rendered visible by the approach. This, Martin argues, positions the approach as a subversive one.

The immediate challenge for the WIR team was to create broad models for the relationship between the language and institutional contexts of junior secondary school and industry. Although subject names and boundaries may have changed over time, one of the most

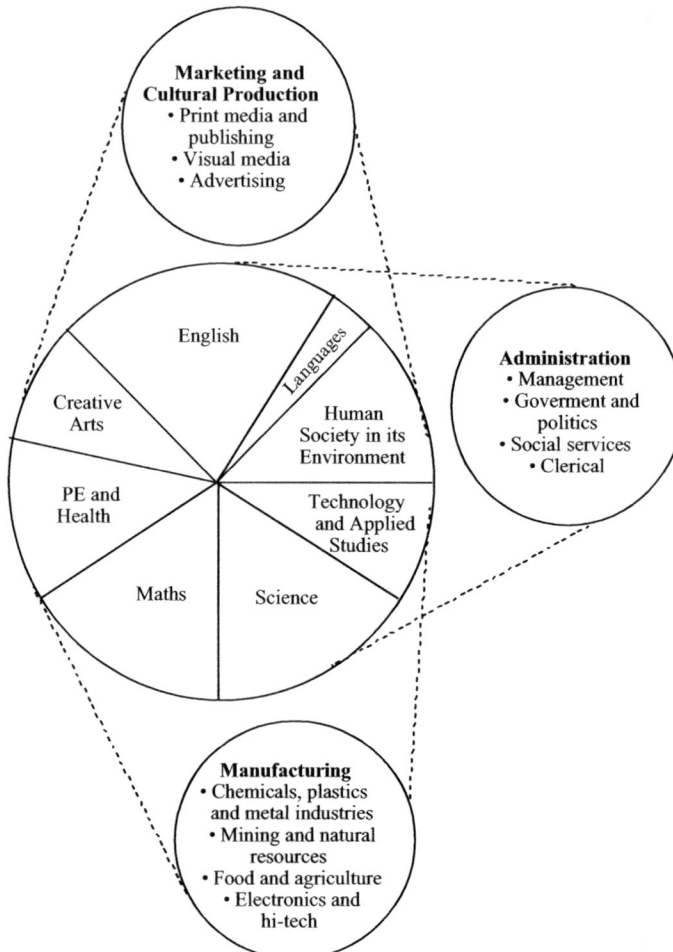

Figure 3.1 Industry sectors and the Key Learning Areas

striking features of junior secondary schooling in Australia remains its role as the point of introduction for discipline-specific knowledge to students. This is most strongly characterized by the organization of time and space in the secondary school. Students entering secondary school find a new world, where boundaries between subjects are strongly framed and paced by timetables, discipline-specific teaching staff and specialized teaching spaces. The divisions between school subjects stem from traditional academic disciplines (mainly the humanities subjects) as well as the specialized organization of the labour in the 'Fordist' industrial age (mainly science and technology subjects). For the purposes of research and materials development,[4]

WIR modelled the relationship between school disciplines and the workplace according to Figure 3.1 (from Rose *et al* 1992: 22).

Rather than assuming that the language of secondary school disciplines is arcane and irrelevant for the workplace, contextual models of language and education suggest that it is reasonable to expect strong similarities between the specialized language of school and the language of specialized labour. This was very quickly confirmed by the team's investigation of manufacturing workplaces and school science, and later in areas of 'symbolic production' such as school English and the media industry. As well as specialization, hierarchies exist within both schooling and the workplace to discriminate between more and less advanced students and more or less powerful/remunerated employees.

The key question for WIR was, therefore, not whether school language was relevant to the workplaces, but rather in what ways it was relevant. Of particular importance was the need to describe the changing literacy requirements of a workforce that was rapidly restructuring towards service-based industries. Whereas the relationship between school science and manufacturing industry was long-standing and well appreciated (if not well understood), the deployment of literacy skills in the fields of media and cultural production was very little researched, despite the fact that this was a growing and economically significant field of economic activity, which Australia had to develop further to remain competitive.

A second important issue was the way in which rapidly developing technology and the formalization of workplace learning were placing increasing demands on Australian workers. Rather than a crisis of 'falling standards' in the school system, Australia faced the challenge of preparing students for the rapidly expanding literacy demands of the post-industrial workplace. More students than ever were being encouraged to undertake post-compulsory education. The implications of such changes were particularly significant for disadvantaged schools, where lower literacy skills lay at the core of educational disadvantage.

3 Modelling institutional contexts

The relationship between context and text is the centrepiece of SFL and its applications in language education. Halliday's ideational, interpersonal and textual grammatical 'metafunctions' (Halliday and Hasan 1985) and the very meaning of grammatical categories in SF grammar spring directly from theories of the variables in context that

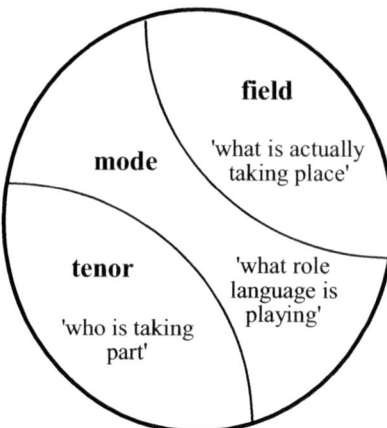

Figure 3.2 Halliday's register variables, as presented in the *Write it Right* science industry report

produce semantic variation and functional varieties of English. Concentrating on the grammar of the clause, Halliday posits a single-level, tripartite model of *Context of Situation*, based around the variables of field, tenor and mode, as in Figure 3.2, from Rose *et al* (1992: 105). The elegant simplicity and broad applicability of Halliday's variables has ensured their longevity, and they were the starting point for modelling work and school contexts in WIR.

In the late 1980s Martin enhanced Halliday's model of context by suggesting an additional stratum of semantic variation – *Context of Culture* – sitting above that of Context of Situation. Whereas Halliday relates Context of Situation principally to the grammar of the clause, Martin relates Context of Culture to genres, 'staged, goal-oriented social processes' (Martin 1992: 505) or linguistic ways of getting things done in a culture. Martin's work was strongly influenced by his involvement in the Language and Social Power Project, which preceded *Write it Right* and focused on primary school language education. At the primary school level, where students are initiated into the broader culture, the descriptions of the social purpose and grammatical features of a range of common written genres in the Language and Social Power project found immediate favour among teachers and soon genre-based teaching programmes sprang up both in New South Wales and most states of Australia. Genre-based approaches were particularly popular among those disenchanted with progressive education models of language education, such as 'Whole Language' (Cambourne 1988). At this time there was heated debate

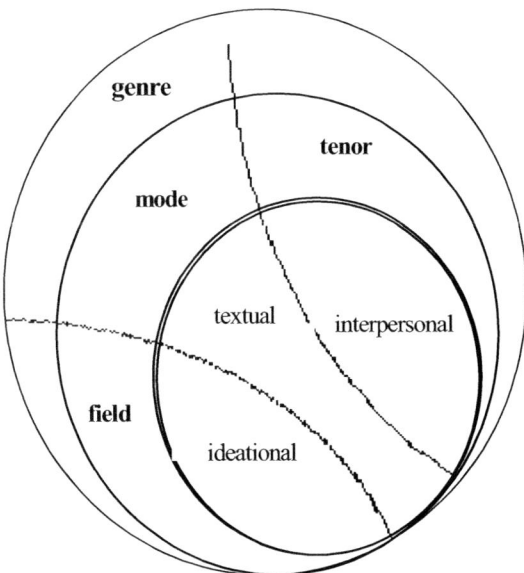

Figure 3.3 Martin's stratified model of context

between proponents of genre-based models and progressive educators, who saw the explicit descriptions of genres and the accompanying interventionist pedagogy as a threat to the child's natural, internal cognitive development and a return to behaviourist models of instruction (see Martin 1999 for a detailed description of this misreading of genre-based pedagogy). Within SFL there were also alternative models of whole-text structure being proposed which offered alternative views to Martin's stratified model of context (as in Figure 3.3, from Martin 1996: 129), notably Hasan's model of generic structure potential (Hasan 1984). Nevertheless, by the mid-1990s, genre-based descriptions of language, if not genre-based pedagogies, were a feature of primary school language syllabuses in most states in Australia.

   In order to develop detailed descriptions of language use in specific *institutional contexts* and to make its work meaningful for school teachers and industry trainers embedded within these contexts, WIR needed to develop more elaborate models of the relationship between text and context at the stratum of Context of Culture. The elaboration needed to occur in two directions: vertically, in terms of hierarchical relationships between written genres, and horizontally, in terms of relationships between written genre types within contexts. The contexts being described were broader than Halliday's Context of Situation (and of a different order), but not as generalized as Martin's notion of Context of Culture. The various descriptions and models of a range of institutional contexts in the workplace and school remain perhaps the most distinctive contribution of WIR.

For example, in a book chapter on the language of school history written well into the project, Veel and Coffin (1996: 194–5) describe a four-stage protocol in the WIR team's school-based research. The stages move from the stratum of genre to that of register and finally to grammar:

1. Analyse the range of written genres encountered by students in their reading practices and demanded of students in their writing requirements, etc.
2. Locate the genres in relation to the syllabus, outcome statements, public examinations, school programmes, school assessment and classroom practice, etc.
3. Analyse register shifts (field, tenor and mode) in genres across subject areas. Link these to broad aims and rationales in syllabuses.
4. Analyse lexicogrammatical shifts in genres across subject areas. Link these to specific learning outcomes in syllabuses.

The second stage, locating genres within their institutional setting, was essential for describing discipline-driven discourse such as those of secondary school subjects and industry sectors. This is very different from earlier models of genre-based language education. In the primary school context it is discourses of psychological and motor development which create the logic through which value and significance is given to particular genres at different stages of the child's progress through primary school. In order to locate texts within institutional contexts, the WIR team first had to gain some understanding of the structure of the institution itself. The first step was of course a careful analysis of the implied literacy demands of syllabus outcomes. However, syllabus outcomes do not emerge from thin air, and so the WIR team read widely outside the fields of linguistics and education in order to gain insight into the institutional logic which was driving syllabus design and, by implication, language practices (e.g. Weber 1948–91 for administration, Windschuttle 1984 for media, Cranny-Francis 1996 for school English, Bazerman 1988 and Latour and Woolgar 1986 for science, Harvey 1989 for geography, etc.).

The physical form of the models of institutional context produced by the WIR team were heavily influenced by Halliday's 'spiral' model of literacy development, itself based on Bruner's helical model of

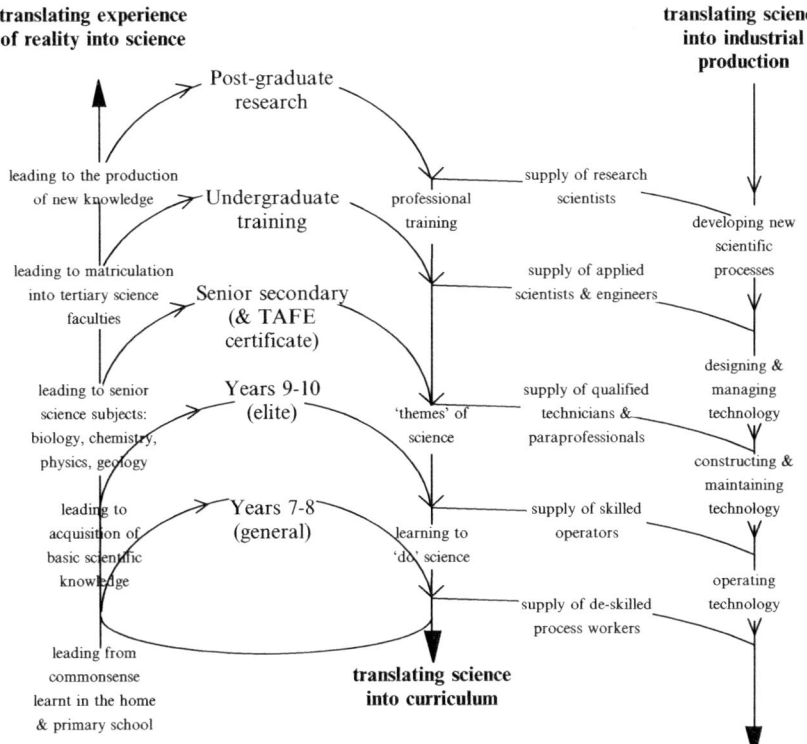

Figure 3.4 Stages in science education and levels in industry

learning, presented at the Australian Systemic Functional Linguistics
Conference in 1990 (Halliday 1996: 368–9). One of the most elaborate
of these models is that of Rose *et al* (1992: 84), reproduced in Figure
3.4, relating the hierarchy of learning in school science to that of
economic production in science industry.

The visual device of the spiral is meant to suggest an iterative style
of language development, in which linguistic resources developed at
one point in the spiral are reused in different contexts at later points.
For example, procedure genres are used in junior secondary science in
order to apprentice students into methods of scientific enquiry and to
illustrate longstanding areas of knowledge. At this level, procedures
appear in the company of report and explanation genres, the linguistic
vehicles par excellence for imparting established scientific knowledge.
Procedures are also used at the very highest levels of research science,
sharing many of the structural and grammatical features of their junior
secondary school counterparts. However, procedures in research
science are used to produce scientific knowledge, and thus appear in

the company of exposition genres, persuading readers of the value and originality of the new knowledge vis-à-vis existing knowledge. Similar argumentation can be used to explain the iterative development of grammatical resources.

The models which were used to present institutional contexts to teachers were not necessarily as elaborate as the research models. For instance, in describing the institutional context of secondary school science, Veel characterizes the field as comprising just four broad functions: 'doing science', 'explaining events scientifically', 'organizing scientific information' and 'challenging science' (Veel 1997: 167). Similarly, Coffin's exploration of the language of school history is based around the categories 'chronicling history', 'reporting history', 'explaining history' and 'arguing history' (Coffin 1996: 13).

Mention should also be made at this point of Macken-Horarick's work in developing a generalized model of register for secondary school teachers (Macken-Horarick 1996). Similar to the discipline-specific models of WIR, Macken-Horarick proposes a model of register for secondary school teachers comprising three rather broad domains in a hierarchical relationship – the everyday, the specialized and the reflexive. Compared to the WIR models, Macken-Horarik's work is more 'teacherly', concentrating on commonalities across school subjects brought about by the systematic recontextualization of knowledge into classroom activity and student assessment in secondary schools, irrespective (though not ignorant) of the discipline.

In seeking to provide meaningful and practical resources, as often as not the project team took an opportunistic approach to the resources of the SF model in describing institutional contexts, rather than following closely the protocol introduced above. Analyses did not always privilege the description and analysis of genres. Emphasis was also given to lexicogrammar and Context of Situation when this best illustrated and explained the role of language in an institutional context, focusing on genre when this suited. In his report on the language of administration, for example, Iedema (1995) sees grammatical variation at the level of clause (but meaningfully distributed across texts) as critical to understanding the hierarchy of bureaucratic institutions. He identifies four different discourse strategies which characterize different levels of social organization and control within bureaucracies. Whereas generalization and technicality are prevalent at all levels, 'demodalized' texts are characteristic of the upper echelons of bureaucracies (Iedema 1995: 18).

Similarly, Veel's (1999) work on the language of mathematics focuses on systematic shifts in the deployment of lexicogrammatical

Table 3.1 Discursive strategies in administrative texts

Discourse strategy	Function	Example	Metafunctional domain affected
Generalization	'collecting' meaning	*to research* { *to organize* *to plan* *to collect data* *to analyse* *to write*	Field
Technicality	constructing uncommonsense taxonomies and accounts of processes	*Abrasion occurs when lots of hard sand particles are carried by desert winds and are thrown with great force against all solid objects in their path.*	Field
Abstraction	organize text	*The Australian Government* was frequently critical of the priorities of American strategy during the war → ... *Australian objections* ...	Mode
Demodalization	background and depersonalize control	*Treasury now believes it is appropriate to provide further impetus to the reform of financial and resource management practices* ...	Tenor

features, particularly grammatical metaphor and nominal groups, rather than on text types. Iedema and Veel's analyses show an important feature of the WIR research. Although the starting point for analysis in an institutional context was the range of written genres, ironically it was the systematic 'micro-level' shifts in lexicogrammar as one moves hierarchically through an institution which reveals the most about the 'linguistic secrets' of power and success within the institution.

4 Expanding descriptions of written genres

Initial research on written genres concentrated, with great effect, on a limited range of written genres which were within the scope of primary school education (Rothery 1986, 1990; Martin 1985; Martin and Plum 1997; Painter and Martin 1986). Just as Martin's stratum of Context of Culture was a broad concept, the 'foundation' genres of recount, narrative, report, explanation and exposition could be applied broadly across cultures, inside and outside of the classroom. Indeed, it was the evident applicability of these genres to a broad range of situations which made them so appealing to teachers, particularly those working in disadvantaged schools.

Along with the more specific description of the context of subcultures in school disciplines and the workplace, the WIR project produced a more detailed and more delicate description of genres and the specific role they played in institutional contexts. The foundational genre 'explanation', for example, expanded to become a range of agnate explanation genres in the WIR project: sequential explanation, causal explanation, factorial explanation, consequential explanation, theoretical explanation. There were two main purposes in developing more detailed descriptions. The first was to make clear to teachers and workplace trainers that linguistic development occurs within broad genre categories, and that it is not sufficient to teach the purpose, structure and language features of a genre on a single occasion (this has significant implications for pedagogy, discussed below). In the discipline of secondary science, for example, Veel (1997) identifies five different types of explanation genre. Although distinctions between these genres can often be blurred, it is apparent that the kinds of explanations students are expected to read and write towards the end of secondary schooling are noticeably more sophisticated than those encountered in the first years of secondary school. When students 'do' the explanation genre in Year 7 science (typically temporally ordered sequential explanations of visible physical phenomena), this does not guarantee that they will be able to independently negotiate theoretical explanations in senior secondary physics (typically atemporal implicational reasoning based around abstract constructs). Describing a range of explanation genres made it possible for teachers and students to explicitly comprehend the development that was expected in their literacy skills within the discipline. 'Apprenticeship' was the metaphor we used to describe this process.

The second reason for providing more detailed and delicate descriptions of genres was to show a clear relationship between language and the learning outcomes in secondary school syllabuses or workplace competency/qualifications frameworks. In the primary school setting, it was sufficient to propose the explicit teaching of commonly used written genres – recount, narrative, report, explanation and exposition – for the broad social benefit this conferred. As primary school education is still sufficiently far from the worlds of work, assessment here is still in terms of success in the acquisition of global skills. In secondary schools, however, the ability to participate in society is measured by the acquisition of one or more sets of *specific* skills, more often than not lying within the boundaries of an academic discipline or workplace (Bernstein 1975, 1990). Academic disciplines in post-compulsory education and institutionally-bounded definitions of success in the workplace govern our ability to gain employment and achieve economic independence in later life. Secondary school syllabuses, and consequently the meaning of 'success', are designed around these disciplinary boundaries, and assessment in secondary school education by and large determines one's level of social and economic autonomy. There is therefore very great pressure in secondary school education to measure success in terms of the acquisition of discipline-specific skills, and this in turn shapes the language of secondary schools and workplaces. A 'global' approach to literacy education through the teaching of five or six foundational genres is not sufficient in this environment, and so the WIR materials sought to locate a greater range of written genres always within the bounds of their institutional context. The example in Table 3.2, from secondary school geography (Humphrey 1996), is typical of WIR's school materials and illustrates this point.

The detailed account of genres, relationships between genres and their embodiment of learning outcomes undertaken by WIR also fulfilled an important 'mapping' function for Australian schools. At

Table 3.2   Genre and social power in secondary school education

Social goal	Discipline	Learning outcomes	Key genres
Allowing for equitable participation in society through success in a school subject by teaching powerful and commonly used written genres *of the subject*	School geography	Describing geographic features	• Descriptive reports • Comparative reports • Macro-reports
		Explaining geographic phenomena	• Sequential explanations • Causal explanations • Factorial explanations • Consequential explanations
		Recording and accounting for change over time	• Historical recounts • Historical accounts • Autobiographical accounts • Biographical accounts
		Exploring issues in geography	• Analytical expositions • Discussions

about the same time as the WIR project, several states in Australia had invested heavily in 'literacy across the curriculum' programmes, recognizing that secondary school subjects had specialized literacy needs. Hitherto, there had been a tendency in Australian schools to expect that either primary schools or secondary English departments would shoulder the burden of students' literacy development, and a parallel tendency to blame students' literacy shortcomings on poor primary school teaching or the inadequacy of secondary English teachers. Similarly, universities, Technical and Further Education (TAFE) colleges and workplaces expected secondary schools to prepare students fully for the literacy demands of higher learning and the workplace, and frequently criticized secondary schools. Literacy materials for secondary teachers, TAFE teachers and industry trainers were long on classroom strategies but very short on guidance as to what kind of language could be usefully taught to students. WIR provided a timely account of the diversity of literacy demands in the secondary school and, by virtue of the way it related written genres to discipline-specific learning outcomes, suggested ways in which literacy skills could be meaningfully taught across the curriculum.

As well as expanding on the descriptions of 'foundation' genres, WIR undertook the description of a range of genres in schooling and the workplace which had not previously received attention within the SF model. In the discipline of secondary school English, for instance, Rothery and Stenglin (see Rothery 1996) described a range of 'response' genres, through which students reacted to text. The range of agnate response genres, from personal to critical response, illustrated how students moved from emotive, personalized reactions to events to the use of socially valid and socially validated categories for deconstructing and evaluating texts. Rothery (1996: 110) argues that response genres, with narrative genres, are at the heart of secondary school English. Certainly they are an important vehicle for assessment – in the Visual Arts as well as English – and deserved thorough investigation.

In the area of workplace research, there had been very little work on functional varieties using the SF model, and so nearly all the descriptions of genres were new. The WIR report on the media industry, for example, undertook extensive analysis of news genres (Iedema *et al* 1994). It was, and remains, ironic that an industry which relies so heavily on a particular text type has little more than anecdotal and mundane explanations of its craft. Discussions with industry representatives revealed that apprentice journalists are assessed on whether or not they have a 'nose' for news stories, with no explicit criteria for evaluating the texts they produce. The dominant structural model of news stories was the clichéd 'inverted triangle', with almost no detail of the organizing principles for news stories, beyond the fact that they began with a 'lead' paragraph. The WIR report of media industry also emphasized the prevalence of media texts in schooling and the importance of 'critical' reading of media texts for participation in society:

> Media texts have already become a significant part of the school curriculum, both as texts used as objects of study in English and Creative Arts as well as sources of information in subjects such as History, Geography and Science. Importantly media texts are appearing in examination papers such as the NSW School Certificate. Media texts are used to make curriculum relevant to an information based society, but the special ways in which the literacy demands of media texts differ from those of the other texts that make up the school curriculum may be overlooked. If this happens media texts could become yet another barrier to students being successful in educational contexts, another culling device, rather than an important extra dimension to the development of the kind of literacy needed to negotiate the demands of late twentieth and early twenty-first century society.
>
> (Iedema *et al* 1994: 73)

5 Development of new ways of modelling genres

For the most part, the techniques for describing genres in the WIR project followed the patterns established in earlier genre-based work. Descriptions were of written texts only, and schematic structures were linear, showing texts moving from stage to stage. During the later phases of WIR, new parameters and techniques were developed for describing written genres. Among them were the inclusion of elements other than written text in the analysis (multimedia analysis) and the development of non-linear techniques for modelling generic structure.

The move into multimedia analysis was necessitated by the research on media texts, and spurred on by friendly criticism that language analysis alone was insufficient to adequately account for meaning-making in many publications. Print media relies heavily on visual images to provide interpersonal meaning and as a compositional device, and of course it is impossible to usefully describe television media without the analysis of visual images. A framework for the functional analysis of visual images came from Kress and van Leeuwen's (1996) grammar of visual images, based around Halliday's metafunctions of field, tenor and mode (rendered by Kress and van Leeuwen as *representation*, *modality* and *composition*). In WIR's school-based work, visual image analysis was used in Geography and Mathematics,[5] with Theo van Leeuwen participating directly in the Geography research. Van Leeuwen and Humphrey (1996: 30) explain the significance of visual image analysis in the following way:

> School textbooks, however, no longer only use language, and have, in the past few decades, become increasingly visual, and the 'language of images', too, should be seen, not as a unified whole, but as a set of registers. There is, for instance, a great deal of 'technicality', not only in the language of school geography but also in the images of school geography, through abstract maps, charts and diagrams. And the apprentice geographer must learn to read images in a specialized way, 'to look through a geographer's eyes', and to read, and in many cases also produce, specialized kinds of visuals ... it has become possible to describe registers of the 'language of images' and hence to outline what is involved in geographical visual literacy. This is all the more important because visual literacies may embody their own discourses and these discourses need not be identical to those realized in language, even within one field, such as school geography.

Stage-by-stage linear descriptions of genres provide a logical and easy to follow account of a text. However, the very structure of this kind of descriptions assumes that texts have a beginning-middle-end logic and reading direction. While this is true of many 'traditional' kinds of writing in educational contexts (e.g. the school essay, undergraduate thesis and academic article), it is perhaps not the most helpful way of characterizing a range of texts in many non-educational contexts. In all branches of the media, for example, it is well known that the 'lead' is the core element of a news story, with all other stages in the text depending upon the way the lead construes the event being reported. To model a news story, then, as if it has a beginning-middle-end structure gives a misleading account of the genre as text which proceeds in a linear fashion.

WIR industry research in media and administration developed visually-rendered 'nucleus-satellite' models to describe genres which did not have a predominantly linear development. In his report on administrative text, for example, Iedema (1995: 79) presents both a linear and a nucleus-satellite model (see Table 3.3 and Figure 3.5).

Iedema's account of administrative texts is centred around the way bureaucracies use language to organize and control the material and social environment. In his analysis he wishes to bring out to readers the discursive resources we use to do this. While the linear model is a useful way for us to read through the text and gain an understanding of its generic structure, it is the visual nucleus-satellite model which makes clear the structural logic of the text.

Table 3.3   Linear model of administrative memo

Analysis	Text
	Memo to all staff
	Conflict of interest
Background	At around this time of year many invitations are received from companies and consultants to Christmas drinks/dinner. Gifts are also sometimes received.
Conciliation	I am sure that such offers only eventuate from a job being well done and it is certainly pleasing to know that the level of service provided by staff is appreciated.
Appeal to judgement: ethics	The acceptance of any offers of entertainment or gifts can however lead to either a real or perceived conflict of interest.
Appeal to consequence: purpose	To ensure that a real or perceived conflict of interest does not arise,
Command	all such offers should be declined and gifts returned.
	[signed]
	Controller, Planning and Building

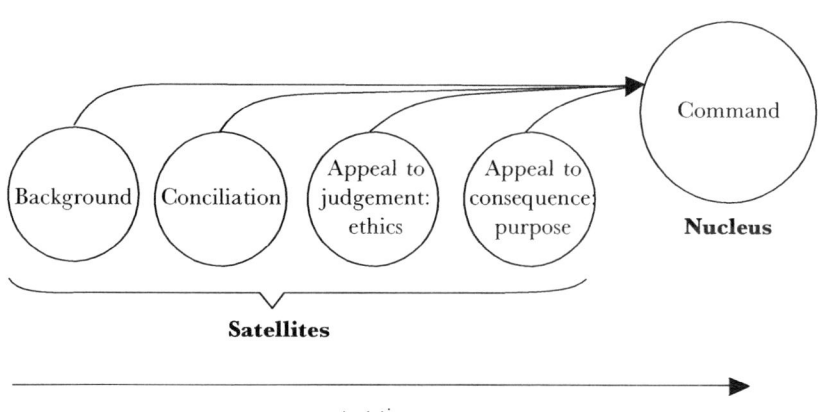

Figure 3.5   Nucleus-satellite model of administrative memo

6 Expanding discourse semantics – appraisal

Much of Martin's linguistic research in the 1980s focused on discourse semantics (Martin 1992; Martin and Rose 2003). Martin provided techniques of analysis for the realization of ideational meaning, conjunction, reference and information flow across texts to account for 'meaning beyond the clause'. In working with teachers and industry representatives during WIR, discourse semantics was a helpful way of moving from generic structure to the grammatical features of a text. Because the emphasis in discourse semantics is on grammatical patterns across texts, they illustrated clearly why it was more effective to teach grammar in the context of teaching about genres, rather than teaching grammar in isolation. Many of the descriptions of 'grammatical features' in genre-based programmes are in fact descriptions of discourse semantics.

Useful as Martin's models were, they did not provide much insight into the development of interpersonal meanings across texts. It was clear from our analysis of media texts, response genres in English and the visual arts, and expository texts in history and geography that interpersonal meaning was critical and had to be highlighted in our published materials. Working closely with Martin, a discourse semantics of *appraisal* was developed by the project. The appraisal system incorporated areas of interpersonal grammar already explored by the SF model, such as projection, modality and graduation, into a broader system, together with new categories developed in response to WIR's areas of research. In media texts, particularly 'analysis' and 'comment' genres, the discourse semantics of *judgement* was an effective tool for describing how points of view and political predispositions could be inscribed in texts through the progressive accumulation of identifiable categories of interpersonal meaning. The model of judgement in Table 3.4 (adapted from Martin and Rose 2003: 62) proposes five broad categories through which people and events are typically judged. Like all interpersonal meanings, judgements can be in positive or negative form and can be graded from 'mild' to 'emphatic' forms.

The analysis of response genres in school English and the Visual Arts led to the development of categories for analysing patterns of *appreciation* in texts, while the analysis of narrative texts led to the development of categories for analysing *affect*. Eventually Martin was able to present the work as a developed system of interpersonal discourse semantics, as in Figure 3.6 (from Martin and Rose 2003: 54).

7 Pedagogy – learning through language and critical literacy

In concluding this account of the *Write it Right* project it is important to make a few brief points about developments which occurred in genre-based pedagogical models during the time of the project.[6] An essential component of the school-based work was the development of an effective classroom pedagogy for introducing knowledge about texts

Table 3.4 Judgement

	Positive	**Negative**
Normality 'is s/he special?'	lucky, fortunate, charmed ... normal, average, everyday ... fashionable, with it, in ...	unfortunate, pitiful, tragic ... odd, peculiar, eccentric ... dated, daggy, retrograde ...
Capacity 'is s/he capable?'	powerful, robust, vigorous ... gifted, insightful, clever ... balanced, sane, together ...	weak, mild, wimpy ... slow, stupid, thick ... flaky, neurotic, insane ...
Tenacity 'is s/he dependable?'	brave, plucky, heroic ... reliable, dependable ... tireless, persevering, resolute ...	rash, cowardly, spineless ... unreliable, undependable ... weak, distracted, dissolute ...
Veracity 'is s/he honest?'	truthful, honest, credible ... real, authentic, genuine ... frank, direct ...	deceitful, dishonest ... bogus, fake, glitzy ... manipulative, deceptive ...
Propriety 'is s/he beyond reproach?'	good, moral, ethical ... law abiding, fair, just ... kind, sensitive, caring ...	bad, immoral, evil ... corrupt, unfair, unjust ... mean, insensitive, cruel ...

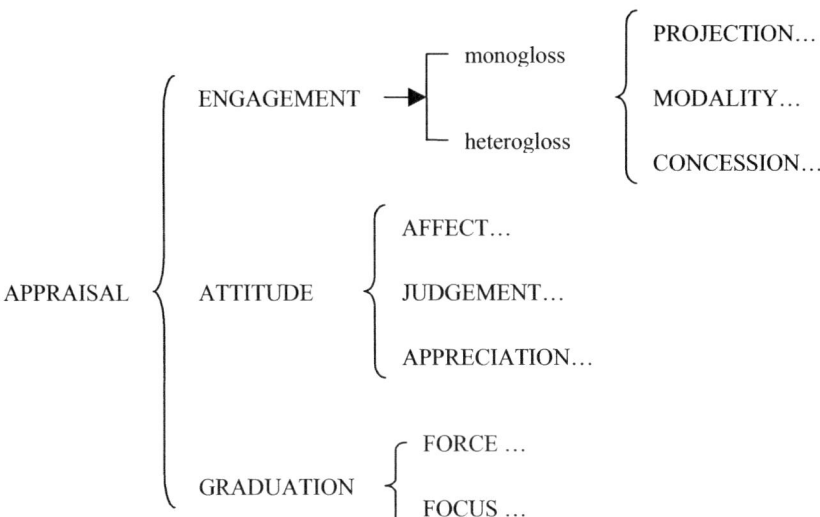

Figure 3.6 Appraisal systems

and their role in learning. Using research on the role of interaction in early child language development (e.g. Halliday 1975; Painter 1984, 1986) and with contributions from language educators around Australia, the Disadvantaged Schools Program had developed a three-stage teaching-learning cycle, which created a classroom environment in which students could move from the examination of the purpose, structure and grammatical features of genres (deconstruction), through a critical phase of guided interaction which provided a context in which the 'constructedness' of texts could be explicitly negotiated, and responsibility for the construction of a new text could be shared among peers and with teachers, through to a phase of independent construction and 'control' of the genre.

Like other aspects of the genre-based work, this primary school pedagogical cycle was a good starting point for our work, but it, too, needed to be adapted to the discipline-driven nature of the secondary school classroom. Whereas in the primary school, teaching writing for its own sake is seen as a legitimate activity and is validated by syllabus documents, in the secondary classroom explicit teaching about text structure and grammar was typically viewed as a distraction from the main task of teaching the content of the subject. The pedagogy developed for secondary schools by WIR therefore needed to emphasize 'learning through language' much more than 'learning about language'. Our immediate aim was for teachers in often stressful classroom situations simply to be prepared to trial language-based materials. If it could be demonstrated that students' learning of content could be enhanced through genre-based activities, then our approach found immediate acceptance. If not, they were very quickly rejected. The longer term aim, to encourage teachers to understand the fundamental role played by language in constructing knowledge in their discipline, was achieved with only a handful of teachers who trialled the materials.

The way of doing this was to emphasize the role of developing content knowledge ('building field') through the deconstruction of texts. The first stage in planning a language-based intervention was to allow the participating teacher to first determine in what sequence content would be presented within a topic and how much time would be allocated to each area of content. Typically this meant that a range of written genres would be encountered; however only one genre was treated in depth – the one which related to the most important learning outcomes. The teaching-learning cycle was then built up around this content oriented framework. Typical content-related activities in the deconstruction phase included translating texts into tables and diagrams and summarizing texts, as well as examination of the structure and generic stages of texts. In a well designed intervention, the language-based activities complemented the sequence of content very well, with deconstruction of texts accompanying preliminary content, and independent construction accompanying

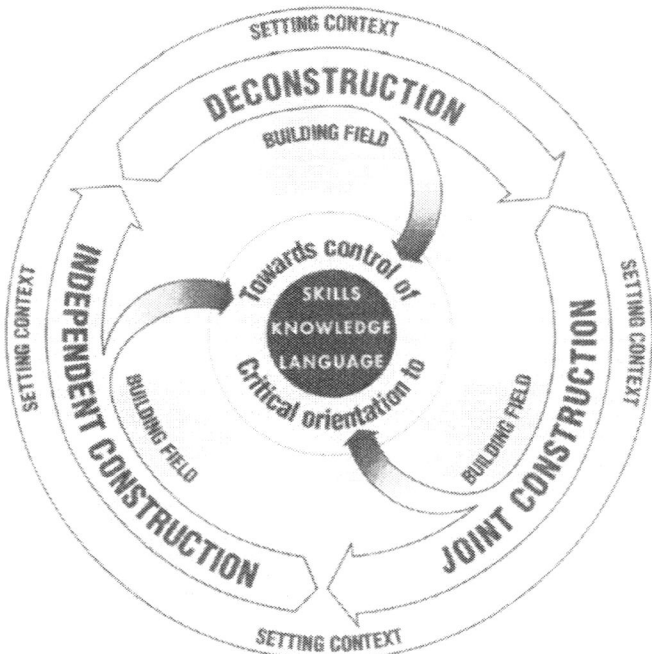

Figure 3.7 WIR teaching-learning cycle

more significant content towards the end of a teaching unit. Thus students were engaged in independent construction of text at precisely the time when the most important content was being covered. Through independent construction of text, students gained independent mastery of key content. Figure 3.7 (from Coffin *et al* 1996: vii) shows a diagrammatic representation of the teaching-learning cycle as it evolved towards the end of WIR.

A second significant modification to the teaching-learning cycle was the introduction of a 'critical literacy' element. Once again this reflects the specific environment of the secondary school where better students in their senior years are expected not only to understand content that is presented to them, but also to deconstruct the basis on which the content is presented – be it a selective tradition of interpretation in history or a dominant reading of a text in English. Thus the centre of the cycle shown in Figure 3.7 includes a 'critical orientation' to text. The explicit inclusion of the notion of a critical orientation in the WIR pedagogical model is also a response to frequent criticism from poststructuralist educators that genre-based approaches to literacy tended to encourage students to reproduce texts, replicating the dominant culture rather than questioning the assumptions in their construction (e.g. Luke 1996). Paralleling WIR's critical orientation to text is Macken-Horarick's (1996: 236) conception of the 'reflexive' domain of secondary education where students 'negotiate social diversity and competing discourses by questioning the contents of specialized knowledge ... deconstructing and reconstructing roles and relationships of different social practices [and] challenging the meanings of dominant discourses'.

8 Coda – whatever happened to equity?

Travelling overseas recently with a group of secondary history teachers, the connection was made by one of the teachers between the writer of this chapter and the *Write it Right* project. 'Oh, I remember those materials', she remarked, 'they *were* great.' She sighed and looked out at the view of the Bay of Naples, as if recalling happier days. Writing this chapter ten years after the conclusion of *Write it Right* has felt rather like anthropological research on a long lost civilization. Several years ago now, a right-wing Labour government in New South Wales 'mainstreamed' the funds allocated to disadvantaged schools, diluting the Disadvantaged Schools Program's resources across schools and effectively denying the possibility of a coherent or prominent approach to addressing issues of socioeconomic disadvantage from public discussion. More recently, a Conservative Federal government has instituted an assessment-driven approach to schooling, based on benchmarking the academic performance of all schools, irrespective of socioeconomic milieux and without regard for the origins of academic underperformance, let alone any reflection of the merits of the regime it has introduced. At the same time, it is advocating models of literacy development based on a phonics approach to reading. In this environment, there is very little scope for engagement on any form of sociologically based or equity-driven approach to literacy education, no matter how effective. Notwithstanding these pressures, the work of the *Write it Right* project continues to influence literacy researchers and teachers especially concerned with the role of language in a specific institutional context. Amid race riots in Sydney and palpable social discontent, one can only hope attention will once again fall on the benefits to society, the economy and democracy of a literate population able to engage through language with the challenges and concerns of the day.

9 Publications of the *Write it Right* project

Some of the research reports produced within the project include:

1. *Workplace literacy reports*: Rose *et al* (1992); Iedema *et al* (1994); Iedema (1995).
2. *Secondary school literacy packages*:
   a. *English*: Rothery (1994a); Rothery and Stenglin (1994a, 1994b, 1994c).
   b. *Science*: Veel (1993).
   c. *Creative Arts*: Rothery (1994b).
   d. *Geography*: Humphrey (1996); Humphrey and Takans (1996); Sikes and Humphrey (1996).
   e. *History*: Coffin (1996); Brook *et al* (1996).

As well as the reports of the Disadvantaged Schools Program, which are not always easy to obtain, a number of books contain extensive contributions by members of the *Write it Right* project team, detailing the description of written genres within institutions and pedagogical approaches to genre. Christie and Martin (1997) contains chapters by Jim Martin on analysing genre, David Rose on science industry, Rick Iedema on the language of administration, Peter White on the news story, Robert Veel on secondary science, Caroline Coffin on school history and Joan Rothery and Maree Stenglin on 'story' texts in school English. Christie (1999) contains chapters by Jim Martin on genre-based literacy pedagogy and Robert Veel on the language of school mathematics. Hasan and Williams (1996) contains chapters by Theo van Leeuwen and Sally Humphrey on visual images in school geography, Joan Rothery on educational linguistics (with a section on narrative and response genres), and Robert Veel and Caroline Coffin on school history.

Notes

1. The term was introduced by Green and Lee (1994). See Martin (this volume, Chapter 4, note 3) for more information.
2. Martin (2000) distinguishes between interdisciplinary and transdisciplinary practices, and describes the relationship between linguistics and education in the Sydney Schools as being fundamentally transdisciplinary.
3. This statement of objectives first appears in the funding submission (unpublished) and is reproduced in all three WIR industry reports.
4. Rose *et al* (1992) provide a background to the selection of the three fields of workplace literacy and their relationship to schooling.
5. Rose *et al* (1992) report on primary school mathematics presents a

multimodal analysis with the semiotic systems of action, symbol, image and language all being incorporated into the analysis. This research was undertaken at the Disadvantaged Schools Program, Metropolitan East Region at the same time as WIR, although it was actually a separate project.

6. For a fuller account of some of the issues, refer to Martin (1999).

References

Bazerman, C. (1988), *Shaping Written Knowledge: The Genre and Activity of the Experimental Article in Science*. Madison, WI: University of Wisconsin Press.

Bernstein, B. (1975), *Class, Codes and Control 3: Towards a Theory of Educational Transmissions*. London: Routledge and Kegan Paul.

— (1990), *Class, Codes and Control 4: The Structuring of Pedagogic Discourse*. London: Routledge.

Brook, R., Coffin, C. and Humphrey, S. (1996), *Australian Identity: A Unit of Work for Junior Secondary History*. Sydney: Metropolitan East DSP.

Cambourne, B. (1988), *The Whole Story: Natural Learning and the Acquisition of Literacy in the Classroom*. New York: Ashton Scholastic.

Christie, F. (ed.) (1999), *Pedagogy and the Shaping of Consciousness: Linguistic and Social Processes*. London: Cassell.

Christie, F. and Martin, J. R. (eds) (1997), *Genres and Institutions: Social Processes in the Workplace and School*. London: Pinter.

Coffin, C. (1996), *Exploring Literacy in School History*. Sydney: DSP, Metropolitan East Region.

Coffin, C., Brook, R. and Humphrey, S. (1996), *Australian Identity* (WIR Teaching Unit) Sydney: DSP, Metropolitan East Region.

Cranny-Francis, A. (1996), 'Technology and/or weapon: the discipline of reading in the secondary English classroom', in R. Hasan and G. Williams (eds), pp. 172–90.

Green, B. and Lee, A. (1994), 'Writing geography lessons: literacy, identity and schooling', in A. Freedman and P. Medway (eds), *Learning and Teaching Genre*. Portsmouth, NH: Boynton/Cook (Heinemann), pp. 207–24.

Halliday, M. A. K. (1975), *Learning How to Mean: Explorations in the Development of Language*. London: Arnold.

— (1996), 'Literacy and linguistics: a functional perspective', in R. Hasan and G. Williams (eds), pp. 339–76.

Halliday, M. A. K. and Hasan, R. (1985), Language, Context and Text. Geelong, Victoria: Deakin University Press.

Harvey, D. (1989), *The Condition of Postmodernity*. London: Basil Blackwell.

Hasan, R. (1984), 'The nursery tale as a genre', *Nottingham Linguistics Circular*, 13, 71–102.

Hasan, R. and Williams, G. (eds) (1996), *Literacy in Society*. London: Longman.

Humphrey, S. (1996), *Exploring Literacy in School Geography*. Sydney: Metropolitan East DSP.

Humphrey, S. and Takans, P. (1996), *Explaining the Weather: A Unit of Work for Junior Secondary Geography*. Sydney: Metropolitan East DSP.

Iedema, R. (1995), *Literacy of Administration (WIR Literacy in Industry Research Project – Stage 3)*. Sydney: Metropolitan East DSP.

Iedema, R., Feez, S. and White, P. (1994), *Media Literacy (WIR Literacy in Industry Research Project – Stage 2)*. Sydney: Metropolitan East DSP.

Kress, G. and van Leeuwen, T. (1996), *Reading Images: The Grammar of Visual Design*. London: Routledge.

Latour, B. and Woolgar, S. (1986), *Laboratory Life: The Social Construction of Scientific Facts*. Princeton, NJ: Princeton University Press.

Luke, A. (1996), 'Genres of power? Literacy education and the production of capital', in R. Hasan and G. Williams (eds), pp. 308–38.

Macken-Horarik, M. (1996), 'Literacy and learning across the curriculum: towards a model of register for secondary school teachers', in R. Hasan and G. Williams (eds), pp. 232–78.

Martin, J. R. (1985), *Factual Writing: Exploring and Challenging Social Reality*. Geelong, Victoria: Deakin University Press.

— (1992), *English Text: System and Structure*. Amsterdam: Benjamins.

— (1999), 'Mentoring semogenesis: genre-based literacy pedagogy', in F. Christie (ed.), pp. 123–55.

— (2000), 'Grammar meets genre – reflections on the Sydney School', *Arts*, 22, 47–95.

Martin, J. R. and Plum, G. (1997), 'Construing experience: some story genres'. *Journal of Narrative and Life History*, 7, 1–4, 299–308.

Martin, J. R. and Rose, D. (2003), *Working with Discourse*. London: Continuum.

McInnes, D. and Murison, B. (1992), 'A model for understanding the literacy demands of mathematics'. Unpublished research report, DSP, Metropolitan East Region.

Painter, C. (1984), *Into the Mother Tongue: A Case Study of Early Language Development*. London: Pinter.

— (1986), 'The role of interaction in learning to speak and learning to write', in C. Painter and J. R. Martin (eds), pp. 62–97.

Painter, C. and Martin, J. R. (eds) (1986), *Writing to Mean: Teaching Genres across the Curriculum*. Applied Linguistics Association of Australia (Occasional Papers 9).

Rose, D., McInnes, D. and Korner, H. (1992), *Scientific Literacy (Write it Right Literacy in Industry Research Project – Stage 1)*. Sydney: Metropolitan East DSP.

Rothery, J. (1986), 'Teaching writing in the primary school a genre-based approach to the development of writing abilities' (Writing Project Report), *Working Papers in Linguistics 4*. Department of Linguistics, University of Sydney.

— (1990), ' "Story" writing in the primary school: assessing narrative type genres'. Ph.D. thesis, University of Sydney.

— (1994a), *Exploring Literacy in School English* (WIR Resources for Literacy and Learning). Sydney: Metropolitan East DSP.

— (1994b), *Exploring Literacy in School Creative Arts* (unpublished report). Sydney: Metropolitan East DSP.

— (1996), 'Making changes: developing an educational linguistics', in R. Hasan and G. Williams (eds), pp. 86–123.

Rothery, J. and Stenglin, M. (1994a), *Spine-Chilling Stories: A Unit of Work for Junior Secondary English* (WIR Resources for Literacy and Learning). Sydney: Metropolitan East DSP.

— (1994b), *Exploring Narrative in Video: A Unit of Work for Junior Secondary English*. Sydney: Metropolitan East DSP.

— (1994c), *Writing a Book Review: A Unit of Work for Junior Secondary English*. Sydney: Metropolitan East DSP.

Sikes, D. and Humphrey, S. (1996), *Australia – Place and Space: A Unit of Work for Junior Secondary Geography*. Sydney: Metropolitan East DSP.

van Leeuwen, T. and Humphrey, S. (1996), 'On learning to look through a geographer's eyes', in R. Hasan and G. Williams (eds), pp. 29–49.

Veel, R. (1993), *Exploring Literacy in School Science* (Unpublished research report). Sydney: Metropolitan East DSP.

— (1997), 'Learning how to mean – scientifically speaking: apprenticeship into scientific discourse in the secondary school' in F. Christie and J. Martin (eds), pp. 161–95.

— (1999). 'Language, knowledge and authority in school mathematics', in F. Christie (ed.), pp. 185–216.

Veel, R. and Coffin C. (1996), 'Learning to think like an historian: the language of school History', in R. Hasan and G. Williams (eds), pp. 191–231.

Weber, M. (1948–91), *Essays in Sociology*. London: Routledge.

Windschuttle, K. (1984), *The Media*. Melbourne: Penguin.

Part Two

SFL Approaches to Literacy in Educational Systems
around the World

4 Metadiscourse: designing interaction in genre-based literacy programmes[1]

J. R. Martin

1 Linguistics for language teaching[2]

The basic question I focus on in this chapter is how to use linguistics, systemic functional linguistics in particular, in language education programmes. From the perspective of genre-based literacy programmes this involves two concerns. One has to do with how linguistics is used to design pedagogy and curriculum; the other has to do with how much linguistics literacy teachers and their students need to share to get on with learning to read and write. I contextualize these issues by briefly reviewing the writing development initiatives associated with the so-called 'Sydney School' in the 80s and 90s (Martin 2000a, Chapter 3 this volume) and then turn to the reading development extensions of this work in Rose's evolving Learning to Read/Reading to Learn programmes (Rose 2003).

2 Scaffolding writing development

Throughout the 80s and 90s the Sydney School[3] drew on systemic functional linguistics both to characterize what needed to be learned and how it could be learned. Drawing for the most part on Halliday's functional grammar (Halliday and Matthiessen 2004) and Martin's discourse semantics (Martin and Rose 2003), functional linguists and their educational linguistics colleagues undertook analyses of writing across primary, secondary, tertiary and adult education sectors[4] – in order to establish the kinds of writing required for success in school (and selected workplace contexts). At the same time, inspired by Halliday and Painter's work on language development (e.g. Halliday 1975, 1993, 2004; Painter 1984, 1986, 1998, 2000), they designed pedagogy which was used to apprentice students into the writing they were expected to control (Hammond 2001). Throughout this process genre theory was developed to interpret curriculum (what students were learning to write) and pedagogy (how they were taught), and so alongside its name (the Sydney School) this action research project has often been characterized as 'genre-based' literacy development.[5]

Space precludes an outline here of our work on school and workplace genres (Christie and Martin 1997, Martin and Rose 2006) and the learner pathways we constructed out of their relations to one another (Coffin 1997; Feez 1998). However, I briefly outline the macro-genre[6] designed by Rothery and her colleagues (Rothery 1994, 1996) to scaffold genre development. (See Figure 3.7 in Chapter 3, this volume.) This teaching-learning cycle consists of three main phases – Deconstruction, Joint Construction and Individual Construction. Deconstruction focuses on a model of the genre being learned; Joint Construction involves the teacher scribing student suggestions as they produce another model of the same genre, but involving a different subject matter; in the Individual Construction stage, students write a text of their own, changing the subject matter once again. Each stage includes activities building up knowledge of the relevant field (the domestic, professional or disciplinary content of the genre); and importantly for the discussion here, each stage both introduces and deploys knowledge about language (KAL) to analyse and produce instances of the focal genre (Rothery 1989, 1996).

Using knowledge about language and genre to scaffold writing development was a radical innovation in Australia at the time, when the writing curriculum was strongly influenced by American progressivism (the process writing and whole language movements). Syllabus designers had interpreted progressivism as prescribing that KAL[7] was useless as far as literacy development was concerned (and harmful, since it took time away from writing). This meant that a generation of Australians, including teachers, had grown up with virtually no knowledge of the structure of their language – so almost any metalanguage we wanted to use we had to introduce. We began with terminology for names of genres and their principal stages ('exposition' with the stages 'Thesis', 'Arguments' and 'Reiteration of Thesis' for example; Derewianka 1990). In some cases, where in-service training permitted, various dimensions of grammar and discourse analysis were also introduced and deployed (Rothery 1989; Williams 2000, 2004). Our interventions at the level of genre were ultimately quite successful, as reflected in primary school syllabus documents and assessment initiatives around Australia. Functional grammar on the other hand had to be spirited in (Derewianka 1998) once New South Wales state politicians and talk-show hosts realized what was going on and legislated for 'conventional' terminology – their knee-jerk 'back to basics' (i.e. back to the 50s) riposte to successful innovation drawing on cutting-edge linguistic research.[8]

Alongside SFL, our work drew on Bernstein's sociology of education, especially his analysis of pedagogic discourse and educational failure (Bernstein 1975, 1990, 1996). For Bernstein, pedagogic discourse embeds an instructional discourse (ID) in a regulative discourse (RD), in a model where instructional discourse is concerned with the classification of what is taught and regulative discourse with the framing of how this is transmitted. As functional linguists we preferred the term projection to embedding, treating the instructional discourse as projected by the regulative one – science discourse projected by varieties of teacher/pupil classroom interaction, for example (Christie 2002). The pedagogic discourse implicated in the teaching/learning cycle explained above is discussed in relation to Bernstein's notions of weak and strong classification and framing in Martin (1998).

We can adapt Bernstein's imagic notation for the projection of instructional by regulative discourse as represented in Figure 4.1(a). In our pedagogy, however, the instructional discourse was in a sense bifurcated, since we projected instructional discourse in Bernstein's sense through our own functional linguistic metalanguage. As this terminology covered both language and social context (i.e. genre and register as well as grammar and discourse semantics), and later on attendant modalities of communication such as image and sound as well (Cope and Kalantzis 1999; Unsworth 2001), it can be referred to as a social semiotic instructional discourse (SSID). This means that as far as students and teachers were concerned, the pedagogy is better represented as shown in Figure 4.1(b).

In our design of curriculum macro-genres, we were of course drawing on the SSID to project the regulative discourse as well; and some educators (e.g. Wells 1999) have argued that teachers and students should be encouraged to negotiate their regulatory discourse with one another, potentially drawing on SSID to do so. This takes us beyond the scope of the present discussion, but this radical possibility is outlined in Figure 4.1(c) (cf. Martin 1998; Martin and Rose 2005). In this chapter, however, I will restrict discussion to the nature of the metalanguage involved in the SSID projecting ID in classroom interaction.

One final step before pursuing this discussion is to position the Sydney School in relation to alternative positions as far as pedagogic discourse is concerned. Bernstein's (1990) topology of theories of

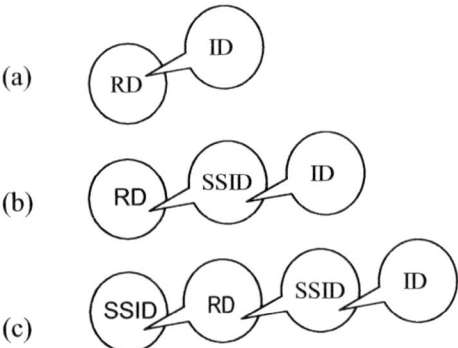

Figure 4.1   Representing pedagogy

instruction has been adapted in Figure 4.2. He outlines the key axes as follows:

> The vertical dimension would indicate whether the theory of instruction privileged relations internal to the individual, where the focus would be **intra-individual**, or ... relations **between** social groups (inter-group). In the first case... the theory would be concerned to explain the conditions for changes within the individual, whereas in the second the theory would be concerned to explain the conditions for changes in the relation between social groups. The horizontal dimension would indicate whether the theory articulated a pedagogic practice emphasising a logic of acquisition or... a logic of transmission. In the case of a logic of acquisition...the acquirer is active in regulating an implicit facilitating practice. In the case of a logic of transmission the emphasis is upon explicit effective ordering of the discourse to be acquired, by the transmitter.
>
> (Bernstein 1990: 213–14)

Read vertically then, Figure 4.2 arranges pedagogies along a scale with psychologically grounded theories focusing on individual development towards the top and more sociologically grounded theories focusing on education as a tool for redistributing power among social groups towards the bottom (individual development vs. social change if you will). Read horizontally, Bernstein's topology arranges pedagogies along a scale, with those emphasizing what we might call discovery learning to the left and those emphasizing mentoring and apprenticeship to the right. I have labelled the four quadrants partitioned by these vectors 'liberal', 'radical', 'conservative' and 'subversive' for ease of reference (for further discussion see Martin and Rose 2005).

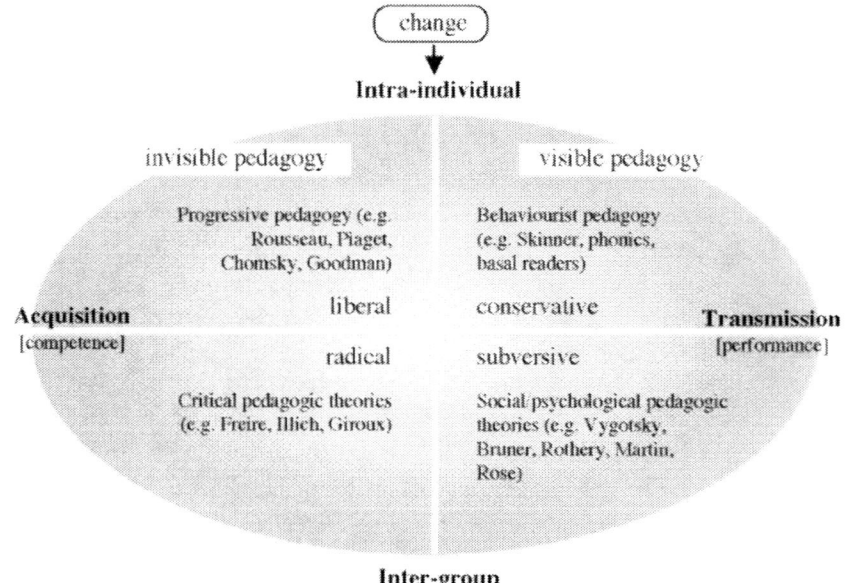

Figure 4.2   Types of pedagogy (after Bernstein 1990)

Bernstein also comments:

> It is a matter of interest that this top right-hand quadrant is regarded as conservative but has *often produced very innovative and radical acquirers*. The bottom right-hand quadrant shows a radical realization of an apparently conservative pedagogic practice ... each theory will carry its own conditions of contestation, 'resistance', subversion.[9]
>
> (1990: 73)

As the matrix implies, our approach in the lower right-hand quadrant has been a visible and interventionist one (Painter and Martin 1986, Hasan and Martin 1989,[10] Cope and Kalantzis 1993), with a relatively strong focus on the transmission of identified discourse competences and on the empowerment of otherwise disenfranchised groups in relation to this transmission. As such, it resonates strongly with the social constructivist position articulated by Mercer and his colleagues in Britain (1994, 1995, 2000), although it has to be said that American implementations of neo-Vygotskian ideals seem at times to slide rather seamlessly into a co-opting upper left-hand progressivist quadrant (see for example Wells' social constructivist manifesto[11] in Appendix I of Wells (1999), in which there is no mention of an agentive teacher). This topology of pedagogies will be further discussed in section 5 below, once Rose's approach to pedagogy and metalanguage has been introduced.

3 Scaffolding reading development

In the 00s, the main innovations to the literacy programme outlined above have been undertaken by David Rose, drawing on his years of experience working in Indigenous communities in Australia, his literacy work with Brian Gray in South Australia (Gray and Cowey 1999; Rose *et al* 1999; Rose *et al* 2004), and his research in the fields of functional grammar and discourse analysis (with special reference to Pitjantjatjara and the discourse of science-based industry; Rose 1997, 2001). Complementing 80s and 90s initiatives, Rose has focused on reading (alongside writing), on the design of micro-interaction in the classroom (alongside the global staging of curriculum genres) and on the use of everyday metalanguage to scaffold literacy instruction (alongside technicality drawn from SFL). These are crucial developments since they address three pressing problems: i) students not being able to read the texts used to model genres ii) teachers interacting with students in ritualized IRF (Initiation, Response, Feedback) exchange sequences no matter where they are in a teaching/learning cycle and iii) students and teachers not sharing specialized knowledge about language with which to analyse and construct texts. Problems of this order, especially when combined with one another, can bring the pedagogic processes outlined in section 2 above to a grinding halt.

Rose's macro-genre[12] for the global organization of his pedagogy is outlined in Figure 4.3 (which correlates stages with metalinguistic foci). The general preparation stage explores the field of the text in question and summarizes its content and sequencing; the teacher reads the text aloud, briefly explaining key concepts where necessary. The detailed reading stage involves a sentence-by-sentence focus on the text; the teacher prepares the students for each sentence with meaning and position cues, the students identify and mark key wordings and the teacher elaborates unfamiliar meanings. I will concentrate on this stage of the pedagogy below. The next stage is note taking, with a student scribe writing dot-points suggested by fellow students and negotiated with the teacher on the board; the metalinguistic focus here is on spelling. Then in the rewriting from notes stage, the students write a new version of the reading passage based on their notes, with the teacher in a guiding role, focusing on text structure, 'grammar', punctuation, spelling.

Alongside this global scaffolding Rose has also designed a generalized more locally focused structure for micro-interaction (see Figure

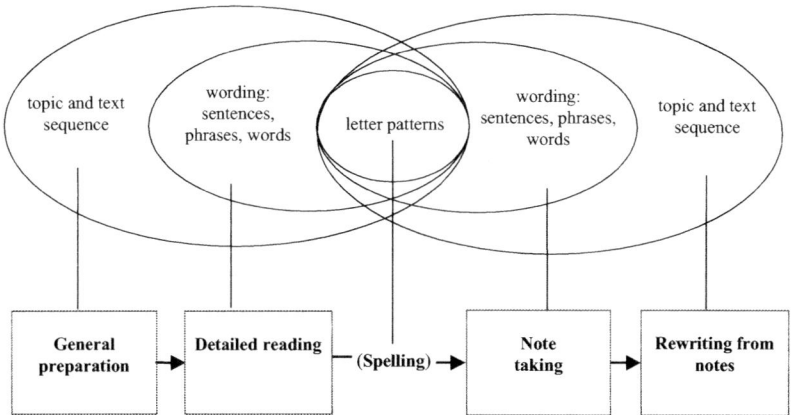

Figure 4.3   Rose's reading-focused curriculum genre

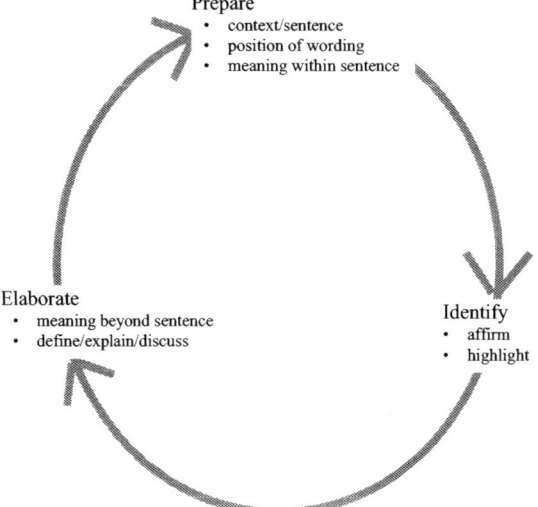

Figure 4.4   Rose's interaction cycle for detailed preparation stage

4.4). 'Prepare' involves cues for learners to identify groups of words, including their meaning in commonsense terms and their position (often probed with a wh- phrase). 'Identify' has students picking out the relevant word or phrase in the text and highlighting it (e.g. underlining or colouring in with a marker pen). 'Elaborate' is used to define technical terms, explain metaphors and abstract language and to relate the text to students' experience.

From a linguistic perspective, what is interesting here is the kind of exchange structure Rose's scaffolding promotes. For this analysis, I draw on Ventola's (1987) exchange structure (as developed in Martin 1992, following Ventola and earlier work by Berry, e.g. 1981). In this model, an exchange consists of between one and five moves, according to the following structure potential – where 'D' stands for delay (a 'test' question[13] or offer of goods and services manoeuvre), 'f' for follow-up, 'K' for knower (in information exchanges negotiating propositions), 'A' for actor (in action exchanges negotiating proposals), '1' for primary knower or actor (the primary knower has authority with respect to the validity of the information exchanged, the primary actor has responsibility for handing over goods or performing the service in an action exchange) and '2' for secondary knower or actor (the secondary knower is seeking information, the secondary actor is seeking goods or services); optional moves are placed in parentheses and '^' stands for sequence.

$$((Dk1) \quad ^\wedge K2) \quad ^\wedge K1 \quad (^\wedge K2f \quad (^\wedge K1f))$$
$$((DA1) \quad ^\wedge A2) \quad ^\wedge A1 \quad (^\wedge A2f \quad (^\wedge A1f))$$

Information and action exchanges of five moves are illustrated below. In the first exchange, someone opens by raising the issue of their name, which is in turn requested by the person needing this information; this information is then given and followed up with two reaffirming moves.

Dk1	You'll never guess who I am?
K2	– Who?
K1	– Rita.
K2f	– Ah.
K1f	– Yeah.

The second exchange begins with an offer of the book by the owner, followed up by a request for such by the borrower; the owner then hands over the book, is thanked for it by the borrower, and then follows up with a closing move further sanctioning the exchange.

Da1	Would you like to borrow it?
A2	– Yes.
A1	– Here you go. (handing over book)
A2f	– Well, thank you very much.
A1f	– No worries, mate.

In a model of this kind, the IRF (Initiation, Response and Feedback) exchange so often explored in classroom-based research (e.g. Sinclair and Coulthard 1975) is treated as a Dk1^K2^K1 sequence. The primary knower, the teacher, delays adjudicating the proposition in question by asking a test question (Dk1), to which students respond as secondary knowers (K2); the teacher then validates 'correct' responses or recycles the Dk1 move until an acceptable answer is proffered. This kind of sequence can function as a useful review strategy, once teacher and students share the knowledge that is being 'tested'. Appropriate consolidation along these lines is illustrated below with a passage taken from the Deconstruction stage of one implementation of the teaching/learning cycle outlined in section 2. The Year 5 class is working on exposition have already completed one cycle, and have been looking critically at some of the individually constructed expositions undertaken by the class. Before moving to another joint construction phase the teacher pulls together some of the key points she wants them to remember next time round.

Teacher	Dk1	What are some of the things I mentioned you are going to try to think about when we do this one today? Filippa?
Filippa	K2	Not to, um, put an argument into the thesis.
Teacher	K1	Good. Right.
Teacher	Dk1	Something else.
Richard	K2	Don't repeat yourself
Teacher	K1	Don't repeat. Excellent
Teacher	Dk1	Something else. Who can think of something? Yes.
Nicole	K2	Don't put any other ideas in the paragraph you are talking about.
Teacher	K1	Good girl. Keep all the paragraph unified. Don't start introducing new ideas into the same one.
Teacher	Dk1	Something else, to think about. Yes.
Linh	K2	The argument that you're doing has to be like the topic or thesis that you choose.
Teacher	K1	Right. So you make sure you mentioned all your arguments in your thesis. Good.

One of Rose's key points is that such IRF sequences work well when students already know the answer to the Dk1 move, but can be extremely frustrating for both teacher and student when they don't. When used to scaffold interaction with poor readers, for example, they can be quite alienating, since they position students to induce something they are trying to learn (Rose 2004a, 2005b). This is the principal motivation for Rose's design of local exchange structure, as presented in Figure 4.4. Following a cycle of this kind, the information students need to know to respond successfully in Dk1ˆK2ˆK1 sequence is front-loaded into the interaction, cyclically, until all members of the class can respond successfully in the Identification phase. Rose sees this as a more democratic approach to teaching reading than one involving just a few select students providing K2 moves in Dk1ˆK2ˆK1 sequences by way of moving the lesson along (e.g. Rose 2004a).

Let's look now at some data from one of Rose's classrooms, breaking the interaction down into exchanges following Ventola's model. The reason I am looking so closely at the interaction is that what is going on in this classroom may not look very different from other classroom routines until we recognize that it is the teacher's conscious focus on language and on the differences between spoken and written grammar in precisely these kind of exchanges that leads the students to success.

For this analysis I've included Ventola's notion of a move complex, namely, two or more clauses selecting independently for mood but jointly realizing a single function in exchange structure. Below, for example, the teacher plays the Dk1 move in the second exchange twice – once as a polar question projecting a wh- question, *Can you see what it is?*, and again as a declarative, withholding words potentially carrying the tonic syllable, *1984 to 1986...?* Similarly the K1 move in the same exchange[14] is accomplished by repeating the K2 move, *Uprising*, and by declaring *that's exactly right!* Note that Rose is working on students' understandings of ideational grammatical metaphors (realized by nominalizations; see Halliday and Matthiessen 2004) in this phase of interaction.

Teacher	K1	And then the next words tell us... it's a word for a rebellion.
Teacher	Dk1 ⎫	Can you see what it is?
Teacher	Dk1 ⎭	1984 to 1986 ...?
Student	K2	– Uprising.
Teacher	K1 ⎫	– Uprising,
Teacher	K1 ⎭	that's exactly right!
Teacher	A2	Do the whole lot, OK, 1984 to 1986 uprising.
Students	A1	(students highlight)
Teacher	Dk1 ⎫	You know why it's called an uprising?
Teacher	Dk1 ⎭	Because what did the people do?
Student	K2	– Rise up.
Teacher	K1	– The people rise up, yes.
Teacher	Dk1	And who were they rising up against?
Student	K2	– The government.
Teacher	K1 ⎫	– The government, that's right.
Teacher	K1 ⎭	that's right.

In Rose's terms, the first exchange above is treated as Prepare, the next as Identify, and the third and fourth as Elaboration (a line is skipped to demarcate exchanges in this and following examples).

From the point of view of exchange structure what seems to be going on here is that exchanges have been organized into exchange complexes, with the Identify exchange as nucleus, and the other exchanges as interdependent satellites (Martin 2000b). Since both Rose's Prepare and Elaboration phases have the discourse semantic function of reformulating the meaning of the word or phrase in focus, I'll revise his terminology here by replacing his term Elaborate with Extend (to avoid confusion when I use Halliday's logico-semantic relation elaboration ('=') below to characterize parts of what is going on). I'll also further specify Rose's phasing by distinguishing two functions, Focus and Highlight, which frequently occur as adjunct exchanges to the Identify Dk1^K2^K1 sequence. Focus orients students perceptually to the word or phrase under negotiation (e.g. *Now have a look at your text*); Highlight gets students to act physically on the text (e.g. *Do that one for me*, prompting the students to highlight a word or phrase).

The text we are in fact working on here is taken from Rose's work with Mike Hart in a secondary school in South Africa (with students aged 15–16); the text involves abstract discourse from the discipline of history which was well beyond the reading level of the class (Rose 2003).

Revolutionary days: The 1984 to 1986 uprising
In the mid-1980s South African politics erupted in a rebellion in black townships throughout the country. The government's policies of repression had bred anger and fear. Its policies of reform had given rise to expectations amongst black people of changes which the government had been unable to meet. The various forces of resistance, which we outlined in the previous section, now combined to create a major challenge for the government.

The townships became war zones, and in 1985 the ANC called on its supporters among the youth to make these areas 'ungovernable'. The army occupied militant township areas. The conflict was highly complex and violent; it involved not only clashes between the security forces and the resisters, but violence between competing political organizations, between elders and youth, and between people who lived in shantytowns and those who lived in formal townships.

(Nuttal *et al* 1998: 117)

Rose's first step is to deal with the Heading, which he contextualizes through a five-move K1 complex functioning as Prepare. He then instructs the students to look at their text (A2^A1-nonverbal realizing Focus). For Identify he uses two exchanges, one dealing with the year beginning the uprising (1984) and one dealing with the end (1986). The first Dk1 exchange involves a three-move complex; once 1984 has been identified, 1986 requires less scaffolding (a simple Dk1^K2^K1 sequence). Rose then gets the students to highlight the dates (A2^A1-nonverbal again), and moves on without an Extend exchange to deal with *uprising* (already analysed above).

Turn Heading	Exchange	Exchange complex
		Prepare
Teacher	K1 ⎞	We'll start off with the heading.
	… ⎠	The heading's called *Revolutionary days*.
		So of course it's the days when the revolution started.
		That's why they call it *Revolutionary days*.
		And then it tells us when the uprising started.
		Focus
Teacher	A2	Now *have a look* at your text,
Students	A1 (nv)	(students look)
		Identify (×2)
Teacher	Dk1 ⎞	and can anybody tell us when it started?
Teacher	Dk1 ⎟	Revolutionary days the …?
Teacher	Dk1 ⎠	What's the first year there?
Student	K2	– 1984.
Teacher	K1	– 1984!
Teacher	Dk1	1984 to when?
Student	K2	– to 1986.
Teacher	K1	– to 1986, OK!
		Highlight
Teacher	A2	Do that first for me, OK?
Students	A1 (nv)	(students highlight)
		… (see preceding text segment for 'uprising' scaffolding)

The first sentence in the text is longer and so takes more work. Rose begins with an exchange complex locating the uprising in time (*in the mid-1980s*). Note that in this complex the Focus and Identify functions are conflated in the Dk1 move *Who can see the words that tell us when?*

Turn	Exchange	Exchange complex

First Sentence

		Prepare
Teacher	K1	Now the first sentence tells us that the trouble blew up in the townships, and that the people were rebelling against the government.
Teacher and Students	K1	*In the mid-1980s South African politics erupted in a rebellion in black townships throughout the country.* (joint reading)
Teacher	K1	Now that sentence starts by telling us when they rebelling.

		Focus/Identify
Teacher	Dk1	Who can *see* the words that tell us when?
Student	K2	– In the 1980s.
Teacher	*check	– Is she right?
Students	*rcheck	– Yes.
Teacher	K1	– OK.

		Highlight
Teacher	A2	Let's all do mid-1980s.
Students	A1 (nv)	(students highlight)

Rose then moves on to deal with *erupted* and the lexical metaphor at stake. Once again Focus and Identify are conflated (*Can you see the word that tells us...*). This exchange involves a dependent move complex (*Is he right? – Yes.*), which is used to affirm and celebrate the successful identification of *erupted*. In Ventola's exchange model this sequence would be treated as dynamic rather than synoptic (i.e. as simply confirming the ideational meaning under negotiation rather than extending the exchange; see Martin 1992 on tracking moves). This is followed by the Highlight function, including Focus (*Can you see...*), and Extend, which mobilizes several knowledge exchanges to explain the metaphor.

		Prepare
Teacher	K1	Then it tells us that South African politics blew up.

		Focus/Identify
Teacher	Dk1	Can you *see* the word that tells us South African politics blew up?
Teacher	Dk1	South African politics ...?
Student	K2	– Erupted.
Teacher	K1	– Erupted!
Teacher	*check	– Is he right?
Students	*check	– Yes.

		Highlight/Focus
Teacher	K2	– Can you see the word that says erupted?

Teacher	A2	Lets do that one, erupted.
Student	A1	(students highlight)

		Extend
Teacher	K1	The reason they use the word erupted is because that's what volcanoes do.
Teacher	K2	Have you heard that before?
Students	K1	– Yes.

Teacher	K2	– A volcano erupts?
Students	K1	– Yes.

Teacher	Dk1)	– So what were the townships like?
Teacher	Dk1)	They were like ...?
Students	K2	– Volcanoes.
Teacher	K1)	– Exactly right,
Teacher	K1)	they were like a volcano,

Teacher	K1	and there was all this pressure inside, waiting to blow up and erupt, with all this anger the people were feeling about the government's repression.

To end the sentence, Rose turns to the nominalization *rebellion*, which he renders verbally in Prepare (*were rebelling*), and then Identifies (including celebration and reinforcement through the checking moves).

		Prepare
Teacher	K1	OK, South African politics erupted and then it tells us that people were rebelling.

		Focus/Identify
Teacher	Dk1)	Can you *see* the word that means people were rebelling?
Teacher	Dk1)	South African politics erupted in a ...?
Students	K2	– Rebellion.
Teacher	K1	– Rebellion!
Teacher	*check	– Is he right?
Students	*rcheck	– Yes.
		...

Obviously there is more analysis to be done. In preparation for this enterprise, I'm suggesting here for Rose's detailed preparation stage of his global teaching/learning cycle that we recognize an exchange complex consisting of five phases. The nuclear phase is Identify, where 'reading' happens. Sandwiching this nucleus there are two elaborating phases, one initial (Prepare) and one final (Extend), whose job it is to shunt to and fro between the written text and spoken discourse that the students can understand. In addition there are two intermodal phases, surrounding the nucleus and connecting the spoken discourse of the classroom to the writing – Focus which ensures students attend perceptually to the text, and Highlight which amplifies this by instructing them to physically highlight the words or phrases under scrutiny.

Identify   nuclear IRF exchange ('reading')
Prepare   prospective elaboration
Extend   retrospective elaboration
Focus   perceive text
Highlight   modify image

These can be organized as a structure potential as follows, with '^' realizing sequence, '()' optionality, '/' for conflation and the 'n' superscript for recursion:

Prepare ^ (Focus)(/) ^ Identify^n (^ check) ^Highlight ^ (Extend)

An alternative imagic representation is offered as Figure 4.5, including turntaking by the Teacher (T) and student/s (S) involved ('nv' stands for non-verbal realization in this diagram, and the arrows show dependency relations between satellite functions and the exchange complex's nuclear Identify exchange).

It is important to stress here that this is a designed interaction, part of the detailed preparation stage of Rose's globally designed curriculum genre. It has been designed to discourage teachers from

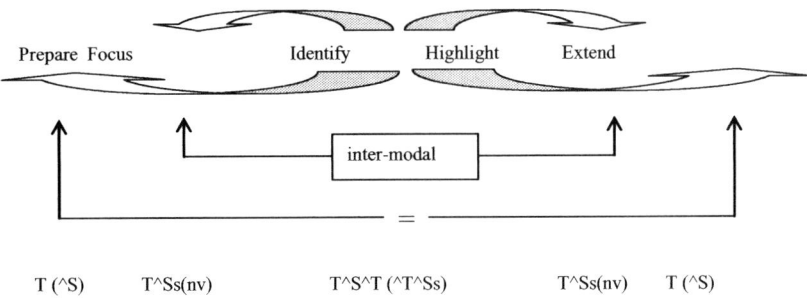

T (^S)   T^Ss(nv)   T^S^T (^T^Ss)   T^Ss(nv)   T (^S)

Figure 4.5   Rose's exchange complex (detailed preparation stage)

teaching reading as they may have been taught, via unscaffolded 'guess what's in my head' IRF (i.e. Dk1^K2^K1) sequences. And it acknowledges in its design that learning to read is not like learning to talk. Domestic interaction will not do.[15] What is required is specifically designed interaction for teaching uncommon sense in institutionalized learning.

4 Metalanguage

One of the most intriguing aspects of Rose's pedagogy in this detailed preparation stage is the way in which he refers to the text he is teaching students to read without using any specialized[16] SFL metalanguage. Let's take a moment to see precisely how this is done.

As far as interpersonal resources are concerned, the key device is wh- interrogatives which focus students' attention on relevant parts of a sentence without having to label participants, processes and circumstances as such:

Dk1:	(who, what, which, when, where, why, how ...)
K2:	= wording
K1:	= repeat wording
Teacher	So who was it that couldn't meet the changes, meet their needs?
Student	The government.
Teacher	– The government.

Textually there are two main resources at play. One was exemplified above, namely withholding the word or phrase containing a tone group's tonic syllable (a supportive 'fill in the blanks' exercise for students – Rose gives the co-text, students supply the rest):

Dk1:	withhold tonic ...
K2:	= wording
K1:	= repeat wording
Teacher	Can you see the word that means policies to make things better?
Teacher	Policies of [...] ?
Student	– Reform.

The other textual resource regularly deployed is the use of exophoric reference to target relevant parts of the text:

exophoric reference to text: *it; this/that, the; next, first* ...

Teacher	OK, let's do all of $\boxed{\textbf{that}}$, *unable to meet.*
Students	(students highlight)

Ideationally, Rose uses behavioural processes of perception to get students to focus on the text, and general material processes to prompt their highlighting.

PERCEPTION	**have a look, look at, watch, see** (Focus)
ACTION	**do, get** (Highlight)

Where metadiscourse is used to name parts of the text, Rose restricts himself to commonsense terms from everyday folk rhetoric (the resources documented by Halliday and Painter in their discussions of the role of talk about talk in early language development; see Painter 1996, 1998, 1999, 2003):

VERBAL	**tell, say; call, mean; read; spell ...**
PREPOSITIONAL	be **about**; word **for** ...

And Rose uses a few relatively familiar terms from traditional school grammar:

NOMINAL	**part; word, words, sentence, text/book ...**
	line, paragraph, heading ...
	comma, full stop, capital, line (under)
	reasons ...

As far as I can see there is nothing here to outrage the presumptuous premiers, meddling talk-back radio shock jocks, overburdened teachers, concerned parents or struggling students who have expressed concern about the introduction of knowledge about language into various Australian language education curricula.

As we have seen, given Rose's carefully designed exchange complexing, these resources are enough to interface his spoken scaffolding with the written word – patiently, cyclically, word by word and phrase by phrase, until he has the whole class reading. Deploying projection, he gets the students to tell him what the text means:

people telling (human sayers projecting meaning):

and can anybody **tell** us (***when*** it started)?
Can anybody at this table **tell** me (***what*** that policy was)?
And who can **tell** me (the **words** that **mean** angry and frightened?)
Who can **tell** me (the **word** that **means** they gave rise to people expecting)?

And he gets the text to talk:

text telling/saying (text sayers projecting meaning):

and then |**it**| **tells** us (that people were rebelling.)
Then |**it**| tells us (**where** that rebellion happened.)
|**it**| **tells** us (**when** the uprising started.)
Then |**it**| **tells** us (that South African politics blew up.)
|**It**| **starts off** by **telling** us (that the government had a policy to make things better)
Then |**it**| **tells** us (expectations of **what**?)
And then |**it**| **tells** us (that the government couldn't meet the people's needs.)
Now |**the first**| sentence **tells** us (that the trouble blew up in the townships...)
Now |**the next**| sentence **tells** us (the **reasons** that you had this rebellion;)
|**this**| sentence... by **telling** us (**which** policy it was.)
And then |**the next**| **words tell** us...
...|**the**| **words** that **tell** us (**when**)?
...|**the**| **word** that **tells** us (South African politics blew up)?

So |**it**| **says** expectations amongst black people.
...|**the**| **word** that **says** erupted?

Via identification, he explores what things are called:

identification (naming):

|**The**| **heading's called** *Revolutionary days.*
That's why they **call** it *Revolutionary days.*
why it's **called** an uprising?

Words are related to their meanings (as Tokens of written text in relation to spoken Values):

word/s meaning (text Token, meaning Value):

|**the**| **word** that **means** people were rebelling?
|**the**| **words** that **mean** angry and frightened?
|**the**| **word** that **means** they gave rise to people expecting?
|**What**|'s the **words** that **mean** they couldn't meet the people's needs?

(|**it**|'s a **word for** a rebellion.)

And meanings are related to one another (unfamiliar words related to more familiar counterparts):

meaning meaning (meaning Token, meaning Value):

So what's reform **mean**? To make things…(students) Better.
Expectations **means** they expected things to get better.

Rose's dialectic tunes the students in to the structure of the written text, and builds bridges between it and the spoken language they already know – until reading becomes part of their verbal repertoire.

From the perspective of multi-modal discourse analysis, what is going on here is that two separate modalities (verbal discourse and written artefact) are reconstructed as dimensions of relatively unified semiotic system (i.e. language). Books and pages don't simply inhabit the classroom as things (alongside waste baskets, desks and pencils); rather they talk – they say things and mean things (they project!). Nudging further, beyond this, books and pages mean; or putting this more technically, they realize meaning, as graphology (the expression form of written discourse). At the same time, spoken and written discourse aren't left to inhabit the classroom as distinct languages, with Rose translating in between. By continually shunting from one to the other Rose reworks separation as complementarity – as registerial difference (transforming intermodality to 'alter'modality if you will). In Rose's experience, every member of the class learns to read, which doesn't otherwise occur. Significantly, in Rose's classrooms this happens by design; it doesn't just happen.

5 Design and practice

What does all this cost? The bottom line is that we have to pay – by finding the money to provide in-service training for practising teachers, and finding the time to change pre-service training (where staff have invested heavily in the very practices we are trying to change). At first blush, a pedagogy that doesn't depend on SFL metalanguage seems an attractive option, since training in linguistics is expensive, and can provoke resistance of various orders (traditional grammar vs. functional grammar, humanities vs. science, 'creativity' vs. technicality – the list goes on). At the same time we have to remember that Rose's pedagogy involves both global and local design. He's not just changing the macro-genre deployed for teaching reading and writing; he's changing the micro-interactions between teachers and students at every stage as well. And teaching teachers to teach differently from the ways they were taught is also costly, and can provoke resistance of a comparable order (teaching vs. learning, authority vs. facilitation, democracy vs. elitism and so on).

Performing Rose's exchange complexing is also dependent on text analysis; it's not just an off the cuff, spur of the moment process but something more professional. When apprenticing teachers, Rose recommends the following text preparation procedure:

Analysing tasks: steps in lesson planning
1. *Select text*: According to **genre** (for modelling writing), **field** (key text in the topic), **mode** (right level of difficulty for grade), **ideology** (message you want to discuss). Blow up a passage for easy reading and lesson preparation. Number sentences.
2. *Identify phases*: Phases are a few sentences long. Types of phases depend on genre, e.g. story phases can include settings, problems, reactions, descriptions, solutions, comments, reflections.
3. *Highlight key wordings in each sentence*: Key information in factual texts and literate language patterns in stories.
4. *Write notes* for general preparation before reading: On a separate sheet. Background knowledge (general field), what the text's about (text field), what happens in the text (how the field unfolds through the text).
5. *Write preparation cues above highlighted wordings*: 'Wh' cues like who, when, where, why or commonsense paraphrases for each wording.
6. *Write notes for sentence meanings and elaborations*: Commonsense summary of the sentence meaning – numbered on separate sheet. Then note words to define, concepts to explain, points to discuss.

(Rose 2005a)

This procedure depends on apprenticeship into at least the rudiments of genre, register and discourse semantics. Unless Rose himself annotates the texts he wants teachers to negotiate with the class, the teachers themselves will have to take control of SFL metalanguage, whether they share this explicitly with the class or not. So there's actually more SFL metalanguage involved in Rose's project than meets the eye when we analyse his classroom interaction without taking into account the preparation that has gone into the Prepare, Focus, Identify, Highlight and Extend exchange complexing.[17]

That said, the basic question I am posing here is whether there is a kind of trade-off between designing micro-interaction and deploying explicit metalanguage. Both the writing pedagogy inspired by Rothery and her colleagues and the reading pedagogy developed by Rose design pedagogy globally – continually refining the macrogenres introduced in Figure 3.7 of Chapter 3 and Figure 4.4 above. The difference comes when we consider metalanguage and exchange structure. Rothery emphasizes the role of sharing explicit metalanguage with students in literacy development whereas Rose does not; at the same time, where Rothery stopped designing pedagogy, Rose pushes on, developing move-by-move interaction in the exchange complexes outlined above. Are local design and explicit metalanguage alternative strategies? Or would one enhance the other whichever pedagogy we are trying to use?

One of Rothery's motivations for sharing metalanguage with students was that we pass on to them the knowledge we use as functional linguists to analyse discourse and to read and write texts. The point of this is to make students more independent readers and writers, once the interactive support offered by the teaching/learning cycle in the classroom is taken away. Metalanguage in other words is intended to function as a permanent ideational scaffolding for text reception and production – a resource to be drawn on when a teacher is not to hand. So we might ask whether Rose's students are in a weaker position, in the absence of such a resource, when they encounter discourse that challenges their literacy repertoire across the curriculum or in other walks of life. Is metalanguage in fact scaffolding that sticks around?

Finally there is the issue of design and fashions of teaching. As the topological overview of pedagogies outlined in section 2 shows, there's more than one pedagogy around; and differences in emphasis are more often than not treated as oppositions rather than complementarities. Alexander, for example, in his brilliant study of pedagogies around the world reports on some progressivist propaganda prominently displayed on the classroom wall of one of his Michigan schools (Figure 4.6).

Important issues to me –
Process orientation vs. product orientation
Teaching students vs. teaching programmes
Teacher as facilitator vs. teacher as manager
Developing a set of strategies vs. mastering a set of skills
Celebrating approximation vs. celebrating perfection
Respecting individual growth vs. fostering competition
Capitalizing on student's strengths vs. emphasizing student's weaknesses
Promoting independence in learning vs. dependence on teacher

Figure 4.6   Pedagogic oppositions (Alexander 2000: 548)

Alexander then comments as follows:

> Try replacing the 'versus' in the list above by 'and' and you create **a refreshingly new and inclusive pedagogy**. That is all it takes, but for many teachers and education ideologues such inclusivity is inconceivable; for what is education without its barricades? This adversarialism lies behind some of the problems in American and British pedagogy to which we have already alluded.
>
> (Alexander 2000: 548–9)

Similarly, Brophy, in his excellent survey of social constructivist pedagogy, argues in relation to 'adversarialism' that:

> ... comparisons are useful (transmission vs. social constructivist pedagogy – JRM), but they must be interpreted carefully to avoid ... implying that one must choose between these two approaches when logic and some data indicate the need for a **judicious blend** and implying that a particular choice or blend will have universal applicability, when there is good reason to believe that what constitutes optimal teaching varies with grade level, instructional goals, and other context factors.
>
> (Brophy 2002: ix)

It is hard not to sympathize with these and comparable words of wisdom. But we do need to be careful here. One common reading of 'inclusive pedagogy' and 'judicious blend' might be that really it's up to teachers to decide what to do when. They're the experts after all and we need to respect their professional practice. If eclecticism is what they require, then that is what we should promote – in pre-service training and in-service support. The danger here of course is that we simply license teachers to teach as they were taught, and continue to produce the stratified literacy outcomes Rothery and Rose are struggling against.

My key point here is that if we want democracy in the classroom, then theory matters. Decisions we make about pedagogy have to be principled, theoretically informed and context sensitive (and this means we need a model of language in context – of what to do when; we can't simply depend on sensitive practitioners). This makes theoretically informed design the key to future developments. Rothery and Rose have opened the door for literacy practices which offer students opportunities they have not been able to access before. And these doors are open because of the ways Rothery and Rose have mobilized the social semiotic theory underpinning their practice. Transcending the practical convenience of eclecticism, we need to foster such practices, and find out more about the kinds of institutionalized learning SFL and affine theories afford.

Notes

1. For reasons of space limitations, the editors have had to abridge the original version of this paper. For the full version, please contact the author at: jmartin@mail.usyd.edu.au.
2. I am much indebted to Jeong Pil Cheon and Ingrid Westhoff for research inspiring this discussion (see Cheon 2004 and Westhoff 2003), and especially to David Rose for 'participating' as both colleague and 'data'.

3. Green and Lee (1994) introduced the term 'the Sydney School', in recognition of the instrumental role played by functional linguists and educational linguists in the Department of Linguistics at the University of Sydney. Ironically, by 1994 the name was already well out of date, since the research was being developed at all the metropolitan Sydney universities, at Wollongong University, at the Northern Territory University, at Melbourne University and beyond. Green and Lee's christening was published in America and has become the name by which the work outlined here is known (e.g. Freedman and Medway 1994a; Hyon 1996; Lee 1996; Johns 2002; Coe *et al* 2002; Hyland 2002).

4. Schleppegrell (2004) provides an excellent overview of this arena.

5. For overviews see Christie (1992), Feez (2002), Macken-Horarik (2002), Martin (1991, 1993, 1998, 1999, 2000a, 2002a, 2002b). Feez (1998) and (2002) include discussion of adaptations for adult education (TESOL). For relevant discussion of ESL learners in mainstream classrooms see Gibbons (2002).

6. For discussion of curriculum genres as macro-genres see Christie (2002).

7. For a British perspective on the politics of KAL, see Carter (1990, 1996), and Chapter 7 here; Martin (1999) and (2000a) review the Australian 'crisis'.

8. Few people would think of challenging innovation in science or mathematics in this way, but when it comes to language, laypersons confidently assert their authority over professional linguists and language educators.

9. At the time of writing this, Bernstein was unaware of our pedagogic initiatives; see Christie (1998).

10. See especially the following chapters: Painter (1989), Rothery (1989) and Jones *et al* (1989).

11. To be fair, there are many places in Wells' book (and in Wells 2002) where teacher-centred activities are acknowledged – but the teacher is completely elided from the manifesto; Brophy (2002) provides a balanced overview of social constructivist teaching initiatives. Muller (2000) critiques the very disturbing 'progressive' implementation of social constructivist principles in South Africa after apartheid (see also Taylor *et al* 2003).

12. For an introduction to Rose's strategies see Rose (2003, 2004b, c, d). To obtain copies of these videos, contact the author at d.rose@edfac.usyd.edu.au.

13. A question the questioner knows the answer to, but delays stating it; for example, as part of a quiz show.

14 Note that the K1 moves in the Deconstruction interaction presented above were all move complexes of this kind.

15 For relevant discussion of social class differences and the relation between reading at home and reading at school, see Williams (1998, 2001).

16. Not that Rose would object to using such metalanguage, if available; but the pedagogy has to work where it is not available.

17. It is also important to note here that Rose typically introduces more metalanguage in the rewriting from notes stage of his macro-genre than in the detailed preparation stage we looked at closely here.

References

Alexander, R. (2000), *Culture and Pedagogy: International Comparisons in Primary Education*. Oxford: Blackwell.

Bernstein, B. (1975), *Class, Codes and Control 3: Towards a Theory of Educational Transmissions*. London: Routledge and Kegan Paul.

— (1990), *Class, Codes and Control 4: The Structuring of Pedagogic Discourse*. London: Routledge.

— (1996), *Pedagogy, Symbolic Control and Identity: Theory, Research, Critique*. London and Bristol, PA: Taylor and Francis.

Berry, M. (1981), 'Systemic linguistics and discourse analysis: a multi-layered approach to exchange structure', in M. Coulthard and M. Montgomery (eds), *Studies in Discourse Analysis*. London: Routledge and Kegan Paul, pp. 120–45.

Brophy, J. (ed.) (2002), *Social Constructivist Teaching: Affordances and Constraints. Advances in Research on Teaching. Volume 9*. New York: Elsevier Science.

Carter, R. (ed.) (1990), *Knowledge about Language and the Curriculum: the LINC Reader*. London: Hodder and Stoughton.

Carter, R. (1996), 'Politics and knowledge about language: the LINC project', in R. Hasan and G. Williams (eds), pp. 1–28.

Cheon, J. P. (2004), *Scaffolding Exchange Structure Model*. Unpublished Honours paper. Department of Linguistics, University of Sydney.

Christie, F. (1992), 'Literacy in Australia', *Annual Review of Applied Linguistics*, 12, 142–55.

— (ed.) (1998), *Pedagogy and the Shaping of Consciousness: Linguistic and Social Processes*. London: Cassell (Open Linguistics Series).

— (2002), *Classroom Discourse Analysis: A Functional Perspective*. London: Continuum.

Christie, F. and Martin, J. R. (1997), *Genres and Institutions: Social Processes in the Workplace and School*. London: Pinter.

Coe, R., Lingard, L. and Teslenko, T. (eds) (2002), *The Rhetoric and Ideology of Genre: Strategies for Stability and Change*. Cresskill, NJ: Hampton Press.

Coffin, C. (1997), 'Constructing and giving value to the past: an investigation into secondary school history', in F. Christie and J. Martin (eds), pp. 196–230.

Cope, W. and Kalantzis, M. (eds) (1993), *The Powers of Literacy: A Genre Approach to Teaching Literacy*. London, Falmer and Pittsburgh: University of Pittsburgh Press.

Cope, B. and Kalantzis, M. (1999), *Multiliteracies: Literacy Learning and the Design of Social Futures*. London: Routledge.

Derewianka, B. (1990), *Exploring How Texts Work*. Sydney: Primary English Teaching Association.

— (1998), *A Grammar Companion for Primary Teachers*. Sydney: Primary English Teaching Association.

Feez, S. (1998), *Text-based Syllabus Design*. Sydney: National Centre for English Language Teaching and Research (NELTR), Macquarie University.

— (2002), 'Heritage and innovation in second language education', in A. Johns (ed.), pp. 43–69.

Freedman, A. and Medway, P. (eds) (1994a), *Learning and Teaching Genre*. Portsmouth, NH: Boynton/Cook (Heinemann).

Freedman, A. and Medway, P. (1994b), *Genre and the New Rhetoric*. London: Taylor and Francis.

Gibbons, P. (2002), *Scaffolding Language, Scaffolding Learning: Teaching Second Language Learners in the Mainstream Classroom*. Portsmouth, NH: Heinemann.

Gray, B. and Cowey, W. (1999), *Book Orientation: The Potential (Scaffolding Literacy with Indigenous Children in School)*. Canberra: Schools and Community centre, University of Canberra.

Green, B. and Lee, A. (1994), 'Writing geography lessons: literacy, identity and schooling', in A. Freedman and P. Medway (eds) (1994a), pp. 207–24.

Halliday, M. A. K. (1975), *Learning How to Mean: Explorations in the Development of Language*. London: Edward Arnold.

—(1993), 'Towards a language-based theory of learning', *Linguistics and Education*, 5.2, 93–116.

— (2004), 'Representing the child as a semiotic being (one who means)', in J. Foley (ed.), *Language, Education and Discourse: Functional Approaches*. London: Continuum, pp. 19–42.

Halliday, M. A. K. and Matthiessen, C. M. I. M. (2004), *An Introduction to Functional Grammar* (third edition). London: Arnold.

Hammond, J. (ed.) (2001), *Scaffolding: Teaching and Learning in Language and Literacy Education*. Sydney: Primary English Teaching Association.

Hasan, R. and Martin, J. R. (eds) (1989), *Language Development: Learning Language, Learning Culture*. Norwood, NJ: Ablex.

Hasan, R. and Williams, G. (eds) (1996), *Literacy in Society*. London: Longman.

Hyland, K. (2002), 'Genre: language, context and literacy', *Annual Review of Applied Linguistics*, 22, 113–35.

Hyon, S. (1996), 'Genre in three traditions: implications for ESL', *TESOL Quarterly*, 30, (4), 693–722.

Johns, A. M. (ed.) (2002), *Genres in the Classroom: Applying Theory and Research to Practice*. Mahwah, NJ: Lawrence Erlbaum.

Jones, J., Gollin, S., Drury, H. and Economou, D. (1989), 'Systemic-functional linguistics and its application to the TESOL curriculum', in R. Hasan and J. Martin (eds), pp. 257–328.

Lee, A. (1996), *Gender, Literacy, Curriculum: Re-writing School Geography*. London: Taylor and Francis.

Macken-Horarik, M. (2002), 'Something to shoot for: a systemic functional approach to teaching genre in secondary school science', in A. Johns (ed.), pp. 17–42.

Martin, J. R. (1991), 'Critical literacy: the role of a functional model of language', *Australian Journal of Reading*, 14.2, 117–32.

— (1992), *English Text: System and Structure*. Amsterdam: Benjamins.

— (1993), 'Genre and literacy – modelling context in educational linguistics', *Annual Review of Applied Linguistics*, 13, 141–72.

— (1998), 'Mentoring semogenesis: genre-based' literacy pedagogy', in F. Christie (ed.), pp. 123–55.

— (1999), 'Linguistics and the consumer: theory in practice', *Linguistics and Education* 9.3, 409–46.

— (2000a), 'Design and practice: enacting functional linguistics in Australia', *Annual Review of Applied Linguistics*, 20, 116–26.

— (2000b), 'Factoring out exchange: types of structure', in M. Coulthard, J. Cotterill and F. Rock (eds), *Working with Dialogue*. Tubingen: Niemeyer, pp. 19–40.

— (2001), 'Giving the game away: explicitness, diversity and genre-based literacy in Australia', in R. de Cilla, H. Krumm and R. Wodak (eds), *Loss of Communication in the Information Age*. Vienna: Verlag der Osterreichischen Akademie der Wissenschaften, pp. 155–74.

— (2002a), 'From little things big things grow: ecogenesis in school geography', in R. Coe *et al* (eds), pp. 243–71.

—(2002b), 'A universe of meaning – how many practices?' in A. Johns (ed.), pp. 269–78.

Martin, J. R. and Rose, D. (2003), *Working with Discourse: Meaning Beyond the Clause*. London: Continuum.

— (2005), 'Designing literacy pedagogy: scaffolding asymmetries', in R. Hasan, C. M. I. M. Matthiessen and J. Webster (eds), *Continuing Discourse on Language: A Functional Perspective*, Vol. 1. London: Equinox, pp. 251–80.

— (2006), *Genre Relations: Mapping Culture*. London: Equinox.

Mercer, N. (1994), 'Neo-Vygotskian theory and classroom education', in R. Stierer and J. Maybin (eds), *Language, Literacy and Learning in Educational Practice*. Clevedon: Multilingual Matters, pp. 92–110.

— (1995), *The Guided Construction of Knowledge: Talk Amongst Teachers and Learners*. Clevedon: Multilingual Matters.

— (2000), *Words and Minds: How We Use Language to Work Together*. London: Routledge.

Morais, A., Baillie, H. and Thomas, B. (eds) (2001), *Towards a Sociology of Pedagogy: The Contribution of Basil Bernstein to Research*. New York: Peter Lang.

Muller, J. (2000), *Reclaiming Knowledge: Social Theory, Curriculum and Education Policy*. London: Routledge.

Nuttall, T., Wright, J., Hoffman, J., Sishi, N. and Khandlhela, S. (1998), *From Apartheid to Democracy: South Africa 1948–1994*. Pietermaritzburg: Shuter and Shooter.

Painter, C. (1984), *Into the Mother Tongue: A Case Study of Early Language Development*. London: Pinter.

— (1986), 'The role of interaction in learning to speak and learning to write', in C. Painter and J. R. Martin (eds), pp. 62–97.

— (1989), 'Learning language: a functional view of language development', in R. Hasan and J. Martin (eds), pp. 18–65.

— (1996), 'The development of language as a resource for thinking: a linguistic view of learning', in R. Hasan and G. Williams (eds), pp. 50–85.

— (1998), *Learning through Language in Early Childhood*. London: Cassell.

— (1999), 'Preparing for school: developing a semantic style for educational knowledge', in F. Christie (ed.), pp. 68–87.

—(2000), 'Researching first language development in children', in L.

Unsworth (ed.), *Researching Language in Schools and Communities: Functional Linguistics Approaches*. London: Cassell, pp. 65–86.

— (2003), 'The use of a metaphorical mode of meaning in early language development', in A. M. Simon-Vandenbergen, M. Taverniers and L. Ravelli (eds), *Grammatical Metaphor: Views from Systemic Functional Linguistics*. Amsterdam: Benjamins, pp. 151–67.

Painter, C. and Martin, J. R. (eds) (1986), *Writing to Mean: Teaching Genres across the Curriculum*. Applied Linguistics Association of Australia (Occasional Papers 9).

Rose, D. (1997), 'Science, technology and technical literacies', in F. Christie and J. Martin (eds), pp. 40–72.

— (2001), *The Western Desert Code: An Australian Cryptogrammar*. Canberra: Research School of Pacific and Asian Studies, The Australian National University (Pacific Linguistics 513).

— (2003), *Reading and Writing Factual Texts at Sobantu*. Teacher Training Video. Faculty of Education: University of Sydney (Learning to Read: Reading to Learn).

— (2004a), 'Sequencing and pacing of the hidden curriculum: how Indigenous children are left out of the chain', in J. Muller, B. Davies and A. Morais (eds), *Reading Bernstein, Researching Bernstein*. London: Routledge Falmer, pp. 91–107.

— (2004b), *Reading and Writing Factual Texts*. Teacher Training Video. Sydney: Learning to Read: Reading to Learn.

— (2004c), *Stories in the Middle Years*. Teacher Training Video. Sydney: Learning to Read: Reading to Learn.

— (2004d), *Early Years Reading and Writing*. Teacher Training Video. Sydney: Learning to Read: Reading to Learn.

— (2005a), *Literacy across the Curriculum*. Teacher Resource Booklet. Sydney: Learning to Read: Reading to Learn.

— (2005b), 'Democratising the Classroom: a literacy pedagogy for the new generation', *Journal of Education*, 37, Durban: University of KwaZulu Natal.

Rose, D., Gray, B. and Cowey, W. (1999), 'Scaffolding reading and writing or Indigenous children in school', in P. Wignell (ed.), *Double Power: English Literacy in Indigenous Schooling*. Melbourne: Language Australia, pp. 23–60.

Rose, D., Lui-Chivizhe, L., McKnight, A. and Smith, A. (2004), 'Scaffolding academic reading and writing at the Koori Centre', *Australian Journal of Indigenous Education*, 32, 41–9.

Rothery, J. (1989), 'Learning about language', in R. Hasan and J. Martin (eds), pp. 199–256.

— (1994), *Exploring Literacy in School English* (*Write it Right* Resources for Literacy and Learning). Sydney: Metropolitan East Disadvantaged Schools Program.

— (1996), 'Making changes: developing an educational linguistics', in R. Hasan and G. Williams (eds), pp. 86–123.

Schleppegrell, M. J. (2004), *The Language of Schooling*. Mahwah, NJ: Erlbaum.

Sinclair, J. McH. and Coulthard, R. M. (1975), *Towards an Analysis of*

Discourse: The English Used by Teachers and Pupils. London: Oxford University Press.

Taylor, N., Muller, J. and Vinjevold, P. (2003), *Getting School Working: Research and Systemic School Reform in South Africa.* Cape Town: Pearson Education.

Unsworth, L. (2001), *Teaching Multiliteracies across the Curriculum: Changing Contexts of Text and Image in Classroom Practice.* Buckingham: Open University Press.

Ventola, E. (1987), *The Structure of Social Interaction: A Systemic Approach to the Semiotics of Service Encounters.* London: Pinter.

Wells, G. (1999), *Dialogic Inquiry: Toward a Sociocultural Practice and Theory of Education.* Cambridge: Cambridge University Press.

— (2002), 'Learning and teaching for understanding: the key role of collaborative knowledge building', in J. Brophy (ed.), pp. 1–41.

Westhoff, I. (2003), 'Learning to Read, Reading to Learn: A Curriculum Genre'. Unpublished research report. Department of Linguistics, University of Sydney.

Williams, G. (1998), 'Children entering literate worlds: perspectives from the study of textual practices', in F. Christie and R. Misson (eds), *Literacy and Schooling.* London: Routledge, pp. 47–73.

— (2000), 'Children's literature, children and children's uses of language description', in L. Unsworth (ed.), *Researching Language in Schools and Communities: Functional Linguistic Perspectives.* London: Cassell, pp. 111–29.

— (2001), 'Literacy pedagogy prior to schooling: relations between social positioning and semantic variation', in A. Morais *et al* (eds), pp. 17–45.

— (2004), 'Ontogenesis and grammatics: functions of metalanguage in pedagogical discourse', in G. Williams and A. Lukin (eds), *The Development of Language: Functional Perspectives on Species and Individuals.* London: Continuum, pp. 241–67.

5   Towards a pedagogical grammar

John Polias and Brian Dare

> ... no literacy education program is worthy of that name if it ignores the richest and most effective resource which resides in the lexicogrammar.
>
> (Hasan and Williams 1996: xvi)

1 Introduction

The systemic functional model of language has had an enormous impact on educational contexts in Australia. From its origins in the work of the 'Sydney School' (Painter and Martin 1986; Cope and Kalantzis 1993), the influence of this model has spread to the point where the curricula of all the states of Australia draw on the theory in some major way. We could also say that despite its controversial beginnings (e.g. Reid 1987), genre-based pedagogy is now a widely accepted part of many teachers' practice, as reflected in curriculum documents and in the kinds of resources produced for teachers. It has been embraced so readily because teachers were convinced by the argument that they needed to teach a much broader range of texts than narrative and personal responses. They have also found invaluable another of its central ideas, making explicit the generic structure of key curriculum texts.

In South Australia, as in other states of Australia, a genre-based pedagogy had a major impact. Helped along by conferences organized around this theme, significant professional development, and the increasing availability of resources such as *Exploring How Texts Work* (Derewianka 1990), teachers began to take on a 'genre approach'. Typically, this meant incorporating a range of factual genres (Martin 1985) in the curriculum and making explicit to students both the purpose and the schematic structure of different genres. Not only were these genres given more prominence but teachers also began to think about when students should be introduced to them. This new discourse around text was a revolution in itself.

Despite this major shift, it cannot be said that another fundamental element of a genre-based approach, the teaching of grammar as part of an explicit pedagogy around language, has been taken up anywhere near the same extent. So while teachers welcomed this new approach to teaching about text, a key piece of the pedagogy went missing. The idea that there was a systematic connection between genres and their lexicogrammar and that these patterns could be taught was ignored by most teachers. Instead, what took its place was a somewhat superficial teaching around 'language features' that was neither systematic, or even functional, though functional annotations in a range of resources were available to teachers. This is not through any lack of intent by those who developed the theory. They clearly intended a focus on the grammar as part of any literacy pedagogy (Martin 1999). However, the educational and political climate of the nineties in Australia made it difficult for teachers to be positively disposed to taking on functional grammar.

This is where the South Australian experience might be useful to those interested in an explicit pedagogy that sees grammar as central. Unlike many other parts of Australia, a significant number of South Australian teachers are engaging with functional grammar in a meaningful way. Considerable interest and expertise in this area has been built up over the last decade and this is reflected in the fact that over 2,000 teachers have done a 27-hour course focusing on the classroom applications of functional grammar, that numerous South Australian teachers have presented at state, national and international forums on how they teach functional grammar, and that a major document for reporting and assessing ESL students is now used by both the state and Catholic sectors. It is also reflected in the widespread and continuing demand for and provision of professional development in literacy that is based in systemic functional linguistics (SFL).

While this chapter focuses on the South Australian context, we address general issues around a linguistically-based explicit pedagogy. We are not concerned here with developing arguments about the value of functional versus traditional grammar, or how useful it is that children and teachers develop a shared metalanguage: this is taken as a given. The focus, instead, is on:

> the means through which teachers might learn to use functional grammar as a professional resource, not only in teaching students about language as part of a literacy curriculum but also for a wide range of other educational purposes, including the assessment of children's language development.
> (Hasan and Williams 1996: xix)

We begin by describing the development of *Language and Literacy: Classroom Applications of Functional Grammar*[1] (Dare and Polias 2004), which has been crucial to building teachers' understanding of the model and metalanguage. This is followed by descriptions of how some of these teachers have recontextualized functional grammar in their classrooms. These range from classes just beginning their schooling to those in the middle years (see Chapter 6 for a description of a school-wide organization of genre teaching). All this points to the rich potential of the educational applications of SFL and gives some sense of what we can teach, where we can teach it, how far we can go, and some possible directions for future research. Finally, we focus on a reporting and assessment tool that is underpinned by SFL and that has been widely accepted by teachers despite its having a certain degree of technicality.

2 Adding to the genre-based pedagogy: *Language and Literacy*

In our view, there appear to be three major reasons for teachers across Australia initially resisting functional grammar, apart from the political ones as mentioned. One lies in the fact that most teachers had limited knowledge of any grammatics let alone functional grammar. Older teachers often had understandings of more traditional descriptions and younger teachers had little or no access to any grammatical descriptions at all. The 'effacement of language knowledge' in Australian education (Rothery 1996: 86) had left its legacy. Another reason can be located in the lack of a pedagogical grammar around functional grammar (Derewianka 2001: 241). Such a complex and elaborate theory would demand considerable recontextualization if it were to be meaningful and accessible to teachers. A third reason relates to the adequacy of the professional development provided. The negative experiences of New South Wales teachers, where only eight hours of professional development were provided to each teacher, showed that a more comprehensive approach was required.

What we did not want in South Australia was a pedagogical grammar that was 'a mere caricature' (Derewianka 2001: 242) of functional grammar theory. For us, the main question was: could a functional model of language with its elaborate and complex theory of language be mediated in such a way that teachers would understand it well enough to apply it meaningfully in their classrooms? A closely related question was: what kind of professional development would give teachers time to understand the theory and help them to apply it in their classrooms?

In order to begin addressing these two key issues, we set up intensive week-long courses tutored by people who we felt could do the 'pedagogic grammar' well. We invited a number of interstate colleagues, Robert Veel, Rick Iedema, Suzanne Eggins and Louise Droga, to present the courses, which filled quickly despite being held during school holidays. These more theoretical courses were then supplemented by workshops run by Geoff Williams and Ruth French, who provided teachers with insights from their own pioneering research in teaching functional grammar to children (e.g. Williams 1998, 2005). Through these early professional development programmes, many teachers were inspired to begin their own explorations in teaching functional grammar and to document these (Athanaso-poulos and Sandford 1997; Hamilton 1998). While the English as a Second Language (ESL) programmes we were part of provided some funding for these activities, we were, to some extent, working at the margins.

To make serious inroads into changing literacy pedagogy in South Australia, we felt we needed to come up with an approach that would allow us to build on the work described above. It would be an approach that would do a number of things. First, it would give teachers the chance to understand all the salient features, including the metalanguage, of the functional model. Second, it would be an approach firmly grounded in practice so teachers could see how this metalanguage could be taken up in the classroom. Third, it would use a model of professional development that would give teachers both the time and the means to learn and then apply what they had learned in the course.

Using a successful model of professional development, one which is delivered in modules over nine weeks and which provides the opportunity to further develop understandings through between-module readings and between-module activities, *Language and Literacy* was developed. The nine modules of the course work systematically through the various strata: genre, register and language. Taking each metafunction in turn, various elements of the lexicogrammar are explored. As these elements are covered, the question of application remains a central concern. Large numbers of teachers in Australia and the rest of the world have now completed the course. The evaluations have been consistently excellent, indicating that teachers find it a valuable professional development programme that significantly enhances their understanding of functional grammar, their ability to apply it in the classroom and that it underlines for them the relevance of a metalinguistic understanding in learning.

As the word spread, increasing numbers of teachers enrolled in the course and many of these teachers later took up key literacy positions. In addition, teacher research projects funded by Language Australia and the Spencer Foundation allowed us to mentor teachers in exploring and reflecting on their practice. It was through these research projects that we began to expand on how the teaching of grammar could be contextualized within an explicit pedagogy. State and national conferences allowed other teachers to learn from and draw on the experiences of these teacher researchers and others (Ashton 1999; Pryor 1999; Williams 1999). Their work dispelled a number of the usual grammar myths being promulgated, such as: it cannot be taught and it has no value even if it is, it cannot be taught to young children and it is boring and dry. These arguments seemed to evaporate as people took on the ideas, tried them out and saw the effectiveness in so many different spheres.

The teachers whose work we describe in the next sections have been chosen in order to illustrate teachers and students working with different areas of the grammar and contexts that include a range of students, in terms of age, social location and whether they are learning through a second language. Another common feature is that the grammar is not taught in isolation but as part of a wider framework of teaching and learning about language. We have tried to capture some of that holistic flavour of the teaching-learning cycles in these classrooms. We believe these examples underscore the value of an explicit pedagogy in which teachers and students build a shared metalanguage as an integral part of learning about language.

3 Explaining how milk gets from the cow to the consumer

In this first example, two teachers in a school located in a low socio-economic area of Adelaide, South Australia, introduced their 7-year-old students to a number of aspects of the grammar as part of a unit of work on milk production. The main aim of the unit was to teach students how to write a sequential explanation. Within this, the classroom teacher, Louise Ferris, and ESL co-teacher, Donna Riethmuller, wanted to introduce the students to some of the key grammatical features of this genre. A characteristic of this class was not only the age of the students but the high proportion of ESL learners in the class, over 70 per cent in fact. There has been scepticism about the value of explicitly teaching any grammar to children of this age, particularly ESL children, but the outcomes of this work surprised many people, not least Donna and Louise.

In the early part of the teaching-learning cycle (about 10 weeks in all), the teachers ensured that the children built the field knowledge needed to write their sequential explanations as 'experts', a term which was used frequently to remind the students of the tenor of the text they would eventually be writing. A range of activities was undertaken, such as watching videos, visiting relevant websites, and cutting out pictures of dairy products and discussing the kinds of products they were made from. They read a big book on how cows produce milk and deconstructed an explanation of milk production. They sequenced photos from a milk factory that they visited later in the unit when the teachers felt they had built up a level of technical understandings to really understand what was happening at the milk factory. They also used flow charts, which they added to as they built up their technical language, such as suction cups, refrigerated delivery trucks, homogenized, pasteurized. Earlier work done on other genres proved very helpful in helping students understand the purpose and schematic structure of sequential explanations. Within that rich context of exploration and slow building of field knowledge, and using set sentences, such as in Table 5.1, Donna and Louise developed the children's abilities to identify and name the functional groupings of participant, process and circumstance.

Table 5.1 Sentence used by the class to analyse for process, participant and circumstance

The trucks	take	the milk	to the factory
Participant	Process	Participant	Circumstance

To identify these elements, the class used prompt questions, starting with the process – What action is going on here? – then participants – Who or what is taking the milk to the factory? The trucks take what to the factory? – and finally the circumstances – Where does the truck take the milk? These and other key questions were revisited on many occasions in order to consolidate the children's understanding, so that, in time, they identified the groupings independently. Colour coding of these three functional groupings – red for participants, green for processes and blue for circumstances – was introduced as an additional way of drawing students' attention to these categories.

Once students had a solid understanding of these categories, they engaged in a number of activities to explore the mobility of each of these groupings. Table 5.2 was used as the basis for looking at what Donna and Louise identified at this point as 'varying sentence beginnings'.

Table 5.2 A sentence to explore the possibility of moving functional groups within the clause

The dairy farmer	milks	the cows	early in the morning
Participant	Process	Participant	Circumstance

After jointly analysing for participants, processes and circumstances, the students wrote each grouping on coloured card; participants on red, processes on green and circumstances on blue. In small groups, they used the cards to arrive at different versions and then, as a class, wrote these versions on the board. This and similar activities served to highlight not only the mobility of circumstances but to introduce the students to the notion of Theme (Halliday and Matthiessen 2004). Donna and Louise decided eventually that it was easier to use the technical term rather than 'what comes at the beginning of the sentence'.

The class moved on to looking at the use of active and passive voice, which Donna and Louise knew had an important role in establishing the flow of information in a sequential explanation. Beginning with *The farmer milks the cow*, the students did a similar exercise to that above, using prepared cards and, of course, realized, to their great amusement, that the version: *The cow milks the farmer* is not possible The students were then asked to turn over the green process card, *milks*, to reveal *is milked*. Flipping the red participant card with *the farmer* on one side, the students saw that it changed to *by the farmer*. They discussed how the process 'got bigger' and also the role of 'helping words' when changing sentences around like this. Donna and Louise then showed how the 'doer' of the action, the farmer, could be removed and you could still have a sentence. As a further step, the notions of 'doer' and 'done to' were introduced in order to consolidate the children's understanding of active and passive voice.

With an understanding of active and passive voice, the class was able to explore thematic choice in sequential explanations: the way the Theme often takes up some element of the previous Rheme. Table 5.3 was used as a means of exploring the 'zig-zag pattern' so common in sequential explanations.

So quickly and easily were the children developing some control of these grammatical concepts, that, towards the end of the unit, the class was shown how to use included clauses (typically, relative clauses that interrupt a clause) to elaborate a technical term. For example, the children were given sentences, such as *Raw milk is pumped to the tankers*, on card, and then shown how to insert a relative clause, such as *which is*

Table 5.3 A text extract used to teach Theme-Rheme patterns in sequential explanations

Theme	Rheme
The milk	flows to the refrigerated tankers.
The refrigerated tanker	delivers the raw milk to the factory.
At the factory	the milk is pasteurized in the pasteurization plant.
In the pasteurization plant,	the milk is heated to kill off germs.

milk straight from the cow, immediately after the technical term, *Raw milk*. They did this by cutting up the card with the original sentence and inserting the included clause, which was written on another coloured card strip.

Text 1 and 2 reveal the very significant gains made over the ten week period by two students. The first is from one of the weaker writers in the class. Before this unit of work, he was only able to make limited, commonsense meanings about milk production. By the end of the unit, his writing is of a very different order.

Before
How milk gets from the Cow to Us
The farmer milks the cow then the farmer bring the milk to the supermute then the people biy them.

After
Cows which are to have had a calf befor been milked by automatic suction cups. After the cow has been milk, the milk is stored and pumped into silos.
Now the milk is delivered to the factory to be homogenized and pasteurized to kill chse and bucteryer. The milk is made into skim milk and flavoured milk. Next the truck is washed before it delivers the milk to the deli and the supermarket. Last the supermarket is selling the milk to the people.

Text 1 A student's writing before and after the unit of work

Text 2 reveals that significant gains were also made by the better writers in the class.

How milk gets from the cow to us
The cow eats grass. The farmer uses suction cups to milk the cow. The raw milk which is milk straight from the cow flows into the vats. The tanker comes and the milk flows to the tanker. The tanker driver tests the milk. The tanker deliveres raw milk to the factory every day. At the factory the raw milk is tested. The tanker is washed inside and outside.

The raw milk is now pasteurised which is heating the milk up and homogenised which is spreding the cream. The milk is flavoud. The milk is placed into cartons. The cartons are placed into crats and puted ino the cold room. Folk-lifs cary the crats to the refrigerated delivery trucks. The truck delivers milk to the supamaket and the deli.

Text 2   A student's writing after the unit of work

These seven-year-old children have a clear understanding of how milk gets from the cow to the consumer and how to express that in a sequential explanation. Both use the language patterns of technical sequential explanations: technical lexis, appropriate use of the passive voice and examples of elaboration through dependent clauses. These significant improvements in the children's texts were replicated across the class and were clearly evident in their sequential explanations written later in the year with much less scaffolding than was provided here.

4 Spooking up narratives

In this context, the English teacher, Monica Williams, scaffolds her 12-year-old students in extending their understanding about how to write a 'spooky story'. Drawing on *Spine Chilling Stories* (Rothery and Stevenson 1994), she focuses on key structural elements of the narrative genre: orientation, foreshadowing, complications and resolutions. Other key features explored were the evaluation stage, which can surface at different points in the narrative, and the notion of building tension. Throughout this unit, Monica drew on the grammar work she had already undertaken with the students (e.g. different process types) and extended that knowledge through a focus on nominal groups.

One of the challenges for Monica with this class of 31 was their wide-ranging abilities in writing narratives. Some already had a high degree of control whereas others would struggle even with the simplest of narratives. As a way of ascertaining the students' capabilities, Monica collected samples of all the students' independent writing of a 'spooky story'. Later, these were compared with the texts produced after explicit teaching of the lexicogrammatical elements outlined above. An early focus in this unit was the dual function of evaluation in a narrative – expressing the thoughts and feelings of the characters and creating tension – and the lexicogrammatical resources for expressing those meanings. The class discussed the role of different process types in a narrative, exploring the function of mental processes in evaluation and the way particular choices of action processes create tension.

This metalinguistic focus then shifted to the nominal group; the function of nominal groups in narratives and in written language, and the structure of the nominal group itself. Examples from various texts were analysed according to the nominal group's functional elements: deictic, epithets, classifiers, the head noun and qualifiers. Monica mediated these more technical terms with more common-sense ones: pointer for deictic and describer for epithet. The class also compared the length of nominal groups from more spoken texts with more written ones. This kind of metalinguistic conversation became a central part of their talk around how particular texts are constructed.

As with other students mentioned here, these students managed the technicality of the metalanguage with ease once they were explicitly taught it, as is evident from Text 3.

Student 1
This story is really terrible. The first thing you notice about it is the orientation. All it tells us is that one night someone called Alana went for a ride on her bike, When was it set? Who is Alana and how old is she? What kind of bike was it? Why was she going for a ride? It doesn't make you want to read on. Also it has no foreshadowing or evaluation.

Student 2
I certainly have quite a few criticisms to make because this particular story does not explain things well such as 'the ghost melted'. I think that they could have added more intense epithets to increase the suspense and horror ... I would've written something like 'the pale terrifying ghost melted away before my eyes into thin air' if I were the author.

Text 3   Student evaluations of narratives

Both these students have started critically analysing the choices of authors and have a grammatical basis for doing so. They have moved beyond commonsense understandings to what Macken-Horarik (1996) calls 'specialized domains', where the students are taking on the role of 'incumbent expert' and are doing so with the confidence developed through their understanding of how the grammar is working to make particular meanings. This ability to reflect on their own and other's use of language was achieved by all the students in the class.

The development of nominal groups, inclusion of evaluation, and repetition to reinforce an unusual event is clear when comparing two narratives by an ESL student, written four months apart (Text 4).

July
One day, her mother was go to the bookroom and get the key. She looking at the door, then she see the fire, she said very loudly 'help! help!' but no-one hear her ...

November
At midnight the horrible, deep wailing sound began again, it was getting louder and louder, deep and deeper. I opened my eye. 'Yh.' The horrible ghastly face setting on my eyes ...

Text 4   Extracts from two narratives written four months apart by an ESL learner

What became apparent to the teacher and students by the end of this explicit linguistic focus on narratives was that all the students had much more control of their narrative writing and were able to create suspense and horror, as an extract from another student shows (Text 5).

The crisp sound of Matt's jumpy feet on the grass and the old rusty swinging chair on the balcony were the only sounds Matt heard through the suffocating darkness of the night. He ignored the thick dripping sound and the sudden warmth of another person at his back.

Text 5   Extract from a student's narrative showing developed command of epithets

How did the students respond to this level of technicality and focus on lexicogrammar from a functional perspective? Did it stifle their creativity, a claim that has been levelled against the teaching of grammar? Text 6 presents one student's evaluation.

I really enjoyed everything we did leading up to writing the story and I believe it did help me a lot to make my second story much more exciting than my first story. In my second story I had built up my nominal groups a heap more than in my first story and that gave it more description and I think more tension.

Text 6   Evaluation by a student after the explicit work on the narrative genre

And the last word from Monica: 'These stories were by far the most imaginative, tightly constructed texts I had read by students in my twenty years of teaching.'

5 Setting up an argument

This next example describes the work of a science teacher, Julie McPhee, who, after working with Monica and then attending the *Language and Literacy* course, set out to support her 12-year-old students improve their written arguments.

The class was looking at the issue of deforestation and, as part of their activities, the students were put in the position of taking a stance, pro or con, with regard to this issue. Time was spent developing the students' field knowledge so that they had more than a commonsense understanding of the main arguments. It was clear that, while the students had a lot to say about the topic, they were unable to organize their ideas into a clear argument. As a consequence, there was a focus on two aspects of the lexicogrammar in this particular teaching-learning cycle (Rothery and Stevenson 1994): introducing the notions of Macrotheme (introduction) and Hypertheme (topic sentence) (Martin 1992) as a way of teaching the organization in the argument genre, and teaching nominalization as a way of moving students' writing to the most written end of the mode continuum.

Text 7 is a typical example of a written argument that the students were producing before any explicit work had been done.

> I'm for deforestation. I believe that we rely on the destruction of rainforests for more land. Land will provide opportunities for farmers and other farming issues including crops which provide food and medicines. Land is also used for housing. The trees of the rainforests provide building products so as trees are cut down, the land provides area for houses which are built from the trees cut down. Houses need to be built for the growing population so that they can have shelter away from the cold winter conditions and the hot summer conditions in Australia's climate
>
> For children to have a good education they need to go to school to learn. To learn you need paper to write on and read from. Paper is made from trees which need to be cut down. Fuel is also provided from the destruction of rainforests. Trees are cut down by loggers. If there was no destruction of rainforests then loggers would be out of a job and would not get paid. Deforestation helps Australia's economy with they buying and selling of rainforests products. Therefore deforestation can benefit many people.

Text 7 Student text before explicit teaching of the argument genre

This student has presented many of the issues around deforestation but the organization of the text is not as we would expect to see in a written argumentative essay. There is no significant ordering of ideas in the first paragraph that signals to the reader the arguments that will be taken up in subsequent paragraphs. Within the paragraphs, the ideas are not organized in an orderly manner with the writer rather expanding on her reasons for supporting deforestation in a superficial way. Also, the student tends to write in a more spoken way. For example, there is a focus on tangible objects (e.g. land, trees, houses), people (e.g. children, they, you, loggers) and actions (e.g. build, go, cut down) rather than issues to be argued.

In addressing these concerns, the class spent a number of lessons analysing their writing, discussing it, deconstructing it and playing with various spoken texts to make them more written. After a number of lessons, the structure of the students' texts improved as did the degree of abstraction (Text 8).

> It is necessary for some rainforest areas to be removed to enable employment opportunities to increase and enable people to support themselves and their families. The clearing would provide more land for farming and housing and countries would benefit economically by the exportation and selling of products such as timber, furniture, medicines, food, firewood, fuel and other products which are produced.
>
> An exceeding amount of employment opportunities would arise with the removal of timber from some rainforest areas. It is essential that people be employed for the removal and processing of the timber. Once the removal and processing of the timber has taken place, the designing, building and supervision of the houses or roads or the planting of the crops and the research of the plants removed needs to be achieved. This requires more people to be employed for these various tasks.
>
> The removal of trees in some parts of the rainforests would produce efficient amount of land for farming and housing. Housing provides homes and farming can provide a wide range of meat, milk, wool and other foods and products. These are all necessities that are very important to the society …

Text 8 Extract from a student's text after explicit teaching of nominalization and the generic structure of an argument

What is clear is the improved organization of the second text where, unlike Text 7, there is a clear Macrotheme with clearly linked Hyperthemes. The opening paragraph signals that the main arguments centre around employment opportunities, more land for farming and housing and the fact that countries would benefit economically. Each of these arguments is taken up in the following paragraphs and the student has made good use of nominalization to synthesize her ideas. So we see abstractions such as opportunities, removal and clearance as head words in nominal groups. In contrast with Text 7, this text unfolds by taking up the issues in the argument. Further analysis of these two texts shows, for example, the overuse of nominalization (an exceeding amount, the exportation and selling), but there is no doubt that, in a short space of time, the students in Julie's class made significant progress in their understanding of how a written argument works. This example highlights what many teachers have found when teaching students about writing arguments; that even a brief exploration of these key linguistic resources is extremely productive in improving students' writing.

6 A reporting and assessment tool: *ESL Scope and Scales*

One of the indicators in South Australia of a system-wide success of all the work in applying a functional model of language, and which is exemplified by the work of the teachers described above, is the *ESL Scope and Scales* (Polias 2003[2]). This document is a resource intended for reporting – to parents, other teachers and the education system – on the language and learning development of second language students. It sets out the scope of that language and learning development and articulates 14 scales across that scope. There are four bands in all, with each band connected to the age of the student: Early Years Band for five- to seven-year-olds, Primary Years Band for eight- to ten-year-olds, Middle Years Band for eleven- to fourteen-year-olds and Senior Years Band for fifteen years and beyond (Table 5.4).

Table 5.4 The relationship between the Scales and the age of a student

Age				5	6	7	8	9	10	11	12	13	14	15
Standards					1		2		3		4			5
Scales														
Early Years	1	2	3	4	5	6								
Primary Years	1	2	3	4	5	6	7	8	9					
Middle Years	1	2	3	4	5	6	7	8	9	10	11	12	13	
Senior Years	1	2	3	4	5	6	7	8	9	10	11	12	13	14

The second row, 'Standards', shows the applicable curriculum standard or benchmark at the given age (used by the state education department to indicate what one could expect of any average-achieving native-speaker child of this age). The 'Scales' on the other hand were derived by looking at the linguistic skills needed by a student in order to achieve all the outcomes of all the subjects across the curriculum within each Standard. However, while the Standards are intended to assess native speakers, the Scales are aimed at assessing ESL students.

With its attempt to link language and learning development, the *ESL Scope and Scales* could be described as a linguistic tool for reporting on achievement in schooling. This resource is a core component of South Australia's curriculum renewal for schooling, South Australian Curriculum Standards and Accountability Framework, begun around 2000.

The *ESL Scope and Scales* uses the SFL model of language and context for its organization and its descriptions of achievement. This has meant that the major organizational strands are 'Text in Context' and 'Language' and both of these are internally constructed according to Genre, Field, Tenor and Mode. Each scale consists of four pages: Table 5.5 shows the page on genre for the Middle Years Band version of the *ESL Scope and Scales*.

It is clear from Table 5.5 that the user of the *ESL Scope and Scales* needs to have a working knowledge of a range of genres and their linguistic elements. This could be seen as being in conflict with one of the two major requirements of the writing brief received from the state education department – that all teachers with an ESL learner in their class should be able to use it – but the trialling teachers demanded at least this level of technicality.

The other requirement in the writing brief was that the outcomes and indicators of achievement described in the document should link closely with outcomes from all the curriculum areas (expressed in the Standards of each curriculum area). This requirement has also had a profound impact on the resource itself and its application in schools. The result is that the learning outcomes of the various subjects are now described in broad linguistic terms and, because of this, the *ESL Scope and Scales* is a tool that connects what ESL students are choosing linguistically to what their first language counterparts are choosing. The *ESL Scope and Scales*, therefore, provides a continuum that links second and first language learning.

The demand that all teachers who have an ESL student in their class use the *ESL Scope and Scales* has had a number of positive consequences. Teachers must now take language into account in their teaching; the language demands across the curriculum are highlighted; and the standards are now described not only in terms of content but also in terms of language demands, although these are not separated into subjects or specific genres. For those involved in ESL programmes, any allocation of resources and intervention strategies to address the

Table 5.5 Extract describing genre from Scale 9 for the Middle Years Band

Scale 9

Text in context	Language

Genre

Outcome 9.1

Communicates in a wide range of social situations and small range of educational genres and reflects on these in an informed way.

Examples of evidence include that the learner:	*Examples of evidence include that the learner:*
• Demonstrates an elementary understanding of genre: – reflects in simple terms on the purposes, the appropriate structure and common features of a range of elementary genres, such as personal and biographical recounts, simple narratives, procedures, descriptive reports, sequential explanations, simple arguments and summaries – begins to reflect on possible variations of the structure of a genre – contrasts texts of the same genre from different cultures in terms of structure but also in simple linguistic terms. • Constructs oral and written examples of a range of elementary genres having a number of stages or a series of events: – writes and draws sequential explanations, such as life cycles and simple flow-charts, which begin to incorporate causal meanings – writes short factual texts drawing from more than one source and using a range of simple cohesive resources (i.e. language elements that make a text hang together) – constructs simple oral and written arguments based heavily on modelled and collaboratively constructed texts – writes and retells examples of story genres which have more than one complication to resolve.	• Identifies and uses a small range of significant language features that set up the structure of a text: – phrases foregrounded (i.e. placed at the front) in a range of genres: – time and place in recounts – time, place and manner in procedures – sub-headings in a report – a new line to mark a change of speaker in a dialogue – conjunctions organizing arguments: *Secondly, In addition, Later, Finally.* • Identifies clauses and expands the information in a text by joining the clauses: – forms complex sentences using a wide range of binding conjunctions: *because, if, since, because if* – uses a small range of relative pronouns with varying accuracy: 'We come from Zagreb, *which is the capital of Croatia*', 'The boy *which writes well is …*' • Uses a range of simple language elements that make a text hang together (i.e. cohesive resources): – uses a narrow range of conjunctions to join sentences or paragraphs in a text: So, *However* – uses reference items appropriately in longer, increasingly complex factual genres such as explanations: 'The woodchips are mixed with water to make a pulp. *This* pulp is …' – uses a small range of synonyms and antonyms.

needs of ESL learners can now be undertaken with a focus on language development, which can be seen as occurring along a continuum with L2 and L1 development connected, and so eliminates the need for multiple, separate continua. For non-experts, such as parents, it is easier to compare what ESL and non-ESL students can do in English.

However, this requirement to use the *ESL Scope and Scales* has brought with it a new set of pressures. The pressures are closely related: teachers who have not studied language and/or second language development are expected to engage with the resource and then understand it; the resource takes on some kind of teaching role; and the technicality of the model of language needs to be reduced. Each of these pressures brings with it a question. What kind of professional development exists to support teachers in their understanding of the resource? Is it appropriate for such a resource to be didactic and does this, and the lower level of technicality, reduce the usefulness of the document for qualified and experienced ESL teachers? In its development and trialling stages, teachers directed the author to retain a relatively high degree of detail and technicality. This degree of technicality at the lexicogrammatical level is illustrated by taking extracts of a specific linguistic element from several consecutive scales. Table 5.6 compares the descriptions of foregrounding (technically known as Theme) from Scales 8 to 11 in the Middle Years Band.

Now that the *ESL Scope and Scales* has been steadily implemented in South Australian schools since 2002, a number of observations can be made. The major one is its positive reception by teachers, including those who traditionally would not wish to use a linguistic document. How has this come about? One factor is the quality and quantity of the support given to teachers prior to and then during the implementation. This is the result of the major state-wide professional development programme, *Language and Literacy: Classroom Applications of Functional Grammar*, described in section 2. This course is substantial, comprehensive and relevant to teachers and students and its ongoing demand after 12 years underlines its importance. Alongside that, new resources are being offered to teachers and the availability of annotated samples of student writing, packaged as *Moderated Evidence*[3], is another factor in the successful implementation.

Teachers comment that the investment of time and energy in understanding and using the resource is worthwhile because the links between programming, assessing and reporting on language are clear, and fundamental to their teaching and their students' learning. With it, programming is simply working forwards and backwards along the detailed descriptions of genre, field, tenor and mode, knowing that

Table 5.6   Descriptions of foregrounding (Theme) from Scale 8 to 11 for the Middle Years Band

Mode

Scale 8	Scale 9	Scale 10	Scale 11
Foregrounds (i.e. places at the front) simple, repetitive patterns most of the time with limited use of alternative elements: – in procedures, primarily chooses to foreground actions: '*Draw the eyes with a fine brush …*' – begins to foreground the means used in an action: '*With a fine brush, draw the eyes …*' – begins to foreground non-human elements in factual genres: '*The leaf* was put in the sun' rather than '*We* put the leaf in the sun'.	Foregrounds (i.e. places at the front) less simple, repetitive patterns: – phrases of time and place are foregrounded on more than one occasion in a recount – topic is not exclusively foregrounded in a report: '*The habitat of snakes* is …' rather than '*The snakes* live …' – foregrounds with some confidence non-human elements in factual genres: '*The lathe* was dismantled carefully' rather than '*We* dismantled the lathe carefully'.	Chooses appropriately most of the time what to foreground in longer independent constructions of texts so that they are coherent: – foregrounds simple phrases of manner, place or time in genres such as procedures: '*After about ten minutes*, take the biscuits …' – foregrounds simple dependent clauses in narratives: '*When the children saw the ghost*, they …' – begins to foreground causal elements in explanations and discussions: '*Because of more rainfall*, floods …' – foregrounds confidently non-human elements in factual genres: '*The pumpkin seeds* were planted 2 cm apart' rather than '*We* planted the pumpkin seeds 2 cm apart'.	Chooses appropriately most of the time what to foreground in longer independent constructions of texts so that they are coherent: – foregrounds a wider range of elements in a variety of genres: – phrases of manner in procedures: '*With a damp cloth*, wipe …' – phrases of place or time in narratives: '*On the edge of the road*, they could see …', '*Later that evening*, they …' – dependent clauses or phrases of cause: '*Because the amount of carbon dioxide is increasing*, scientists …' – foregrounds appropriately in explanations and taxonomic reports – foregrounds confidently generalized noun groups in factual genres such as explanations, arguments and reports: '*The diet of the brown bear* is …' rather than '*The brown bear* eats …' – constructs more complex topic sentences and introduction in arguments and discussions: begins to use rhetorical questions in written texts – constructs less basic concluding paragraphs in arguments and discussions.

these are linked directly to the standards of the general curriculum. The scope part of the *ESL Scope and Scales* describes what teachers should be focusing on in their programming. It, too, is organized according to 'Text in Context' and 'Language', and, further, according to genre, field, tenor and mode.

With respect to assessment, the criteria for assessment are based on the descriptors in both the scope and the scales. Although anecdotal evidence suggests that teachers need at least a couple of years to really understand the materials, what is observable is that teachers now rely much less on using accuracy (tenses, punctuation and spelling) as the main if not the only feature they assess.

Lastly, it has been remarked by teachers and consultants that the success of the implementation in each school is not only dependent on what happens institutionally but also on the personnel in each school. Those schools that have availed themselves of the professional development and been involved in research projects are invariably those that are at the forefront of the successful implementation. That should not be a surprise but it does highlight the need for the other schools to catch up quickly now that the *ESL Scope and Scales* is mandated.

7 Conclusion

In all of the contexts described above, we can see a serious engagement with language and its role in teaching and learning, by teachers, teacher educators and students. One common feature of all these contexts is that as language is addressed, 'the richest and most effective resource', the lexicogrammar, is addressed at the same time. We would say that this is perhaps the most heartening thing to come out of the work here in South Australia.

In elaborating on the work begun over ten years ago in our state, we hope that we have shown some of the potential of the functional model for influencing and shaping pedagogy that has knowledge about language as a fundamental principle. In particular, we hope that through the examples we have outlined above, others can be inspired to take up the challenge of developing understandings of the lexicogrammar as a central part of developing a set of semiotic tools for both teachers and students alike.

Notes

1. Refer to www.unlockingtheworld.com for details on the course and its availability.
2. Contact John at john@lexised.com for an electronic copy. A hard copy is available from www.unlockingtheworld.com.
3. Available at www.sacsa.edu.au.

References

Ashton, R. (1999), 'Last night, Mrs. Shepherd ate worms: Teaching circumstances with fun', *English as a Second Language Educators' Journal*, 15, (2), 10–12.

Athanasopoulos, V. and Sandford, D. (1997), 'Teaching the argument genre in a year 6/7 class', *English as a Second Language Teachers' Association Journal*, 13, (1),10–12.

Cope, B. and Kalantzis, M. (eds) (1993), *The Powers of Literacy: A Genre Approach to Teaching Writing*. London: Falmer Press.

Dare, B. and Polias, J. (2004), *Language and Literacy: Classroom Applications of Functional Grammar*. Adelaide, South Australia: DECS Publishing.

Derewianka, B. (1990), *Exploring How Texts Work*. Sydney: PETA.

— (2001), 'Pedagogical grammars: their role in English language teaching', in C. Coffin and A. Burns (eds), *Analysing English in a Global Context*. London: Routledge, pp. 240–69.

Halliday, M. A. K. and Matthiessen, C. M. I. M. (2004), *Introduction to Functional Grammar* (3rd revised edition). London: Hodder Arnold.

Hamilton, A. (1998), 'Yak Yak Yak!', in S. Gapper (ed.), *Learning about Literacy as Teacher-Researchers*. Language Australia and The University of South Australia, pp. 177–9.

Hasan, R. and Williams, G. (eds) (1996), *Literacy in Society*. London: Longman.

Macken-Horarik, M. (1996), 'Literacy and learning across the curriculum: towards a model of register for secondary school teachers', in R. Hasan and G. Williams (eds), pp. 232–78.

Martin, J. R. (1985), *Factual Writing: Exploring and Challenging Social Reality*. Geelong: Deakin University Press.

— (1992), *English Text: System and Structure*. Amsterdam: John Benjamins.

— (1999), 'Mentoring semogenesis: genre-based literacy pedagogy', in F. Christie (ed.), *Pedagogy and the Shaping of Consciousness: Linguistic and Social Process*. London: Cassell, pp.123–54.

Painter, C. and Martin, J. R. (eds) (1986), *Writing to Mean: Teaching Genres Across the Curriculum*. Applied Linguistics Association of Australia (Occasional Papers 9).

Polias, J. (2003), *ESL Scope and Scales*. Adelaide, South Australia: DECS Publishing.

Pryor, G. (1999), 'Introducing functional grammar in a new arrivals classroom', *English as a Second Language Educators' Journal*, 15, (3), 4–9.

Reid, I. (ed.) (1987), *The Place of Genre in Learning: Current Debates*. Geelong,

Victoria, Australia: Deakin University Center for Studies in Literary Education.

Rothery, J. (1996), 'Making changes: developing an educational linguistics', in R. Hasan and G. Williams (eds), pp. 86–123.

Rothery, J. and Stevenson, M. (1994), *Spine-Chilling Stories: A Unit of Work for Junior Secondary English (Write It Right Resources for Literacy and Learning)*. Sydney: Disadvantaged Schools Program Metropolitan East.

Williams, G. (1998), 'Children entering literate worlds: perspectives from the study of textual practices', in F. Christie and R. Misson (eds), *Literacy and Schooling*. London: Routledge, pp. 18–46.

— (2005), 'Grammatics in Schools', in J. Webster, C. M. I. M. Matthiessen and R. Hasan (eds), *Continuing Discourse on Language*. London: Equinox, pp. 281–310.

Williams, M. (1999), 'Does the teaching of Systemic Functional Linguistics make narrative writing more spine chilling?', *English as a Second Language Educators' Journal*, 15, (1), 23–7.

6   Whole-school genre maps: a case study in South Australia

Bronwyn Custance

1 Introduction

This chapter outlines the process undertaken to develop a school-wide framework for genre-based explicit teaching of grammar. The process was undertaken by the staff of St Brigid's Primary School, a small South Australian Catholic school in a disadvantaged area with a high ESL population. Through the process, the staff developed a 'whole-school genre map', which specified the genres to be explicitly taught at each year level, and the language features to be focused on within each genre. The language features to be taught were chosen according to the variables of genre, field, tenor and mode as outlined in the *ESL Scope and Scales* (Polias 2003) which form part of the *South Australian Curriculum Standards and Accountability (SACSA)* framework, and are described in Chapter 5.

Beyond outlining the project undertaken at St Brigid's and the resulting product, the chapter covers the initial stages of implementation. It provides overviews of language-focused teaching of the explanation genre at three levels of primary school, including a sample student text and comments made by students following the unit. The chapter ends with a summary of the early reactions to, and consequences of, this whole-school approach to the explicit teaching of functional grammar.

2 Background

2.1 The school

St Brigid's is one of the ten schools of lowest socio-economic status in Australia. Its students come from diverse language and cultural backgrounds. In 2002, the Reception class (5-year-olds commencing school) of 22 pupils included ten minimal speakers of English from five different language backgrounds. ESL students across the school range from second generation Australian migrants and refugees to new arrivals including refugees from Sudan, and Afghani students on temporary protection visas.

The school had an ESL teacher, Beverley White, who worked there four days a week and was appointed by Catholic Education South Australia (CESA) as part of a network of ESL teachers. Throughout the project, Beverley, Mark Hennessey (the school-appointed Key Literacy teacher who had two days per week to support literacy development across the school) and Ray Klecko (the principal) played key roles in ensuring the success of the project and the type of support necessary for such an undertaking, as Chapter 5 concluded.

2.2   ESL Scope and Scales

The *ESL Scope and Scales* (Polias 2003) were made available mid-2002 and CESA began a professional development programme with its ESL teachers in preparation for a move to adopt the scales as the system assessment and reporting tool in 2003. Scales data would then be used to allocate ESL teacher placements according to levels of need.

The *ESL Scope and Scales* are described more fully in Chapter 5. Broadly speaking, they are programming and reporting support materials for all teachers of learners for whom English is an additional language or dialect. They describe English literacy proficiency levels and are aligned to 'SACSA standards' and year levels. The descriptions of literacy levels are organized according to genre, field, tenor and mode and provide detailed description and examples of language at various levels, based on understandings of the systemic functional linguistic (SFL) model.

3 Development and implementation of the genre map document

3.1   Preparation

Beverley, the ESL teacher, had been in the group which trialled the final draft of the *ESL Scope and Scales* document and recognized its potential not only as a tool for assessment of learning but also as a framework which could inform the teaching and learning programme for the whole school. This insight led her to propose extending the use of the document: it should not only be used by ESL teachers, or merely to collect data for funding purposes. Instead, she wanted all teachers in her school to be able to understand and use the document to maximize the benefits for ESL students.

With the support of Mark, the literacy teacher, and Ray, the principal, she arranged for the staff to undertake the teacher development course: *Language and Literacy: classroom applications in functional grammar* (Polias and Dare 2003). The course was run by a CESA ESL consultant during staff-meeting time after school in the third and fourth terms of 2002. The course is organized as nine three-hour workshops and takes teachers through those aspects of genre, field, tenor and mode which are most relevant to the development of language and literacy in schools.

Early in 2003, Beverley ran a staff-meeting session introducing teachers to the *ESL Scope and Scales*. From this, teachers understood the process of scaling for funding, its timeline and their role in providing Beverley with two work samples, a recount or narrative and a factual text, for each ESL student in their class.

The following term, Beverley carried out the task of scaling each ESL student using the samples supplied by classroom teachers. Based on this, she provided teachers with feedback on their students' performance and areas of need. Alongside this process, Mark worked with staff to gather a picture of the genres they were currently teaching across the school.

Beverley, Mark and I also met to plan for two pupil-free days that had been set aside for staff to gain an understanding of the programming potential of the *ESL Scope and Scales*. From our meetings came the vision of the product which could result from these days: an agreed whole-school genre map, specifying four genres to be explicitly taught at each year level, and the language features to be focused on within each genre.

Most primary teachers in Australia are familiar with the genre approach and the major schooling genres identified through the *Write it Right* project, carried out in Australia during the 1990s (as outlined in Chapter 3). As the school year is divided into four terms, each of about ten weeks, teachers also often choose to focus on one genre per term. However, they are not always familiar with the links between genres and their purposes, contexts and language features and rarely teach anything more than the structure of the genre.

3.2   Developing the genre overview

Working from this knowledge base then, the day began with considering various SACSA outcomes across the learning areas and determining which genres would be appropriate to demonstrate achievement of the learning described in the outcome. Staff were also asked to consider which learning areas were most likely to use the genres of description, explanation, exposition narrative, recount, report and response.

Once the idea of teaching genres related to context and purpose had been established, teachers were asked to work in 'Bands of Schooling' groups: Early Years (5–8 years old), Primary Years (8–11 years old) and Middle Years (11–13 years old). Within Band groups, each teacher took on specific responsibility for one year level. They were then to

- skim the scale relevant to their year level
- highlight the genres mentioned
- decide which four would be explicitly taught
- identify learning areas/topics where each could be taught.

During this process, they could also refer to the list showing which genres were currently taught in the school. The *ESL Scope and Scales* also contains tables outlining the typical genres at each Band of schooling. Together with the other teachers in their 'Band group', they then checked whether they had covered each genre listed for their Band and made any necessary adjustments so that they were satisfied with the coverage.

A large genre overview was then drawn up on the whiteboard, with the genres to be taught at each year level filled in. This enabled everyone to see at what points each genre would be explicitly taught. Some minor adjustments were made, after which all were in agreement that teaching according to this overview would ensure that each genre was introduced, taught and developed at appropriate stages across the school (see Table 6.1).

In the years prior to a genre being explicitly taught, teachers would expose students to examples through reading and at times exploring it in oral work or perhaps by modelling how to write an example. Once a genre had been explicitly taught, teachers would in following years consolidate this teaching by reading examples with reference to the genre type, purpose, structure and features and engaging students in written and oral tasks requiring the genre after revising its structure and features.

Table 6.1 The agreed genre overview for St. Brigid's: from Reception to Year 5

	Reception	Year 1	Year 2	Year 3	Year 4	Year 5
Description	Teach	Teach	Consolidate	Consolidate	Consolidate	Consolidate
Explanation	Expose	Teach	Teach	Consolidate	Teach	Teach
Exposition	Expose	Expose	Teach	Teach	Teach	Teach
Narrative	Expose	Teach	Teach	Consolidate	Teach	Teach
Procedure	Teach	Consolidate	Teach	Teach	Consolidate	Teach
Recount	Teach	Consolidate	Consolidate	Teach	Consolidate	Consolidate
Report	Teach	Teach	Consolidate	Teach	Teach	Consolidate

(adapted from White and Custance 2003: 5)

3.3   Including the language features

Each teacher had been provided with a 'year level planning chart' and had recorded the four genres for their year level and ideas for topics within which they could be taught. As most of the staff had undertaken the *Language and Literacy* course the previous year, the teachers were guided through a number of activities to revise, or in some cases explain and teach, key aspects of grammar outlined in the *ESL Scope and Scales* under the organizers: genre, field, tenor and mode. The activities chosen not only revised aspects of grammar, but modelled types of activities which could be used with students.

In the *ESL Scope and Scales*, the aspects of grammar considered under the heading of genre include use of conjunctions and reference. Once these aspects had been revised, teachers were then asked to refer to the 'Genre Language Strand' for the scale relevant to their year level, and select and record three or four relevant language features to be explicitly taught for the four chosen genres. As the teachers worked in their band groups, Beverley, Mark and I were each able to work with a group to develop teachers' understandings of which language features would be most relevant to their chosen genre, linking language choices back to the social purpose of the genre.

This process was then repeated, revising aspects of grammar related to field: types of processes (verbs), participants, circumstances (adverbials) and expanding noun groups; tenor: modality and attitudinal lexis; and mode: Theme (foregrounding) patterns, passive voice and tense. In addition to the *ESL Scope and Scales* (Polias 2003) and the *Language and Literacy* course materials (Polias and Dare 2003), three other key resources were drawn on and recommended to teachers to help them understand aspects of grammar, their relevance to particular genres and ideas for teaching activities: the *English K-6 Syllabus* (Board of Studies NSW 1998), *Grammar in Teaching* (Collerson 1997) and *A Grammar Companion for Primary Teachers* (Derewianka 1998).

Two factors which were critical to the success of these two days were the support of the principal and the way in which teachers' current practice was acknowledged, shared and built on. The principal, Ray, demonstrated his support of the project, not only by designating the pupil-free days for this purpose, but also by being an active participant throughout the two days.

Mark, the literacy teacher, was keen to ensure that the work teachers were already doing was acknowledged and shared throughout the process and so we had decided to ask teachers to share their successful practices in teaching grammar. I had provided Mark and Beverley with an overview of the aspects of grammar which would be revised over the two days, and they approached teachers asking them to nominate an area for which they could share an example of classroom practice. With prompting and encouragement, which Beverley was able to give because she taught collaboratively in each class, each teacher was scheduled in for sharing. This gave them opportunities to prepare and then present their successful practices at relevant points throughout the two days.

3.4   The product: St Brigid's whole-school genre map

At the end of the two days, the staff of St Brigid's had developed an agreed overview of genres to be taught at each year level and a draft plan of which language features would be explicitly taught with each genre. They had also decided that it would be important to record some details about the learning area and topic, or theme, within which the genre had been taught, to prevent students, for example, only ever writing reports about animals. The principal worked on a proforma for recording this information which would be passed on with the students from year to year. The proforma also allowed for teachers to provide comments which could, for instance, indicate aspects of grammar which the students had not grasped well and would need further development, as well as aspects they had excelled in.

Beverley and I then spent a day working together on the drafts to achieve consistency of language and format. We also wanted to ensure that there were a manageable number of language elements to be explicitly taught while working on a genre, which sometimes meant reducing the number of points the class teachers had listed and shifting language features between genres, to ensure they were being addressed at the most relevant points. In any given year level, we then looked across the four genres and the language items, and checked that, in covering those, a teacher would have taught – and provided opportunity for a student to demonstrate – all of the items considered evidence of achieving the scale for their year level as regards writing.

As we worked on the year level planning charts that the teachers had completed, we noticed that they had used the ideas for topics in a variety of ways. Some had listed a topic and learning area, while others had noted ideas for activities they might use to teach a particular language element. We decided to complete the proposals for activities to cover all language features listed for each genre.

While a number of decisions had been made by the end of our day together, and several genre teaching guides had been completed as models (see Table 6.2), much work remained to be done. Beverley continued the process, dedicating many hours to the completion of the document in electronic form. In addition to the changes we had made, Beverley also included an assessment proforma for each of the four genres named at each year level, which she developed by taking the structural and linguistic elements specified in the teaching guide.

In place of suggested topics, and to ensure that teachers planned to teach genres within meaningful contexts across the curriculum, the list of suggested related SACSA outcomes was used. Mark prepared an overview of the SACSA outcomes for each learning area at the appropriate Standard, to be included with each teaching guide. The final addition to the document was an appendix of grammar handouts (originally developed by myself and/or Tony Hole, a CESA Literacy Consultant) which had been used for revision purposes during the sessions, as well as some material on tense. The result is an extremely practical document to assist teachers to programme, teach and assess writing in a thorough and systematic way.

3.5 Implementation phase

The staff of St Brigid's began using the document, which they had been instrumental in developing, to guide their programming, teaching and assessment in 2004. Beverley found that her practice of collaboratively planning and teaching with class teachers had become much easier and more straightforward, as the document now provided them with the framework and much of the focus of their teaching. Together, they would decide which of the designated genres and topics

Table 6.2   An example of a completed genre teaching guide

Year 2 Scale 6 **Sequential Explanation**	**Ideas for Activities**
Genre structure: phenomenon identification, sequence of events.	Use proformas to scaffold the structure. Complete a flow chart to sequence the events and to use as a guide for writing.
Genre language features to be explicitly taught: • Conjunctions that organize the text: *First, then* • Binding conjunctions to form complex sentences: *because, before, when, after* • Reference items: The tadpole's back legs grow longer. Now it can jump.	Sequence pictures from the explanation with the captions focusing on the time of the event. Write sentence beginnings on cards with binding conjunctions, students complete: *Before the frog can breathe air* . . . Cloze activity for reference items.
Field language features to be explicitly taught: • Uses a narrow range of technical vocabulary: *frogspawn, froglet* • Expose to a range of common nominalizations (words that have been formed by changing verbs, adjectives or conjunctions into a noun: *growth, development*	Make charts with words and pictures to introduce and provide access to technical words. Discuss nominalizations as they arise in texts/ discussions.
Tenor language features to be explicitly taught: • Appropriate tenor for a factual text, i.e. *the cute little tadpole, one day the frog*. . . is not appropriate. Keep it factual.	Give a list of sentences from a narrative e.g. *The Frog Prince* and an information book on frogs. Sort under fact/fiction headings. Discuss appropriateness in terms of writing an explanation.
Mode language features to be explicitly taught: • Present tense used for factual writing: focus on final s in present tense i.e. *Frog**s** hop, A frog hop**s*** • Phrases of time to organize the text: *At two weeks*	Emphasis on pronouncing the ends of words when reading aloud. Cloze activity with a known text: blank the present tense verbs.

(adapted from White and Custance 2003: 27)

they would teach each term, and then map out the language focus lessons and activities. Beverley was able to allocate to each class one lesson per week in which she took the lead role to explicitly teach aspects of grammar and their role within texts. The class teacher focused on the learning area objectives to be covered and the teaching of the corresponding key concepts and skills. In addition, class teachers taught aspects of grammar they felt comfortable with, and reinforced the parts Beverley had taught.

4 The development of a genre: explanation at Years 2, 5 and 7

As Beverley and several teachers were keen to track, in some way, the impact of this whole-school focus on the explicit teaching of grammar within a genre-based approach, it was decided to examine the teaching of one genre: explanation at three different levels of schooling: Early Years: Year 2 (7-year-olds), Primary Years: Year 5 (10-year-olds) and Middle Years: Year 7 (12-year-olds). A snapshot of the work covered is provided here.

4.1 *Year 2 explanation: The life cycle of a sea turtle*

The first language focus lesson of this unit took up the notion of maintaining an appropriate tenor for a factual text, with the aim that students would understand that explanations are factual texts. After the teacher had read a narrative about a turtle, the class discussed the book with the teacher asking questions such as: Is it fact or fiction? How do you know? What are the differences between a factual text and a fiction text? The students were then asked to sort sentences about turtles under the headings 'Fact' or 'Fiction'.

The language lessons over the next two weeks focused on developing aspects of field: technical vocabulary to label parts of a turtle and talk about the life of a turtle. Together, the class built a glossary chart for the classroom wall.

The following four weeks focused on grammatical aspects associated with genre and mode: present tense, conjunctions, reference items, circumstances of time and sequencing conjunctions to organize the text. Students were involved in activities such as:

- using conjunctions to add information and expand sentences
- circling reference items (pronouns) and drawing arrows from them to the referents

- deciding which pronoun (singular or plural) should be used to refer to a given noun
- underlining in blue all the time words in a jumbled text and using these to re-order the text
- completing a present tense cloze activity.

In the language lessons of the last weeks of term, the teacher and students jointly constructed a text as a model, prior to students independently constructing their explanation. This final stage included the processes of drafting, conferencing and publishing.

4.2   Year 5 explanation: The respiratory system

A major aspect of language focused on by the Year 5 class was Theme and Rheme patterns and the role that passive voice plays in maintaining this pattern. Students completed an activity in which they identified the zig-zagging Theme-Rheme pattern of an explanation and practised changing sentences from active voice to passive.

Figure 6.1 depicts a sample student text in which boxes again highlight how this student was able to take up, in her independent construction, language features which had been explicitly taught. At times there is an overuse of the Theme-Rheme pattern but this is often a developmental stage in the appropriation of a linguistic device. The sample also shows the proforma which Beverley had provided students to scaffold their writing, providing structural, linguistic and editing prompts.

4.3   Year 7 explanation: A rainforest ecosystem

In addition to reference and passive voice, the Year 7s were also introduced to nominalization and revised subject verb agreement in the present tense, a problem area for many ESL students. The following are examples from a nominalization worksheet. The instructions were 'Rewrite the following sentences by replacing the underlined words with nominalizations (the words in brackets)'.

1. Leaf litter is rapidly broken down with the help of insects and fungi. (decomposition)
2. Some trees grow their roots into the leaf litter to directly absorb water and nutrients. (growth)
3. Tiny microbes help maintain all life in the rainforest. (maintenance)

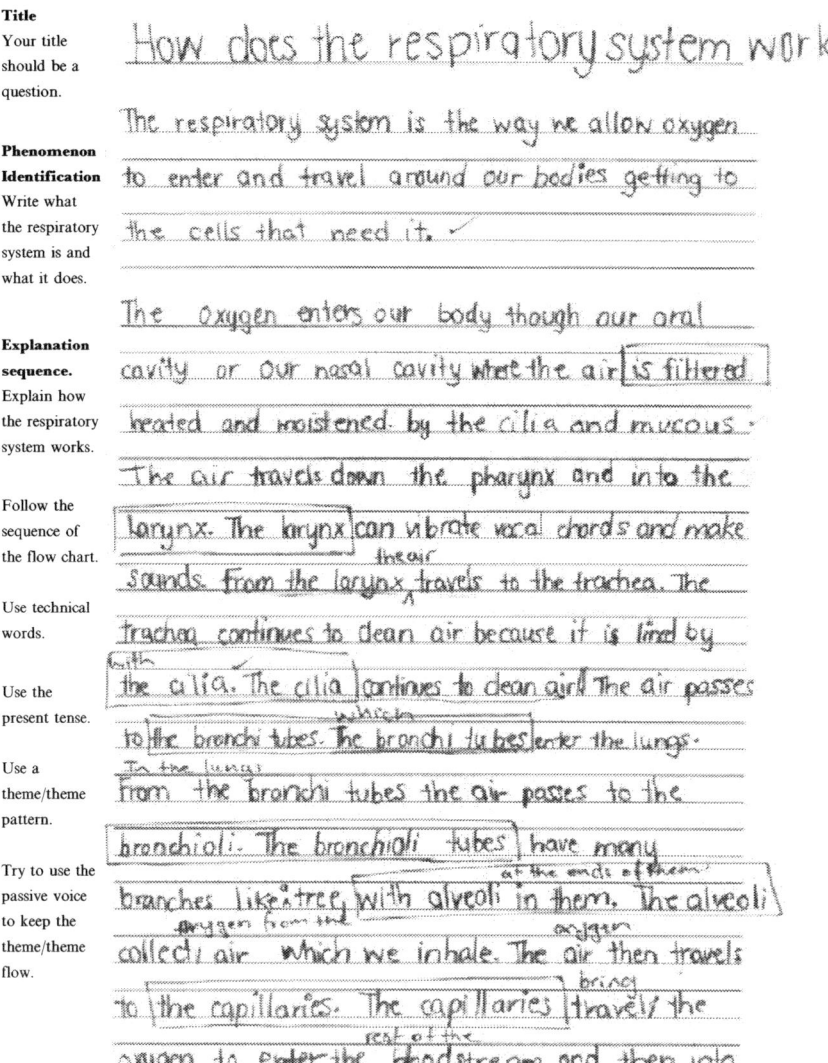

Title
Your title
should be a
question.

**Phenomenon
Identification**
Write what
the respiratory
system is and
what it does.

**Explanation
sequence.**
Explain how
the respiratory
system works.

Follow the
sequence of
the flow chart.

Use technical
words.

Use the
present tense.

Use a
theme/theme
pattern.

Try to use the
passive voice
to keep the
theme/theme
flow.

How does the respiratory system work

The respiratory system is the way we allow oxygen to enter and travel around our bodies getting to the cells that need it.

The oxygen enters our body though our oral cavity or our nasal cavity where the air is filtered heated and moistened by the cilia and mucous. The air travels down the pharynx and into the larynx. The larynx can vibrate vocal chords and make sounds. from the larynx the air travels to the trachea. The trachea continues to clean air because it is lined by with the cilia. The cilia continues to clean air. The air passes to the bronchi tubes. The bronchi tubes which enter the lungs. In the lungs from the bronchi tubes the air passes to the bronchioli. The bronchioli tubes have many branches like a tree with alveoli in them at the ends of them. The alveoli collect air which we inhale. The air then travels oxygen to the capillaries. The capillaries bring travel the oxygen to enter the rest of the bloodstream and then into

Figure 6.1   Student independent construction: Year 5

4.4   Student reactions

At the completion of the units, Beverley chose two students of non-English speaking backgrounds from each class to talk about their learning experiences. The students were told that someone would be going to Spain to tell other people about their work. They had their workbooks to refer to and remind them of the various activities they had done throughout the unit and Beverley videoed their responses. Extracts of the transcripts are included here.

Two Year 2s (7-year-olds)

T	What did you do with these cards?
S1	We did conjunctions about these cards. Like um put them like to see what could go with it. Like 'Before turtles swim to the water every few minutes ...' (rising tone indicating incomplete sentence)
T	What are the blue words? (pointing to words underlined in workbook)
S2	They're time words.
T	What else can you tell me about these blue words?
S2	They start at the beginning of a sentence.
T	And how do they help us to organize the text? They help us keep the text in the right ... ?
S1 and 2	Order.

Two Year 5s (10-year-olds)

S1	Theme-Rheme is ..., if for an example you're using a ... taco, it's a easier for you guys in Spain, so you say 'Mr Mexico ate a taco'. And then the next one would (be) 'The taco was full of rice.' Theme-Rheme, there you go, you learned it already there, guys.
S2	And the passive voice is that when you use Theme–Rheme because if you were to write 'The nose cleans the air.' (Next) You have to say 'The air ... What does the air does? So you can't say anything so you have to say, 'The air is cleaned by the nose.' And the next sentence would be, 'The nose filters, moistens and heats the air.' And that's passive voice and Theme-Rheme.

Two Year 7s (12-year-olds)

Both of these girls are of Vietnamese background and had only been in Australia learning English for two and three years respectively. While they were still having difficulties with pronunciation of some technical terms and their English at times sounded quite broken, they clearly understood the grammar which had been taught and its applications.

S1	Present tense. Like when the participant have an 's' and we're been given this 'give and gives', so we have to add give um gives instead of give because in there they're talking about sunlight and it doesn't have any 's'.
S2	And it's not plural. We also did reference items. We drew

| | an arrow from the underlined word back to its . . . referent or the word it's referring to them. For example, 'these plants' I drew an arrow to epiphytes because it's referring to epiphytes. |
| S2 | The rainforest explanation was not easy. We had to use a lot of information and we had to use the correct participants: grammar, and we had to use technical words as well and Theme-Rheme. |

5 Outcomes

5.1 For teachers

Towards the end of the first six months of implementation, I met with the staff and asked them to reflect on what they felt had been the impact of the whole-school genre map. All of the teachers commented positively that the document provided clarity of expectations. Interestingly, this was voiced most strongly by those teachers new to the school who had not been a part of its development. Teachers felt that it was reassuring to know that all genres would be covered across the school. This also eased some of the pressure, as they knew that they needed to cover only a few genres in depth in any one year and, even then, they knew that this work would be revisited and further developed in later years.

While clarity of expectations and a sense of a whole-school systematic and developmental approach to teaching literacy were directly related to the aims of the project, there were also other positive outcomes which had not been foreseen. The move to this whole-school approach was encouraging greater documentation and sharing of practice. This was not at the request or directive of school leaders, but came from the teachers themselves.

5.2 For students

The main aim of the project had been to improve ESL student achievement, in particular English literacy levels. While there was no specific testing or data collection to measure this, some conclusions can be drawn both qualitatively and quantitatively. Anecdotally, students appeared to be engaged, willing and successful participants in language-focused lessons. They were able to produce texts at a length and complexity above a level generally expected for their age, and were using metalanguage with ease and confidence as they spoke about their learning. It should be noted that the students selected for the interviews, and the one whose sample text is included here, were representative of the class, not those who performed at the highest level.

Quantitatively, the ESL Scaling data collection can be used to attain an indication of changes in English proficiency levels. As explained earlier, Beverley had assigned each ESL student an ESL scale. This data was then submitted to CESA where it was used to determine ESL teacher time allocations. Students whose current ESL scale level is furthest behind the 'Standard' scale level, and hence have the greatest need, attract the most time.

ESL scale data collected at St Brigid's in 2002 indicated a level of need which translated to just over one full-time ESL teacher (Beverley worked four days per week and another teacher worked one and a half days). Data collected in 2003, using samples of student work produced at the end of units which had explicitly taught the genre required, including the relevant language features, indicated a level of need which translated to an allocation of one half-time ESL teacher. While it could be argued that other factors were at play, no other school in the sector had anything like such a dramatic improvement in student performance. Because CESA staff were aware of the pivotal role that Beverley was playing in this improvement of student performance, her position was maintained there at four days per week.

5.3 Moving beyond St Brigid's

What began as one school's development of a whole-school approach to the teaching of literacy has spread to many other schools. One teacher, who had been at St Brigid's and part of the initial development of the document, transferred to another school the next year and took a copy with her which she used to guide her planning, teaching and assessment. Others in the school were soon interested and copying the portions relevant to their year level/s.

Word also spread through ESL and Key Literacy teacher networks both within Catholic schools and inter-sector networks. With a growing interest in the document, the school and CESA jointly managed an 'in-house' publication of the document. It is sold at a minimal fee to recover printing costs with a small amount per copy returned to the school to be spent on literacy. At the time of writing, over 600 copies have been sold.

6 Final reflections

While problems of implementation have not arisen at this stage, attention needs to be paid to the questions of development of teachers' understandings of systemic functional linguistics, the *ESL Scope and Scales*, and their applications to the classroom teaching and learning programme. On the one hand, teachers feel the need for ongoing support to develop their understanding and confidence in teaching grammar and on the other, given the constant changes in the staff, new teachers will need help if they are to become familiar with, and progressively gain deeper understanding of, the school's document and the theory behind it. To date, we have found that most teachers are keen to learn the approach to language teaching adopted by the school, which means that the work on the genre map will remain in focus, and ensures that the document and the practices it advocates are continually revisited.

References

Board of Studies NSW (1998), *English K-6 Syllabus*. Sydney: Board of Studies New South Wales.
Collerson, J. (1997), *Grammar in Teaching*. Sydney: Primary English Teaching Association.
Derewianka, B. (1998), *A Grammar Companion for Primary Teachers*. Sydney: Primary English Teaching Association.
Polias, J. (2003), *ESL Scope and Scales*. Adelaide, South Australia: Department of Education and Children's Services.
Polias, J. and Dare, B. (2003), *Language and Literacy Course: Classroom Applications of Functional Grammar*. Adelaide, South Australia: Department of Education and Children's Services.
White, B. and Custance, B. (2003), *Genre Mapping across the Curriculum in SACSA*. Adelaide, South Australia: Catholic Education South Australia.

7 The impact of genre theory and pedagogy and systemic functional linguistics on National Literacy Strategies in the UK

Paddy Walsh

1 Introduction

1.1 Background

In 1998, the recently elected New Labour government in the UK launched the National Literacy Strategy in infant and junior schools – Key Stage 1 (KS1, ages 5 to 7) and Key Stage 2 (KS2, 8 to 11) – in response to serious concerns about poor literacy standards nationally. In 2001, the Strategy was extended to the early years of secondary school, KS3 (11 to 14), and in 2005, to KS4 (14 to 16). The project offers a sustained, funded programme of professional development for teachers, with comprehensive support materials in print and online, which aims to raise standards and transform the life chances of school students in the UK. The Strategies are clearly influenced by the work of Vygotsky, Bruner and Australian genre theory and pedagogy, without explicitly acknowledging their provenance. At primary and secondary level, the teaching of grammar is given prominence; but while there are some references to systemic functional linguistics (SFL), the model of grammar adopted is a hybrid version of formal or traditional, descriptive grammar, which draws on Greenbaum and Quirk (1970) and is mediated by the Strategies' grammar consultants, Professors David Crystal and Richard Hudson.

1.2 The ineffability of the subject 'English'

In order to contextualize the problems of attempts to improve literacy in the UK, I begin with a number of views on the subject of English.

First, then, a summary by Peter Medway (1980: 3), currently of King's College London, which presents the problem:

> English teachers do not describe what happens in their lessons as 'learning' and what their pupils end up with as 'knowledge'; or if they do, it is only when referring to subsidiary aspects of the work such as spelling or literary facts and not what they regard as the central activity. 'Knowledge' and 'learning' are tied in people's mind to facts and information, and the reason teachers avoid the terms is that they do not see themselves as dealing with facts. Indeed it is sometimes said that English is a subject without a content.

This view can be contrasted with the evaluation, 25 years later, of a 13-year old boy, Alex, from an Islington secondary school in London, after explicit teaching in the SFL genre model. He and his fellow students had been working with his English teacher and a government Department for Education and Skills (DfES) Secondary Strategy Literacy Consultant as part of an inclusion project to raise the attainment of white working class boys in English lessons. The teacher and consultant had worked with the class on producing rhetorical texts, deconstructing, in the Secondary Strategies' terms, the text, sentence and word level features of the writing. In SFL terms, they were working on the discourse semantics and lexicogrammatical features of persuasive texts. Applying key strategy pedagogies which draw upon neo-Vygotskian approaches, the teacher, together with the class, jointly deconstructed, modelled and shared the reading and writing of examples, before the students were guided to a better understanding of the linguistic resources for producing their own persuasive texts. Presenting the results of their work to a conference of teachers and DfES consultants, Alex was asked what he had most enjoyed about the project's specific work. He replied: 'I now know what English is.'

Presumably, until that point, for him, the subject of English was the indeterminate entity that Peter Medway had described 25 years earlier, more recently defined by John Yandell (2004) of London's Institute of Education (IoE) in these words: 'English, in comparison with other subjects, is always going to be strange and elusive'. In my view, it is precisely this strangeness and elusiveness that leaves the boy, who represented a targeted group i.e. 'underachieving white working class boys', adrift.

Influential teachers at major teacher training institutions in London, such as the IoE and Goldsmith's College, provide consistent robust criticism of National Strategies which are aimed at improving the life chances of inner city children. These criticisms represent the continuing playing out of tensions between what Ian Hunter (1997) has called 'aesthetico-cultural' and 'neo-rhetorical' discourses in English teaching. Coles (2004) of Goldsmith's claims that:

> The current political imperative, that of a literacy quick fix, propelled by bands of objectives and predetermined outcomes is inimical to the conditions needed to foster the sort of reflexive linguistic interaction which is the prerequisite of the social construction of classroom learning.

She asks:

> What hope have my students in making sense of constructivist learning theory as explored in college, when it is continually set against the warped version of Vygotsky's 'zone of proximal development,' or Bruner's 'scaffolding' as served up by literacy strategy devotees in the shape of tedious teacher dominated compositions written up longhand on the whiteboard followed by overly constructed writing frames which bleed pupil's writing of its individual voice?

These comments are echoed by such celebrated British children's writers as Phillip Pullman and Anne Fine (Ashley *et al* 2003: 2), who claim the Literacy Strategies are mechanistic and stultifying, recalling the words of Margaret McMillan (1904: 98–9) – more than a hundred years ago – who said:

> I have seen a class of very dulled and stupefied children, who could understand only a very small range of words, begin to live at once when they were allowed to dramatise even a word.

In the same line, Pullman, in his famous Isis lecture at the Oxford Literary Festival in 2003, suggested that:

> When you come to the end of the story, stop. Turn away from it. Let it do its own work in its own time; don't tear it into rags by making the poor children analyse, and comment, and compare, and interpret. Good God, the world is full of stories, full of true nourishment for the heart and the mind and the imagination; and this true nourishment is lying all around our children, untouched, and they're being force-fed on ashes and saw-dust and potato-peelings.

Anne Fine deplores a real drop in the standard of children's writing – not in grammar, construction or spelling, but in creativity. She no longer accepts invitations to judge children's writing

competitions, since: 'The standards, even of the best, are generally so
truly awful that I rarely think we should give a prize at all' (Ashley *et
al* 2003: 2). In what she calls the 'untestable quality of creativity,'
(ibid.) there are echoes of Newbolt's (1921) post-World War I
description of the 'pedagogical use of literature' as: 'a possession and
source of delight, a personal intimacy and the gaining of personal
experience, an end in itself and at the same time, an equipment for
the understanding of life'. Obviously, little has changed. In the same
line, John Dixon in his seminal *Growth through English* (1967: 8)
anticipates present-day writers, Fine and Pullman, and echoes those
of the nineteenth and early twentieth century, Stow (1850),
McMillan (1904), Green (1913) and Newbolt (1921), when he
constructs the English teacher as: 'The person to whom pupils turn
with a sense of trust. The sensitivity, honesty and tact of his response
to what pupils say will confirm their half-formed certainties and
doubts in what they have said'. I now turn to the period between
Dixon's words and those of Fine and Pullman.

2 The 1970s and the Bullock Report into the Teaching of English

I began my career as an English teacher in 1968, the year after Dixon's
influential book appeared. I had been a school student at a time when
the discourse of English teaching was tired and reaching its end. The
teaching of rhetorical, analytical resources to respond to Shakespeare
and nineteenth-century texts, to debate a point of view, or to make an
oratorical presentation were very important, as were the regular daily
doses of traditional Latin-based grammar. Dixon blew away the
cobwebs of archaic and dreary pedagogies for newly qualified teachers
like me, who were, inevitably, forged in the white heat of progressivist
ideology. The curriculum had been stale, but for a recent migrant
from a working class Irish background, my grammar school education
in a fee-paying Catholic college had, ironically, given me the linguistic
resources to both critique the old, and advocate the new.

I was, however, in a messianic pother. Having failed the 11+
selection exam and been saved – much to my disgust – from the dead
end school at the dead end of the street by ambitious migrant parents
whose own education had been curtailed, I wanted to attack the
pernicious nature of traditional grammar. Research evidence had
demonstrated incontrovertibly that it had no impact on improving the
writing of those upon whom it was inflicted. Yet traditional grammar
had a social function, in addition to pedantry:

The logic of the traditional curriculum was to serve up a universal 'standard,' with pretensions to factualness and cultural universality, pass those who found the standard and its underlying cultural logic congenial, fail those who didn't, then ascribe the consequent differences in social and educational outcome to individual 'ability'.

(Cope and Kalantzis 1993: 4)

The Bullock Report (1974: 170) in the UK had reached the same conclusion:

Pupils not too certain of their ability with language would thus be looking for the gins and snares, to the equal detriment of their confidence and writing. This kind of teaching has often inhibited a child's utterance without strengthening the fabric of his language. It has nurtured in many the expectation of failure and drilled others in what they already know.

The paradigm of progressivism that emerged and achieved official and institutional dominance in Australia in the 1970s, owing much to Dewey and Montessori, was more coherent and stable than that which was prevalent in the UK, but many of the principles were the same. Both were influenced by the Plowden Report (1967). Students were now to be active learners, to learn by doing, to learn through practical experience rather than assimilate facts by rote. Effective learning was relevant and child-centred, and not institutionally imposed. Process was more important than content. Texts that students wanted to read and write, and which were of relevance to their own lives, were used instead of textbooks. Student ownership became an exalted concept; teachers were facilitators rather than a source of knowledge about language. As there would be no imposed notion of 'proper language' there would not be 'disadvantaged students.' The notion that there might be a standard of correct English was deemed to be sheer prejudice; what was central to the progressivist vision of literacy was the 'student voice'. The teacher facilitator gave students space to voice their own interests.

Teachers contributing to the Bullock report, when asked about what was then generally known as 'personal writing' – a loose term distinguished from impersonal uses by which knowledge is acquired and recorded – articulated a healthy scepticism about this emphasis at the expense of other kinds of writing. They observed:

Many teachers see 'creative writing' as the high point of literacy. We need to rethink this: overemphasis on such writing has distorted a whole view of language. It usually means colourful or fanciful language. It is often false, artificially stimulated and pumped up by the teacher, or written to an unconscious model given to the children. It is often divorced from real feeling.

(Bullock 1974: 163)

3 The 1980s and events in Australia

By the mid-1980s I had begun to question my own commitment, and that of my English Department's, to progressivism in English teaching. We had begun to sense that progressivism's prescriptions for individual control, student-centred learning, student motivation, purposeful writing and individual ownership did not provide the success for the predominantly working class students with whom we worked. We were beginning to conclude that the power of voice, in fact, matched the moral temper and cultural aspirations of middle class students from child-centred households. This is when I became aware of critiques of progressivism offered by genre theorists from the Sydney School in New South Wales (NSW), Australia. They described genre theory and pedagogy as a post-progressive discourse. For them, progressivism's pedagogy of immersion favoured students whose voice is closest to the literate culture of power in industrial societies; it was no more motivating than the traditional curriculum, particularly for students who do not see the immediate point of learning literacy, or even being at school. Progressivism reproduces educational inequities, given the inequities of the social value placed on 'different voices in the world outside school' (Cope and Kalantzis 1993: 6). Far from elevating teachers to the role of expert professional it reduces them to the role of manager. The obsession with starting where the child is, and from his or her language, leads to a pedagogy which encourages students to produce texts in a limited range of genres, mostly personal recounts or narratives. This may explain why English teachers are often disappointed, given that exhortations to 'choose your own topic' or 'say what you feel like saying' often produce work that is monotonous and repetitive. And, most importantly, those texts which are furthest from the student's own voice – the powerful, culturally valued genres, which are generically and grammatically most complex, the interpretative, rhetorical and persuasive in the English classroom – remain beyond those who most need the social and cultural capital they bestow.

The complete overturn of traditional pedagogies by progressivist regimes in Australia produced no evidence that the life chances of those traditionally marginalized groups whom they were intended to benefit were in fact improved. This perhaps explains why genre theory and pedagogy has proved such an attractive and persuasive pedagogy in Australia, developed as it was in New South Wales in the early 1980s to meet the needs of marginalized ethnic groups.

Immediately, genre-based pedagogies were attacked simultaneously by progressivists as well as proponents of a traditional curriculum. Progressivists saw a transmission pedagogy in the mould of the traditional curriculum. Traditionalists distrusted the way genre theorists lean towards cultural inclusivity. Advocates of genre theory and pedagogy and SFL were equally strong in their rejection of both progressivism and traditionalism.

By 1988, working as Head of an English Department in a UK comprehensive school in Peterborough I had, with my colleagues, embarked on a re-evaluation of our KS3 English curriculum. We were aware of the fierce debates that were raging, and the Conservative government's determination to outflank Donald Graves' progressivist disciples who believed children were programmed naturally to write without support, or adult intervention, providing the stimulus was right. Norman Tebbitt, the Conservative Party Chairman, put the Tories' fears starkly, on BBC Radio 4 in 1985:

> We've allowed so many standards to slip ... teachers weren't bothering to teach kids to spell and to punctuate properly ... if you allow standards to slip to the stage where good English is no better than bad English, where people turn up filthy ... at school ... all those things cause people to have no standards at all, and once you lose standards there's no imperative to stay out of crime.
>
> (Tebbitt quoted in Carter 1996: 4)

Tebbitt had made a link between poor punctuation and rising crime. More seriously, tucked away in a Curriculum Matters document (DES 1984, Section 3.8), intended to lay down the principles for a National Curriculum, was the following:

> There is much confusion over whether grammar should be explicitly taught. It has long been recognised that formal exercises in the analysis and classification of language contribute little or nothing to the ability to use it. One consequence of this, however, is that many pupils are taught nothing at all about how language works as a system, and consequently do not understand the nature of their mistakes or how to put them right. We suggest that if some attention is given to the examination and discussion of the language pupils speak, write, read, or listen to for real purposes their awareness of its possibilities and pitfalls can be sharpened. In the course of this, it is reasonable that they should learn such grammatical terminology as is useful to them for the discussion of language. But what and how much

terminology they should be taught at any given stage must depend on how much they can assimilate with understanding and apply to purposes they see to be meaningful and interesting. The least able at using language are the least likely to understand the terminology, let alone use it in any useful way.

So great was the clamour amongst English teachers, the press, and many other groups that the Government asked the Kingman Committee (1979) to 'recommend a model of language, whether spoken or written, which would serve as the basis of how teachers are trained to understand how the English language works' (Dean 2003: 19).

It was a time when Conservative politicians and their advisers pursued a narrow and dogmatic definition of standard English, grammar and literary heritage. The influence of right-wing pressure groups and think tanks on the shaping of the English curriculum was strong. Conservatives argued that the teaching of English had become the main ideological battleground in Britain for those who wanted to politicize education in a left-wing direction. However, the evidence suggested that any politicization of education was in far less danger from the left than from the right.

4 The 1990s and the Language in the National Curriculum project (LINC)

The Conservative ministers of the time were to drop a further bombshell. They had commissioned a national project under the leadership of Ronald Carter at Nottingham University. The main aim of the project was to produce materials and conduct activities to support implementation of English in the National Curriculum in the light of views on language expressed by the Kingman and Cox reports, and by *English 5–16*, a response to criticism of Cox. The LINC (Language in the National Curriculum) project supported these views expressed in the 1989 Cox report:

> Language is a system of sounds, meanings and structures with which we make sense of the world around us. It functions as a tool for thought; as a means for social organisation; as the repository and means of transmission of knowledge; as the raw material of literature, and as the creator and sustainer – or destroyer – of human relationships. It changes inevitably over time and, as change is not uniform, from place to place. Because language is a fundamental part of being human, it is an important aspect of a person's sense of self; because it is a fundamental feature of any community, it is an important aspect of a person's sense of social identity.
> (Cox report quoted in Carter 1990: 5)

The LINC project was much influenced by Michael Halliday's functional model of language. Halliday has always placed meaning at the very centre of theories of language and LINC endorsed that position. Such a functional theory of language was a complement to influential theories of language development constructed in the 1970s by James Britton and others at the London IoE (see Chapter 1). These theories make clear the centrality of context, purpose and audience in language use, and the salience of this understanding for children's learning.

So, M. A. K. Halliday, one of the architects of genre theory and pedagogy in the SF framework in Australia, was about to become the theoretician whose work would dominate the teaching of English in the UK from 1990 onwards. However, the seeds of LINC's own destruction could be anticipated in the explicit acknowledgement of Halliday's views on language in the document's introduction. Teachers, English advisers and those close to the project, anticipating the massive act of academic vandalism committed through the Tory government's decision not to publish the project's work, surreptitiously photocopied anything of the materials that they could salvage. But not all English teachers had been as disappointed as I was that all we had left were samizdat copies. The teaching of grammar proposed was not easily understood by a generation of English teachers who had been taught little about the subject, or those who had been exposed to traditional descriptive grammar. The subject of grammar remained a controversial one. The outcome was that English teachers, the majority of whom were situated within personalist and progressivist discourses, were certain about what they did not want to teach, but could not establish any consensus about what they did want students to know.

5 Australian Genre Theory and Pedagogy in the UK in the 1990s

5.1   Genre and the National Literacy Strategy

The Qualifications and Curriculum Authority (QCA)'s *The Grammar Papers – perspectives on the Teaching of Grammar in the National Curriculum* (1998) appeared the same year that the National Literacy Strategy in Primary schools was introduced. This document encouraged grammar teaching that should:

- involve teacher exposition
- encourage pupil investigation
- focus on individual pupil's needs
- refer to previous grammar teaching
- include responses to, and assessment of, pupils' oral and written work.

QCA then proposed grammar tests which reminded teachers of decontextualized grammar tests administered some 30 years earlier; they certainly did not reflect the suggested teaching styles quoted above. Moreover, at the same time, the Primary Literacy Strategy, with its focused one hour of literacy teaching each day, was launched at the same time in primary schools to teachers who were uncomfortable at the prospect of teaching grammar.

The Primary Strategy owed much to the work of David Wray and Maureen Lewis who were at the time at Exeter University. They, like the authors of the Strategy, were very concerned about the dominance of narrative and personal recount texts in the primary curriculum, along with the lack of teaching of writing and reading of what they and the Strategy called 'non-fiction texts'. Wray and Lewis (1997: 8) proposed a curriculum and pedagogy to address the weaknesses they perceived. They claimed the model they found most useful 'owes a great deal to that put forward by Australian theorists such as Frances Christie and Joan Rothery' (as presented in Derewianka 1990) and based upon a curriculum cycle of:

- teacher modelling/demonstration
- joint activity
- independent activity.

They advocated a further stage which they called 'assisted activity'. It is dismaying to note the reductive nature of their representation of the Sydney School's 'text in context model'. Within the Australian model, 'negotiating field' takes account of the student's engagement with ideational meanings, and points out that the learner needs to identify the 'field' or the 'what' of the text: what Halliday called 'the text-generating activity'. Students need to identify the part of the field to be explored, which means their prior knowledge of the field should be activated before the range of experiences and activities which form the exploration are embarked upon, and the method of organizing and recording information from the activities is taught. This has been described, for example, by Beverly Derewianka, a Sydney School academic, in the UK LINC reader (Carter 1990), in an account of how an Australian teacher apprenticed her class of 7 year-olds into the language of geological discourse. Derewianka makes clear the role of Halliday's notion of register, a way of describing how the context influences the language produced in a particular situation for this Year 3 teacher.

However, the Australian curriculum cycle that Wray and Lewis found 'most useful' was entirely stripped of any reference to its provenance, with the theoretical complexity of Malinowski, Firth, Halliday, Martin, etc. reduced and rendered 'accessible' – the criterion placed above all others, it seems, in professional development in the UK. The Australian curriculum cycle has Firth's notions of 'context of culture' and 'context of situation' at its heart, along with Martin's notion of 'genre' as social process – texts patterned in relatively predictable ways according to patterns of social interaction in a particular culture. Rather than simply listing, as Wray and Lewis do, 'the 'structures of the main non-fiction text types', genre theory explains where they come from and why students need them: 'genres give their users access to certain realms of social action and interaction, certain realms of social influence and power' (Cope and Kalantzis 1993: 7, summarizing Kress 1989).

After listening to Professor Wray address an audience of over 120 primary and secondary Literacy Coordinators in Croydon in 2003, on the 'structures of the main non-fiction text-types', I asked him why he had not drawn attention to the work of the Sydney School. He claimed it was 'too complex'. Similarly, on my first day of Strategy Consultant training in May 2001, I asked the same question of a National Strategy Regional Director. After his exposition on the 'the six main non-fiction text types', I asked would we explore Halliday's notion of 'register variables' – field, tenor and mode – and was informed that it was 'too difficult.'

5.2   1990: Grammar teaching and the Labour government's Qualifications and Curriculum Authority

In 1999, three QCA papers offered exciting and challenging opportunities to moving considerations of grammar into the mainstream of English teaching. Firstly, *Not Whether but How: Teaching Grammar at KS3 and 4* (QCA 1999a) claimed to reflect the 'changing debate and addresses concerns about how best to teach grammar'. Then, *Improving Writing at Key Stage 3 and 4* (QCA: 1999b) and *The Technical Accuracy Project* were the outcome and summary of projects begun in 1996 designed to investigate 'the accuracy and effectiveness of pupils' writing in post-16 examinations'.

Now, English teachers were able to see detailed linguistically principled analyses of students' work, which helped to indicate where a student could be placed in relation to a National Curriculum writing level. The student texts were used for analysis of text organization, the effectiveness of openings and closures, the way a reader-writer relationship is established and maintained and coherence. Whether teachers need an acquaintance with Halliday's three metafunctions and particular resources in language, such as mood, modulation and modality, when discussing writer/reader or speaker/listener relationships is the question at stake. Some detractors from a position described as 'approaching writing through this kind of limited linguistic analysis' baulked at the Technical Accuracy Project's encouragement to systematically teach 'clause structure'.

Meanwhile, the government was committed to the teaching of grammar within the Primary National Literacy Strategy launched in 1998. While QCA and the DfES were aware of the work of the Sydney school – Michael Halliday, in fact, enjoyed very good relations with QCA and 'was asked one or two questions about grammar by them' – the rationale for *Grammar for Writing* (DfES 1998), the flagship Primary Strategy grammar teaching and professional development resource was left to Professor David Crystal, whose view is:

> Grammar is what gives sense to language ... sentences make words yield up their meanings. Sentences actively create sense in language and the business of the study of sentences is the study of grammar.
>
> (Crystal 1998)

Predictably, research was mobilized to point out the futility of teaching grammar. Colin Harrison (2002) and more recently Andrews *et al* (2004), warned policy-makers that, while they thought explicit knowledge of grammar should be taught, and taught early, according to Harrison: 'Research reviews have consistently failed to provide evidence that grammar teaching makes any difference to the quality of students' writing' (quoted in Dean 2003: 37). At the same time, advocates of personalist discourses in English were reiterating that:

> The aim is not to impart knowledge about language, but to develop each child's individual writing voice. Having something to say – and knowing whatever it is will be valued by the reader – is the first step to effective communication in writing.
>
> (Hilton 2001, quoted in Dean 2003: 37).

The National Strategies were started, with their huge financial investment in resources and professional development, to address, in my view, the failure of progressivist discourses to improve the life chances of pupils, in particular marginalized groups. But at no point did the DfES or QCA offer a critique of personalist and progressivist methodologies; instead, they pointed out, in 1997, the consequences of low levels of literacy for societies in the late twentieth century:

- unskilled occupations and low pay
- lack of advancement and training at work
- poor health and depression
- rented housing – as distinct from home ownership
- higher divorce rate
- less likely to take part in public activities such as voting
- characteristic of more than one in two prison inmates – one in six in the general population.

As a Literacy Strategy Consultant, I find all of the above powerful and persuasive. But, I would add, that the 'hows' of language need to be brought to the foreground in education because of schooling's unique mission to provide equitable access to as broad a range of social options as possible for historically marginalized groups – marginalized for reasons of culture, gender, socio-economic background or the social meaning ascribed to race. Even in its most conservative moments, schooling in a democratic society boasts about creating equality of opportunity, and as an educator I am duty bound to take this injunction at its word. The National Strategies at their best offer the visible and explicit curricula, and pedagogies that are needed by those outside the discourses and cultures of certain realms of power and access: the ways in which the 'hows' of text structure produce the 'whys' of social effect. This is what Cope and Kalantzis (1993: 8) asked for some years ago: 'Students from historically marginalised groups need explicit teaching more than students who seem destined for a comfortable ride into the genres and cultures of power'.

6 Inclusion and the role of language in learning in the new century

The UK government is, in 2006, rightly concerned about marginalized groups. Within the complex architecture of the National Strategies, there are a number of highly visible, high priority, well funded programmes to address the exclusion and lack of attainment of targeted groups: the Minority Ethnic Achievement Project; the Black Pupil Achievement Project; Ensuring the Attainment of High Mobility Pupils Project; the Low Attainers Project and the White Working Class Boys Underachievement Project.

The government's Strategies and its inclusion projects acknowledge that language is the main medium we use for teaching, learning and developing thinking; thus it is at the heart of all teaching and learning. It is therefore important to link literacy and learning because good literacy skills contribute to learning, whereas poor literacy skills are a barrier to learning. The Strategies claim that literacy skills need to be taught systematically and consistently, and that pupils should be given regular opportunities to consolidate their literacy skills by using them purposefully in order to learn within all subject discourses.

Williams and Hasan (1996: xix) expand on this imperative for literacy education, focusing explicitly on grammar:

> Literacy education will remain incomplete until pupils have a conscious understanding of how patterns of language are systematically used in the construal of our social universe, and this means not just being able to write 'correct' sentences, or to reel off definitions of noun and verb or to parse correctly. Above all this, it means, as the ultimate goal, the ability to realise how invidious systems of relations are developed, how they are maintained, and what part our discourses play, and where they derive their power from for playing those parts. An understanding of the role of grammar is a necessary step in engaging with problems of exploitation.

So far, there is no National Literacy Strategy in Australia as there is in the UK, although a number of Australian States have embedded genre theory and pedagogy and SFL within their curriculum documents. (See Chapters 3 and 5.) Yet there is an irony here. The UK Strategies are profoundly influenced by the work of the Sydney School – Halliday, Martin, Rothery, Christie and Macken-Horarik, etc. – whose work is clearly and always explicitly related to the theories of such thinkers as Vygotsky, Luria, Whorf, Malinowski, Firth and Bernstein. UK Strategies owe much to genre theory and pedagogy and SFL. However, they never acknowledge their theoretical background – I have shown earlier how Wray and Lewis, for example, simplify Australian developments for an English context.

In Australia, genre theory and pedagogy provided a sustained critique of progressivist and personalist discourses, which was supported by Hunter's (1988) analysis of the history of subject English, and the perceived failure to address the needs of marginalized groups in particular. This did not mean that advocates of 'growth models' in Australia acquiesced. Far from it. There have been sustained objections in Australia from AATE (Australian Association for the Teaching of English), Sawyer, Watson and Terry Threadgold, amongst others. In the UK, these have been endorsed by Michael Rosen, the poet, one of the group of UK writers which includes Phillip Pullman, Anne Fine, Alan Gibbons and Jamila Gavin who are dedicated to reversing 'the prescriptive and stifling' nature of the Strategies (Ashley *et al* 2003: 2). But criticism in the UK comes not only from children's writers. Sections of NATE, Higher Education Institutions – I cited London IoE and Goldsmith's College earlier – teachers' unions such as the ATL (Association of Teachers and Lecturers) and sections of the national press, whether from traditionalist or progressivist perspectives, all feel that the Strategies are flawed (see Chapter 9 for the beginning of a similar debate).

Marshall (2002), in an *English in Education* editorial, presents a particularly intemperate, but widely representative criticism: 'The fact that the initiative(s) are merely a half-baked set of reactionary prejudices overcooked by expensive PR should have been enough for them to be thrown into the slop bin by now'. 'Half-baked', objectionable as it is from a respectable journal, is in some senses legitimate, since, as I have said, the enormous National Literacy Project with its billion pound funding and unprecedented professional development opportunities failed to provide a critique of progressivist discourses in English schools since the mid-60s or of their inability to address educational failure amongst low socio-economic and marginalized groups. There has been mention of 'key research', but there has been no sustained and explicit acknowledgement of the importance of understanding Vygotsky and Bruner, or Halliday, Bernstein and Kress, mediated by the radical, post-progressive theorizing of the Sydney School, or examples of applications in schools. The LINC project, in 1989, explicitly acknowledged the influence of Halliday's SFL as the framework for its model of the role of language in learning, after which the documents it produced were suppressed.

Finally, I will make reference to some personal experiences in UK classrooms where literacy was being taught. The roles of grammar and language in learning have been my great interest from the time I migrated to Australia in 1990 (I stayed for five years), and since then I have immersed myself in the debates about the teaching of English. Since 2001, I have been what some see as a 'New Labour apparatchik', or Literacy Strategy Consultant, working in classrooms in culturally and linguistically diverse contexts, with teachers and students, with the aim of raising standards of attainment, in particular, but not exclusively, for marginalized groups.

I see the Strategies as visible and explicit pedagogies, with what Basil Bernstein (1990) called strong framing and classification, offering the best opportunity for those excluded from realms of cultural and linguistic capital. Some brief examples illustrate the dilemmas I face as a result of the way the teaching of grammar in the secondary programme has been made vulnerable by not being aligned theoretically to a particular view of grammar.

The *Framework for Teaching English: Years 7, 8 and 9* (DfES 2001), based closely on the Programmes of Study for English in the revised National Curriculum of 2000, represents 'the teaching objectives for pupils in Key Stage 3 which will ensure they build on their achievements in primary school' (p. 9). The Framework arbitrarily separates word and sentence level objectives in 7, 8 and 9 whereas SFL proposes a lexicogrammar which focuses on lexical items making meaning within clauses. An objective such as 'Extend use and control of complex sentences by recognizing and using subordinate clauses' has the potential to lend itself to narrow interpretation – I have seen it on many occasions – and, in turn, to draw the worst possible criticism.

In Year 8, a key objective concerned with the 'stylistic conventions of non-fiction' exhorts teachers to teach students how to 'identify the key alterations made to a text when it is changed from an informal to a formal one, e.g. change from first to third person, nominalization and use of passive verbs'. In five years working for the Literacy Strategy, I have not seen one teacher who has taught students how nominalization – a form of grammatical metaphor (Halliday 1994), the substitution of one grammatical class and function for another, e.g. eroded for erosion – works to construct the specialized texts which students need to read and write every day, if they are to move their language along the mode continuum, from producing spoken to written sounding discourse.

Similarly, a Framework objective that deals with teaching students to 'vary sentence structure' ignores the SFL notion of Theme and Rheme (Halliday 1994). Theme/Rheme configurations and their relation to hypertheme – topic sentences – and macrotheme, together with nominalization, are critical resources to understand Halliday's textual metafunction, and the potential such understanding offers in the writing of abstraction and technicality in a range of curriculum contexts, typically a characteristic of written language above level 5 in the UK National Curriculum.

In a recent conversation with some Year 11 students 'redrafting' their essays on Othello, we looked at lists of adjectives they had, with their teacher, attributed to characters in the play. The girls told me that Iago was 'dishonest'. We identified this abstract quality as 'dishonesty', then I suggested constructing a clause in which the nominal group 'Iago's dishonesty' was deployed as topical Theme in a hypertheme. The girls quickly came up with: *Iago's dishonesty deceives Othello*. By thematizing the nominal group, the student writers gave authorial confidence to the text. They easily understood that the remainder of the paragraph should develop and explicate coherently this confident, critical assertion. (See McDonald, Chapter 11 and Marshall, Chapter 12.)

Like Alex, the 'white working-class boy' from the Islington school quoted at the beginning of this chapter, the girls were opening a door to a visible understanding of the rhetorical capacities that grammar, as a complex system of choices, offers students in the English curriculum.

References

Andrews, R., Beverton, S., Locke, T., Low, G., Robinson, A., Torgerson, C. and Zhu, D. (2004), *The Effect of Grammar Teaching (Syntax) in English on 5 to 16 Year Olds' Accuracy and Quality in Written Composition*. York University, Toronto: EPPI Review Group for English.

Ashley, B., Fine, A., Gavin, J., Powling, C. and Pullman, P. (2003), *Meetings with the Minister: Five children's authors on the National Literacy Strategy*. UK: National Centre for Language and Literacy.

Bernstein, B. (1990), *The Structuring of Pedagogic Discourse: Class, Codes and Control. Vol. IV* London: Routledge.

Bullock, A. (1974), *A Language for Life*. London: HMSO.

Carter, R. (1990), 'Introduction', in R. Carter (ed.) *Knowledge about Language and the Curriculum: The LINC Reader*. London: Hodder and Stoughton, pp. 1–20.

— (1996), 'Politics and knowledge about language: the LINC project', in G. Williams and R. Hasan (eds), *Literacy in Society*. London: Longman, pp. 1–28.

Crystal, D. (1998), Video accompanying Module 3 of the NLS 1998 training materials. UK: DfES Publications.

Cope, B. and Kalantzis, M. (1993), *The Powers of Literacy*. London: Falmer Press.

Coles, J. (2004), 'Much ado about nationhood and culture: Shakespeare and the search for an "English" identity' *Changing English*, 11, 2 (October), 47–58.

Dean, G. (2003) *Grammar for Improving Writing and Reading in the Secondary School*. London: David Fulton.

DES (1984), *English from 5–16 (report) – Curriculum Matters 1*. London: HMSO.

DfES (1998), *Grammar for Writing*. UK: DfES Publications.

DfES (2001), *English Key Stage 3, National Strategy Framework for Teaching English in Years 7 8 and 9*. UK: DfES Publications.

Derewianka, B. (1990) *Exploring How Texts Work*. NSW, Australia: PETA.

Dixon, J. (1967), *Growth through English*. London: Oxford.

Green, J. (1913), 'The Teaching of English', *Journal of Experimental Pedagogyand Training College Record*, 2, 14–25, 201–9.

Greenbaum, S. and Quirk, R. (1990), *A Student's Grammar of the English Language*. London: Longman.

Halliday, M. A. K. (1994) *Introduction to Functional Grammar*. London: Arnold.

Harrison, C. (2002), *Key Stage 3 English – Roots and Research*. London: DfES.

Hilton, M. (2001), 'English in Education', *Writing Process and Progress*, 35, 4–11.

Hunter, I. (1988), *Culture and Government: The Emergence of Literary Education*. London: Macmillan.

— (1997), 'After English: Towards a Less Critical Literacy', in P. Freebody, A. Luke and S. Muspratt (eds), *Constructing Critical Literacies*. New York: Hampton Press, pp. 315–35.

Kress, G. (1989), 'Texture and meaning', in R. Andrews (ed.), *Narrative and Argument*. Milton Keynes: Open University Press, pp. 9–21.

Marshall, R. (2002), 'Editorial: Revolting Literacy', *English in Education*, 36, (2), 1–6.

Medway, P. (1980), *Finding a Language: Autonomy and Learning in School*. London: Writers and Readers in association with Chameleon.

McMillan, M. (1904), *Education through the Imagination*. London: George Allen and Unwin.

Newbolt, H. J. (1921), *The Teaching of English in England (The Newbolt Report)*. London: HMSO.

Plowden, M. (1967), *The Plowden Report: Children and their Primary Schools*. London: HMSO.

QCA (1999a), *Not Whether but How: Teaching Grammar in English at Key Stages 3 and 4*. London: Qualifications and Curriculum Authority.

—(1999b), *Improving Writing at KS3 and 4*. London: Qualifications and Curriculum Authority.

—(1998), *The Grammar Papers – Perspectives on the teaching of Grammar in the National Curriculum*. London: Qualifications and Curriculum Authority.

Stow, D. (1850), *The Training System, the Moral Training School, and the Normal Seminary*. London: Longman, Brown and Green.

Williams, G. and Hasan, R. (1996), 'Introduction', in G. Williams and R. Hasan (eds), *Literacy in Society*. London: Longman, pp. xi–xxi.

Wray, D. and Lewis, M. (1997), *Extending Literacy: Children Reading and Writing Non-fiction*. London: Routledge.

Yandell, J. (2004), 'Sermons in stones, or how many kick-ups can you do?', *Changing English*, 11, 2 (October), 175–82.

8 Language, literacy and cultural politics: the debate on the new language curriculum in Portugal

Carlos A. M. Gouveia

1 Introduction[1]

This chapter discusses the cultural politics of a genre-based approach to Portuguese language teaching in the context of secondary schooling in Portugal, where the implementation of a new language curriculum has drawn fierce criticism from public opinion leaders. What attracted the attention of writers and newspaper columnists in particular and the public in general was the new language curriculum's explicit openness to different text types and genres, together with a restructuring and reduction of the literary canon in use during the three years of secondary education (15- to 17-year-old students). Since it was understood that literary texts would no longer have the same privileged status in the school curriculum as they used to have, most of what people wrote was centred on the role of literature both in society and in the characterization of the country's culture as being unique. In this respect, arguments were based on the belief that whoever is competent in reading the literary classics is also competent in producing all types of texts.

More than discussing the curriculum, people were actually engaged in a politics of representation, whereby an ideology of the subject was being shaped and transmitted, received and contested. From this understanding of what happened, I analyse the views presented in the arguments put forward during the discussion, in an attempt to show that the criticisms raised in the public arena of the newspapers aimed in fact at the reorganization of the cultural hegemony.

In order to achieve these goals, I will start by briefly describing the present state of affairs and problems raised in the public discussion of the new curriculum, moving on in the second section to the identification of some of the issues that were involved in the politics of representation that was actually taking place. In section 4, I will briefly discuss some linguistic approaches to language learning and teaching and how they are related to different theories of language, and finally, in section 5, I draw some conclusions.

2 The new curriculum

Even if not presented as such, the new curriculum for language teaching in primary and secondary education in Portugal is inspired by what one may consider a text or genre-based approach. Adopted in 2001 in the new curriculum for the seventh, eighth and ninth grades (12- to 14-year-old students), this same approach was followed in the development of the curriculum for grades 10, 11 and 12 of secondary education (15- to 17-year-old students), which is now being implemented, having started with grade 10, in 2003/2004 (Coelho *et al* 2001/2002).

The implementation of the new curriculum was amply publicized in the newspapers, with some opinion-makers bringing into the public arena the idea that Portuguese language teaching and learning is a matter of national interest and, as such, it should not be dealt with lightly. During the discussion, which involved teachers, linguists, literary writers and some political leaders, the idea that something was wrong with the teaching and learning of Portuguese was constantly stressed, with the curriculum and its *never-ending* restructuring being held responsible for this undesirable situation. And, even if this was not exactly an image activated by linguists, they were also contributing to the general feeling of frustration concerning the situation of Portuguese language teaching and learning by bringing into the forefront of the discussion the undeniable fact that Portuguese students were assessed below the average of EU and OEDC students in the *Programme for International Student Assessment* (Ministério da Educação 2000).[2]

Actually, it was the acknowledgement that many students do face difficulties when expressing themselves in a written form that promoted, as one of the main goals of the curriculum, the production of different types of texts, following textual typologies that are valid for the development of all the skills (Coelho *et al* 2001/2002: 3). This new pedagogy of writing expressed in the curriculum was specifically targeted in the criticisms expressed in the newspapers, but along with it came the criticism of the 'reduced' importance that such pedagogy attributes to literary genres in the teaching and learning of Portuguese (see, for instance, Pedrosa 2003; Guerreiro 2004; Graça Moura 2004a, 2004b; Seixo 2004). Even though the attacks on the curriculum did not single out this last aspect as the main cause for the poor performance of Portuguese students, it was quite clear that what was behind the attacks was an attempt to discredit the new focus on the communicative function of language. As I have already noted elsewhere (Gouveia 2004), the idea that one cannot learn to speak Portuguese properly without knowing about the great legacy that is made up of all the literary authors in the canon (Graça Moura 2004a: 7) is more an attack on the communicative function of the language than a defence of literature. This attack was explicitly expressed by one of the main protagonists in the discussion, Vasco Graça Moura, a member of former governments, a poet and a translator. By assigning linguists the authorship of the curriculum, Graça Moura held them directly responsible for the chaotic state of Portuguese language teaching and learning:

> Os responsáveis dos programas são linguistas e os linguistas têm ódio à literatura. Esse é o principal problema. Preocupam-se com a questão comunicacional e não com o valor da própria língua.
>
> (Graça Moura 2004a: 6)
>
> (*The authors of the curriculum are linguists and linguists hate literature. That is the main problem. They concern themselves with the communicative aspect and not with the value of the language itself.*)

What one can read in this statement is an accusation directed not only at linguists but also at any teaching methodology that emphasizes the communicative function of language. It is as if the value of the language in itself, attributed particularly by the literary use writers make of it with complete disregard for the communicative function, could be sufficient for the teaching and learning of Portuguese. Such a position unquestionably denies principles of equal access of students to the systems of opportunity at play in society. Also it recalls Bernstein's (1981) work showing how certain groups are disfavoured by processes of social stratification and cultural reproduction, a theory thus summarized by Halliday (1990: 16): 'while the *system* of the language construes the ideology of society as a whole, the *deployment of resources within the system* differentiates among different groups within a society'.

The use of the resources of the system is therefore both a consequence of social stratification and cultural reproduction, helping to differentiate groups, and a means for social and cultural discrimination, helping to evaluate those social groups differently. Explicit teaching of the language as a system of communication and an instrument for power will help students in the deployment of the correct resources to fight their disempowerment.

The argument against teaching language from the perspective of its communicative function, then, disempowers students right from the start, since it denies them access through the education system to the whole range of resources of the linguistic system. By not favouring the development of all the students' pragmatic and discursive abilities to produce different types of texts, such an argument ends up favouring principles of social and cultural discrimination. It is an argument that does not take into account the consequences that the development of those abilities has for opening up opportunities for students in their lives, since it does not recognize Bernstein's assumption that codes and other linguistic constructs take over from socio-economic structures as the most important factor in determining the actions of individuals. Since texts get their value from the particular contexts or markets in which they are produced, part of the practical competence and knowledge of speakers is to be able and to know how to produce texts and other linguistic constructs which may be valued in the markets they want to have access to (Bourdieu 1991). The linguistic market-place is, then, just a part of the economic marketplace. As Bernstein (1981: 327) says, one has to bear in mind that 'class relations [inequalities in the distribution of power and in principles of control between social groups] generate, distribute, reproduce and legitimate, distinctive forms of communication, which transmit dominating and dominated codes; and that subjects are differentially positioned by these codes in the process of their acquisition'.

Taking into account the type of ideological stance involved in the discussion of the curriculum, it is not surprising, then, that almost all the other arguments against the implementation of the curriculum were centred on the general perception of degeneracy in standards of language learning and use. Contributing to that fall in standards was also, of course, the curriculum's disrespect for the literary canon and for the symbolic value of the language. To counteract this, the need for standard models (standard language vs. non-standard forms; literary genres vs. non-literary genres; written language vs. spoken language; etc.), for absolute rules of correctness in grammar and pronunciation and the defence of formal grammar teaching and learning came to be presented as the only right and possible solution.

3 Cultural hegemony

From the short description presented so far, one can easily conclude that, more than a discussion of different approaches to language teaching, what was actually happening in the newspapers was a fight for power, a fight for legitimacy. This is not new and it is certainly not exclusive to Portugal. In fact, as Alan Luke (1996: 309) argues, literacy education has always been a site of struggle:

> The history of literacy education thus is about power and knowledge. But it is about power not solely in terms of which texts and practices will 'count' and which groups will have or not have access to which texts and practices. It is also about who in the modern state will have a privileged position in specifying what will count as literacy.

The imposition of a specific cultural design on the basis of the power possessed by a dominant group, whereby that group's culture is reproduced and distributed through the school, is a fundamental characteristic of the development of systems of opportunity, means of production and modes of representation, and constitute what Bourdieu and Passeron (1970) have defined as cultural hegemony. As a successful attempt of a dominant class to establish its view of the world as an all inclusive and naturalized reading, cultural hegemony exercises its power via control over the resources of the state and civil society, such as the mass media and the educational system. Therefore, the history of literacy is also, to use Luke's expression, the history of cultural hegemony and the fight to impose a specific cultural design.

An appraisal of the Portuguese discussion shows that power (and cultural hegemony with it) was being reconfigured in all three dimensions referred to by Luke: i) which texts and practices count; ii) which students have or do not have access to which texts and practices and iii) who specifies what counts as literacy. It is interesting to notice, though, how the three dimensions are interrelated, and how the first one cannot be separated from the other two. In fact, choosing between giving students access to the different means of functional variation in the production and reception of texts, so that they may also have access to the literary canon, a position defended by linguists, and giving them access to the literary canon, because this automatically guarantees them access to other types of texts, a position defended by many of the detractors of the curriculum, is not only to make a stand on which texts and practices count (first dimension), but also one on which students have access to which texts and practices (second dimension). In a country where 45 per cent of young adults aged between 18 and 24 have not finished their secondary education, almost two and a half times more than the average for the EU (19 per cent)[3], support for the latter solution seems, at the least, offensive, such is the principle of exclusion it presupposes. In the end, the specification of what counts as literacy does not depend on scientific and validated criteria. It depends on the force of certain political solutions and the ideological motivations behind them (third dimension), that is, on the specific cultural and educational designs being imposed and on whether those designs give people the possibility to have access to education or not, considering not only language learning, but also the role of language in learning and in education in general.

Once again, Luke's words (1996: 309) put the point very clearly:

> Viewed sociologically, literacy training is not a matter of who has the 'right' or 'truthful' theory of mind, language, morality or pedagogy. It is a matter of how various theories and practices shape what people do with the technology of writing – and of how, once institutionalised, these selections and constructions serve particular class, cultural and gendered formations.

The connection referred to by Luke between the implementation of a language curriculum and class, cultural and gendered formations is of paramount importance here. Life in society is a configuration of systems of opportunity, means of production and modes of representation, whose access is regulated and monopolized via the production, distribution and consecration of knowledge and capital. Access to literacy is, therefore, access to those systems of opportunity and the right to master the genres of power of the dominant culture.

Thinking of the classics as 'all those who constitute the great patrimony of the Portuguese language without whom one cannot learn to speak Portuguese properly' and resorting to a solution of failing all the students who do not speak Portuguese properly, as Graça Moura (2004a: 7) proposes – and one should read here the assumption that proper Portuguese is that Portuguese learnt through the reading of the classics – seems to me to favour a principle of exclusion that will reduce future life opportunities for students. Also, it involves an idea of the language as some entity crystallized somewhere in the past, in the literary canon, as if the natural evolution of the language and the needs speakers ask it to fulfil do not exist, an idea any linguist would reject.

4 Approaches to language teaching

Curriculum design is not only a matter of developing a coherent plan for a course of study based on explicit objectives. It involves also beliefs about what the nature of language is and what one thinks learning is. It is exactly this aspect that is stressed by Nunan (1988: 10), when he says that while selecting curriculum components from the set of options available, we make judgements that 'are not value free, but reflect our beliefs about the nature of language and learning'. It is a fact that over the past forty years we have been witnessing a proliferation of different approaches to language teaching in the fields of applied linguistics and language teaching methodology. It is also a fact that these approaches have been informed by an increasing knowledge of the nature of language and language learning. Whether based on theories that construct a natural language as a set of sentences and language as the capacity to generate those sentences, or on theories that consider situational aspects extremely relevant for the production and exchange of meaning, each of these new approaches challenges the legitimacy of the previous one. According to Feez (1998: 13), this has had three consequences whose negative impact one should consider: first, 'People assume that language teaching is based on fads and fashions rather than on an evolving body of knowledge'; second, 'Language educators are divided between those who support the latest approach and those who reject it' and third, 'Language educators lose access to valuable aspects of the approaches which have gone before'.

While these consequences may not be true of all the approaches to language teaching developed during the past decades, it is certainly true of most of them. And it was surely this that came out in much of the public discussion that has taken place in Portugal. Most of the approaches to language teaching, in Portugal at least, have been implemented by drawing on theories developed within linguistics, but the results have not always been satisfactory. Linguists frequently mistrusted the use of their theories and data by teachers in the classroom and teachers mistrusted the type of knowledge linguists were producing, mostly seen as hermetic and highly specialized (cf. Castro 2003: 211; Gouveia, 2004). In fact, communication has always been problematic, with general linguists constantly dissociating themselves from anything connected with language teaching (Castro 2003: 213) and almost all of the research in language teaching being produced by applied linguists. The latter nevertheless have been producing their own theoretical body based on findings from general linguistics on the nature and functioning of language, while bringing along contributions from psychology, sociology and language didactics.

Despite the dependency of applied linguistics in relation to general linguistics, the two fields have always threaded their ways along parallel paths, as if applied linguistics could offer nothing to general linguistics, but, on the contrary, had everything to gain from it. While bringing in notions of text and discourse, thus somehow contributing to the idea that they are all about fads and fashions, some modern approaches to language teaching seem to have failed in their mission, because the final outcome has been the integration of learners' pragmatic ability to produce texts with the learning of the grammar in formal terms. Many of those approaches end up evolving in a dual manner, with the teaching of grammar on one side and the teaching of pragmatic competences on the other, in a strange and unproductive attempt at conciliation of what, in the end, are two opposing views of language. And even if this kind of false conciliation is not stressed in the curriculum, it is exactly what happens, considering that teacher-training programmes in Portugal still hold a formal view of language, with the metalinguistic competence being taught in mere structural terms and with the description of the sentence as its main goal. Notice here that I am not denying the importance of developing metalinguistic alongside pragmatic or discursive competence. But we have to bear in mind the conception of language that teachers hold when teaching grammar. As Macário Lopes (2004) has stressed when taking position in the discussion reported here, 'the reflection on language is not reducible to the grammatical knowledge that traditionally has been considered its structuring core: morphology and syntax' (my translation). The type of language teaching expressed and defended in the curriculum does not hold a traditional view of grammatical knowledge and, therefore, does not choose morphology and syntax as the structuring core of language; however, the teachers implementing the curriculum do in fact hold such a view. And that is understandable, since they have not been given the instruments and support to change it.

Language teaching is no longer the product of views of 'language as an accumulation of separate building blocks, e.g. individual grammatical forms and structures, vocabulary items or pronunciation items' (Feez 1998: 4). Therefore, we cannot go on exemplifying the rules for learners for putting those building components together in contrived, isolated sentences and insisting on their learning of forms and rules 'through repetition, drills and other kinds of intensive practice'. While no longer the product of such views of language, language teaching nevertheless needs to be the product of a view of language; and one where the description of the linguistic system and the developing of the students' metalinguistic competence go along the same paths as the description of the language products and processes. Such a view is presupposed in the new Portuguese curriculum, but no one seems to notice it or care to explain it to the teachers involved in the teaching of the curriculum. Furthermore, no one seems to be interested in addressing the problem of implementing such a curriculum using as agents for that implementation teachers who hold a view of language as being constituted by grammatical forms and structures, vocabulary items and pronunciation items that are learned through the repetition of decontextualized and detextualized grammar exercises.

5 Conclusion

To conclude, let me just stress that there are reasons to be apprehensive about the situation in Portugal; not only because of the discussion generated by the implementation of the curriculum, but also because of that implementation and the problems I have referred to concerning the students' metalinguistic competence. While I am totally in favour of the textual typologies introduced in the curriculum, presented as 'having a praxiological dimension, allowing for the production of texts that, fitting into one of the categories of textual prototypes, prepare young citizens for integration in socio-cultural and professional life' (Coelho *et al* 2001/2002: 4), I actually fear the practical results of the work to be undertaken in the classroom. This is because I feel that the views and beliefs about language that motivate the praxiological dimension of the curriculum will end up submersed by the radically different practices and beliefs of the teachers. Notice, though, that I am not here blaming the teachers, I express compassion towards them, on the one hand and praise them, on the other: compassion, because even though they are the social actors involved in the teaching of the curriculum, they have not been given the instruments and the institutional and social conditions to teach them, and praise because once again they will have the courage to go ahead with the teaching of this new curriculum without the necessary training and support. Thus, again, unfortunately, teachers will become the scapegoats for whatever problems may be identified in the future evaluation of the curriculum implementation.

In fact, a text or genre-based approach to language teaching is not only a way of designing and developing and implementing a school curriculum, it is also a response to changing views of language and language learning. The question that remains refers to the way university courses and teacher-training programmes are responding to these changing views. It seems they continue as before: teaching future teachers to master syntax and morphology, understood as the core components of the system, in a decontextualized manner. In the majority of teacher-training programmes, foreign language ones excluded, neither notions of text and discourse variation nor aspects of representation associated with the production of texts and discourses are taken into consideration. By representation I mean the capacity of relating 'two qualitatively different types of phenomenon – an expression and a content – to each other so that the significance of one is understood in terms of the other', as Hasan (1996: 379) puts it, which is 'a necessary condition for using any semiotic system whatever'. So, the use of language is the use a semiotic system whereby the significance of the world is understood in terms of the language used, that is, the texts and discourses produced. Involving register choices of a representational nature, those texts and discourses vary according to the nature and content of the social action that is taking place.

What, then, distinguishes a text or genre-based approach to language teaching from other possible approaches? Is it the approach in itself, or the theory of language behind it? Or is it both? In contrast to the sort of text or genre-based approach one can read in the Portuguese curriculum, the genre-based approach to language teaching developed within the framework of systemic functional linguistics is also a fundamental part of its theoretical body of knowledge and of its particular way of looking at the nature of language.

As Halliday put it as far back as 1990, language teaching needs to reconcile two conflicting but complementary themes:

> Our practice as language teachers depends more on our being able to adopt the complementary perspectives of two conflicting themes, that of 'learning' and that of 'meaning', than on putting together pieces from linguistics with pieces from psychology and sociology.
>
> (Halliday 1990: 8)

Learning a language is thus learning how to mean, to echo a title of Halliday's (1975), that is, learning to make appropriate choices from the meaning potential that is made available by the system, or in other words, considering register and genre, learning the means of functional variation, of the difference between texts and the contextual motivations for that difference. In contrast with many other approaches, a systemic genre-based approach to language teaching evolves alongside the linguistic theory, not from it. With Eggins and Martin (1997: 237), one may say that a genre-based approach to language teaching 'involves both a detailed account of language, *and* a theory of context and the relationship between context and language'. Is this the case of the Portuguese curriculum? I fear it is not.

Notes

1. I would like to acknowledge the helpful comments of Luísa Azuaga and Sandra Barcelos on an earlier draft of this text.
2. Vd. 'Nos três domínios de literacia em estudo – leitura, matemática e ciências – os alunos portugueses de 15 anos tiveram um desempenho médio modesto, uma vez comparado com os valores médios dos países do espaço da OCDE.'
   (*In the three assessed domains of literacy – reading, mathematics and science – 15-year-old Portuguese students had a modest average performance, when compared with the average values of the countries in the OECD area.*)
   (Ministério da Educação 2001: 47).
3. Source: Ministry of Education: www.min-edu.pt/Scripts/ASP/destaque/numeros.asp

References

Bernstein, B. (1981), 'Codes, modalities and the process of cultural reproduction: a model', *Language and Society*, 10, 327–63.

Bourdieu, P. (1991), *Language and Symbolic Power*. Cambridge: Polity Press.

Bourdieu, P. and Passeron, J. C. (1970), *La Réproduction. Eléments pour une Théorie du SystÒme d'Enseignement*. Paris: Editions de Minuit.

Castro, R. V. de (2003), 'Estudos linguísticos e ensino do português: conjunção, disjunção, rearticulação', in I. Castro and I. Duarte (eds), *Razões e Emoção: Miscelânea de Estudos em Homenagem a Maria Helena Mira Mateus. Vol. I.* Lisbon: IN-CM, pp. 203–17.

Coelho, M. da C., Seixas, J., Pascoal, J., Campos, M. J., Grosso, M. J. and Loureiro, M. de La S. (2001/2002), *Programa de Língua Portuguesa. 10°, 11° e 12° Anos. Cursos Gerais e Curso Tecnológicos. Formação Geral.* Lisbon: Departamento do Ensino Secundário, Ministério da Educação.

Eggins, S. and Martin, J. R. (1997), 'Genres and registers of discourse', in T. A. van Dijk (ed.), *Discourse Studies: A Multidisciplinary Introduction, Volume 1: Discourse as Structure and Process*. London: Sage Publications, pp. 230–56.

Feez, S. (1998), *Text-based Syllabus Design*. Sydney: NCELTR, Macquarie University.

Gouveia, C. A. M. (2004), 'Syllabuses, textbooks and teaching practices: literacy and language teaching in Portugal'. Paper presented at the *First Regional Latin American Conference of Systemic Functional Linguistics: Systemic Functional Linguistics in Language Education*, Universidad Nacional de Cuyo, Mendoza, Argentina, 8–10 April.

Graça Moura, V. (2004a), 'Ideias fortes: entrevista com Vasco Graça Moura', *Pública*, 1 February, 5–7.

— (2004b), 'O padrão da cena do ódio', *Expresso-Actual*, 13 March, 17.

Guerreiro, A. (2004), 'Ensino do português: um longo e obscuro desastre', *Expresso-Actual*, 13 March, 14–16.

Halliday, M. A. K. (1975), *Learning How to Mean: Explorations in the Development of Language*. London: Edward Arnold.

— (1990), 'New ways of meaning: a challenge to applied linguistics', *Journal of Applied Linguistics*, 6. Thessaloniki: Greek Applied Linguistics Association, 7–36.

Hasan, R. (1996), 'Literacy, everyday talk and society', in R. Hasan and G. Williams (eds), *Literacy in Society*. London: Longman, pp. 377–424.

Luke, A. (1996), 'Genres of power? Literacy education and the production of capital', in R. Hasan and G. Williams (eds), *Literacy in Society*. London: Longman, pp. 308–38.

Macário Lopes, A. C. (2004), 'Reflexões sobre o lugar da gramática'. Paper presented at the workshop *Ensino do Português para o Século XXI* (The teaching of Portuguese for the twenty-first century), Faculty of Arts, University of Lisbon, 25 March.

Ministério da Educação (2001), *Resultados do Estudo Internacional PISA 2000 – Programme for International Student Assessment*. Technical Report. Lisbon: Gabinete de Avaliação Educacional, Ministério da Educação.

Nunan, D. (1988), *Syllabus Design*. Oxford: Oxford University Press.

Pedrosa, I. (2003), 'Crónica feminina. A obra em si', *Expresso-Única*, 15 November, 14.

Seixo, M. A. (2004), 'Escolas do paraíso'. *Expresso-Actual*, 6 March, 21–2.

9 Implementing the genre approach in a South African school

Carol Thomson and Mike Hart

1 Introduction

In this chapter we describe and evaluate a genre teaching and learning project (the Classroom Literacy Project) which we implemented in five secondary schools in KwaZulu-Natal, South Africa. We will focus on one school which we will call Khanyise High School, a rural school of isiZulu mother-tongue speakers, 95 km northwest of Pietermaritzburg in a district called Impendhle. This initiative must be seen against the backdrop of the debilitating effects of past apartheid policy on the one hand, and the post-1994 policy of transformation, reconstruction and development on the other. A central thesis of this chapter is that the hopes of the majority of students for equal access to high levels of literacy are in danger of disappearing into a 'Bermuda triangle' of systemic poverty engendered by apartheid; the tenacious hold of inadequate teacher training on teacher practices and attitudes in the classrooms; and the excessive influences of both traditional and progressivist approaches and curricula. This chapter thus:

- describes what research has indicated is happening in South African classrooms like Khanyise High School, and how this is shaped by past and present policies and practices; and
- describes and evaluates our initial, tentative steps to implement a genre approach to the teaching of literacy with teachers in their classrooms in the light of the constraints mentioned above.

2 Historical framing: the legacy of apartheid and post-1994 curriculum policy

Apartheid created an extremely negative environment for literacy development in schooling in South Africa. As a result, there continue to be low levels of literacy nationally: 24 per cent of African adults in South Africa over the age of 20 are illiterate, while 7.4 million adults

(34 per cent of all adults) are functionally illiterate (*ERA Initiative* 1999: 34). As regards teachers, a 2001 audit found that 17 per cent (58,000) of teachers were underqualified (Sukhraj *et al* 2000). Furthermore, many rural and urban African schools have inadequate infrastructure. Over 50 per cent of schools lack school libraries, and overcrowded classrooms and poor school management, coupled with a lack of learning materials such as exercise books and textbooks, create a situation far from conducive to the development of effective literacy practices. Furthermore, school-based teaching of reading and writing in the vast majority of black South African primary and secondary schools is dominated by traditional authoritarian approaches and rote learning. Literacy education has therefore suffered for decades from the inequities of apartheid education ideology and, despite the transition to a democracy in 1994, the legacy of these experiences lives on.

A focus on the issue of textbooks illustrates the impact of apartheid education policies and practices on literacy development. Textbooks are crucial to the development of students' ability to read and write effectively in the specialized domain of the language of schooling, which is the basis for engagement in reflection and critique. However, in South African schools it has been found (Macdonald 1990) that the gap between the students' language competence and frames of reference, and those presented in the textbooks, is so vast that students are unable to read these books or manage the tasks and exercises in them. In the face of these difficulties, many South African teachers resort to classroom interaction dominated by teacher-talk, chanted responses by the students, rote learning and memorization. This pedagogy is self-perpetuating: teachers resort to these methods because students cannot read and, as a result, students do not learn to read effectively. Vinjevold (1999) found that teachers either do not use textbooks, or use them unsystematically, because of their own poor content knowledge and reading skills. The tasks 'often do not engage students in progressively more demanding activities aimed at developing reading, writing and numeracy skills' (184). There is, thus, a crippling neglect of the basic skills on which the future academic progress of students depends. As Taylor and Vinjevold (1999: 231) observe:

> Our researchers found that what students know and can do is dismal ... the conceptual knowledge of students is well below that expected at the respective grades ... the development of higher order skills is stunted. Books are very little in evidence and reading is rare. Writing is also

infrequent and, when practised by students, hardly ever progresses beyond single words or short phrases.

It is against this backdrop of dearth and inadequacy that the aspirations of South Africa's new, post-1994 curriculum should be understood. The pressing imperatives for the radical transformation of apartheid education, and the need to be seen to be doing so, led educational officials to Outcomes-Based Education (OBE) practised in some developed countries. The subsequent introduction of OBE, known officially as Curriculum 2005 (C2005) in South Africa, was an inadequately conceptualized decision driven by the demands of transformation and the need to signal a shift from apartheid education.

A number of criticisms of the implementation and the theoretical foundations of C2005 have emerged. Jansen (1999) and Taylor (2001), for example, argue that C2005 is a curriculum borrowed from contexts which assume highly qualified teachers operating in classrooms with favourable teacher-pupil ratios in well resourced schools and thus was based on '... flawed assumptions about what happens within schools, how classrooms are organized and what kinds of teachers exist within the system' (Jansen 1999: 149). Furthermore, the language of OBE and C2005 and its mechanisms of implementation are too complex and inaccessible for most teachers, and are thus unlikely to be translated into classroom practice.

A further criticism concerns the progressivist theoretical and pedagogical model underpinning policy of the new curriculum which manifests itself in a number of ways (Harley and Wedekind 2003). Firstly, the heavy emphasis on the concept of the teacher as a facilitator, illustrated by the training slogan that teachers are now 'the guide on the side rather than the sage on the stage', signals a radical shift in identity for the majority of South African teachers. Learning now takes precedence over teaching, and constructing meaning by students takes priority over teacher intervention. Secondly, there is the movement to an integrated curriculum, a change from a strongly classified collection code curriculum to a weakly classified integrated code (Bernstein 1990). Official documents proclaim that South Africa has '... embarked on transformational OBE. This involves the most radical form of integrated curriculum ...' (cited in Taylor 2001: 5). These shifts present a number of challenges to the majority of teachers in South Africa. Teachers are now expected to be independent curriculum and materials developers, promoting and developing a cooperative learning environment with students and other teachers for the achievement of integrated learning outcomes. Harley and

Wedekind (2003), using examples from other parts of Africa, warn that the uncritical importation of progressivist, learner-centred pedagogies is unlikely to achieve their goals of educational and social equity because teachers struggle to understand and implement the new roles foisted on them.

Macdonald (2002) illustrates this confusion by pointing out that in designing the new curriculum, the processes of early literacy were effectively ignored. Foundation phase teachers were told that students '... can learn to read and write by themselves. You don't have to explicitly teach this – they will pick this up incidentally.' (Macdonald 2002: 131). Taylor commented that textbooks, even if they are available, are rejected by teachers, principals and provincial officials because they are 'not OBE'. He also observed that 'children sit in groups and talk about their everyday experiences, often with little or no conceptual content or direction to this activity' (2001: 6), indicating the extent to which OBE has encouraged an oral learning method at the expense of literacy.

There is accumulating evidence of literacy attrition as a result of the implementation of C2005 (Macdonald 2002; Pretorius 2002). Many Year 3 students are already two years behind their counterparts in developed countries (JET 2000). As there is no provision for training in the development of reading skills in schools after Year 3, many children are likely to be locked into a cycle of inadequate literacy development. The magnitude of the problem is evident in the test results recorded by Year 12 English second language applicants to Technikons in the Gauteng province in a longitudinal study of functional literacy (cited in Pretorius 2002), shown in Table 9.1. Other research (Webb 1999) indicates that many school leavers applying for tertiary education places are reading at levels below Year 8.

The likely outcome of this situation is widening inequality across school contexts, the very antithesis of the declared aims of C2005.

Table 9.1 Year 12 ESL applicant literacy results

Year	Student number	Functionally literate
1990	568	51%
1994	1314	28%
1998	621	20%
2000	451	18%

Privileged schools, with highly qualified teachers and strong frameworks of knowledge, will be able to fill the gaps created by the
unsystematic approach to knowledge and learning of C2005. However,
for the majority of teachers and students in South African schools, the
reality is starkly different. Extreme poverty means that the majority of
students come from either illiterate and semiliterate homes or homes
with little or no access to empowering literacy resources such as books,
newspapers or libraries. Many teachers are first generation literates
and therefore lacking in knowledge and the types and levels of literacy
that would enable them to develop their students' literacy skills
effectively. Taylor (2001) usefully sums up the disjunction between the
social equity agenda of C2005 and its likely outcomes. He argues that,
in a context where most learners come from low socio-economic
backgrounds, a constructivist, learner-centred curriculum such as
C2005 is more likely to result in widening social inequality. His
argument is borne out by the research presented above and provides
the context and impetus for the Classroom Literacy Project.

3 The Classroom Literacy Project

The Classroom Literacy Project is a research project, conceptualized
and coordinated by the authors, and located in the School of
Education and Development at the University of KwaZulu Natal
(UKZN) in Pietermaritzburg, South Africa. The five teachers in the
project tutor in an Education Honours module, coordinated by the
authors, which teaches and models the genre approach to language
across the curriculum. In a model of 'expanding expertise', these
teachers are taking their experiences and knowledge of the genre
approach into their own classrooms. This chapter focuses on one
school, Khanyise, and describes an initial six-week process of reading
and writing around the history of the school.

Khanyise High School represents a complex and challenging
context to the project as it suffers from all the problems presented in
the last two sections. The school lies deep within a rural area. The
physical conditions in the school reflect those of thousands of schools
across South Africa: overcrowded classrooms (11 for 567 students), no
library or laboratory, chipped and rugged classroom floors, broken
windows, and minimal numbers of textbooks. There are, however,
clean and sufficient numbers of pit latrines, and running water.
Electricity was supplied to the school last year but it cannot be used, as
all the electric cables, light switches and globes have been stolen. From
a pedagogical perspective, the school appears strong. It has had 100

per cent Year 12 pass rates for the past three years. However, such a laudable record is maintained by holding back 'weak' students in Year 11 until they are considered ready to proceed to Year 12, creating a bottleneck in Grade 11 (189 students), and a very small Year 12 cohort (36). In addition, English language proficiency in the school is generally very low, as English (the medium of instruction) is not the primary language of any learner, teacher in the school or member of the community. Despite all these difficulties, staff commitment remains exceptionally high. Almost all 16 members of staff have spent ten years or more at Khanyise, and all except three travel the 190 km return trip from Pietermaritzburg by public transport every day.

There are a number of reasons why the genre approach has been adopted for the project. By drawing on theory that understands language use to be social, never neutral, and intimately related to relationships of power and identity, the genre approach in a classroom can be considered both a political as well as a pedagogical intervention. In the context of South African education, and the transformation agenda it must serve, such a balance is a critical necessity. Of particular importance to the project is the comprehensive and explicit methodology of the genre approach. It provides a highly scaffolded cycle of modelling, criteria development, joint construction and guided and scaffolded practice, all leading to independent construction. This offers teachers an explicit and flexible process to work with, and provides a contextual model and vision of what it means to teach literacy across the curriculum. Furthermore, in the progressivist climate of C2005, the positioning of the teacher as authoritative in the genre approach will be more likely to create 'buy in' from South African teachers than the retreating, facilitative role posited by C2005. At the same time, the authoritative role of the genre approach does demand a change from both the authoritarian traditionalist or progressivist roles that many teachers in South Africa have adopted.

A further development of the genre approach, relevant to South African classrooms, and one on which the project draws substantially, is Rose's (2004) *Learning to Read: Reading to Learn* methodology (see Chapter 4 this volume). Drawing on the models of Vygotsky's learning as social process, Halliday's language as text in social context, and Bernstein's education as pedagogic discourse, Rose has developed a set of strategies for the explicit and highly scaffolded teaching of reading (alongside writing). The *Reading to Learn* approach is a six-stage curriculum cycle represented in Figure 9.1 (Rose 2004: 12).

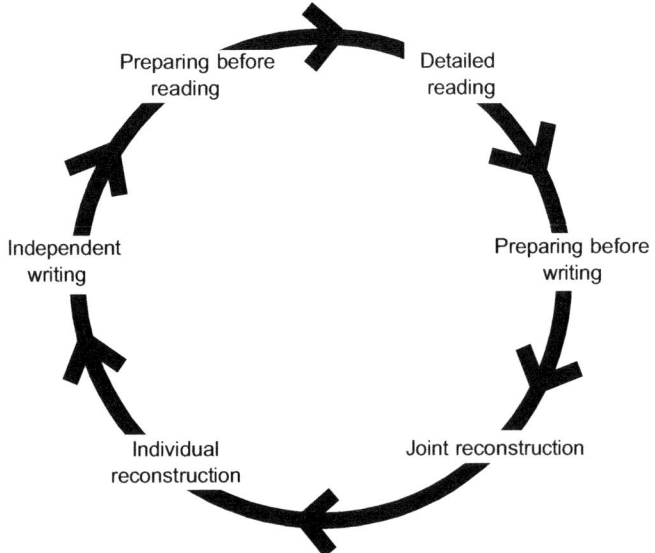

Figure 9.1 *Learning to Read: Reading to Learn* curriculum cycle

This process addresses a potential problem with the genre approach, whereby reading is made 'marginal to the central goal of learning to write for assessment' (Rose 2004: 4). Rose argues that the primary functions of writing are to reinforce the knowledge acquired through reading and to assess that acquisition. Students who came from backgrounds where reading is not a significant part of their early socialization are unlikely to be able to read and use model texts, and will not get enough support from genre pedagogy to benefit from the process. The approach thus addresses three major problems in the teaching and learning of literacy in the historical, socio-economic and educational contexts of South African schools like Khanyise. These contexts do not provide students with the ability to read texts used to model genres, constrain teachers into classroom interaction patterns dominated by ritualized and discriminatory Initiation-Response-Feedback exchange sequences (or chanted choruses in many South African schools), and deprive teachers and students of the specialized knowledge about language needed to analyse and construct texts, as discussed in Chapter 4.

The aims of the project are thus to implement and model genre-based literacy teaching and materials development, and to evaluate their appropriateness and efficacy in the South African context.

4 Process of the project

As a result of our consultations with the tutor-teacher from Khanyise, Ms Ntombela (pseudonym), in keeping with project policy, chose the class she wanted to work with, her Year 8 class (50 students) – for two reasons. The first was that the Year 8 timetable and curriculum allow teachers greater choice and flexibility in terms of what content can be used in order for students to achieve the stipulated learning outcomes, more so than that of grades further up the school. Secondly, she felt that if students entering high school could be 'captured' right at the start of their secondary school years, their possibilities of success higher up the school were more likely. As regards conditions in the classroom, her Year 8 class sits in groups of nine with three desks per group, making the physical act of writing very difficult. Students have access to a recently published English language textbook, although there is only one book per five students. However, despite this book being written specifically for speakers of English as a First Additional Language (FAL), it is far too difficult for these particular students to read, or find interesting. In this regard, when choosing to introduce the Classroom Literacy Project at Khanyise, we did so with the express intention of demonstrating that one's own community or locality is rich in possibilities, even if the school itself cannot afford much material for literacy teaching. As a result, we were able to demonstrate to Ms Ntombela and her colleagues how materials can be generated quickly, easily and at very little expense. Another more long-term aim would be to enable teachers and students to use the textbooks available more effectively.

Our modus operandi throughout the six-week process was to work in consultation with Ms Ntombela in developing materials, and then model teaching the materials in her Year 8 class. She then used this experience to teach another Year 8 class. She also acted as a translator, explaining in isiZulu at the beginning and during the class, so that the students clearly understood what was required of them. The students' home language was thus used as a bridge to understanding the content and process of the lessons, as well as the genre and language issues we focused on. This process gave us a rich source of insights to evaluate lessons and make adjustments.

In keeping with our focus on literacy across the curriculum, we decided to teach the writing of a history of Khanyise school as a context with which the students could identify. We asked both Ms Ntombela and one of the first teachers at the school, Mrs. Zuma, to write the history of the school as they remembered it. These two histories were then used for a number of related purposes. First, the authors used the texts to write a model history text in consultation with Ms Ntombela. She gave the class the task of interviewing her to develop their knowledge of the history of the school and used the text as a source of information. In the process she helped the students develop notes on the blackboard. The authors then used the text to develop a number of activities to scaffold students' writing of the history of the school.

Before we focused on the actual history of Khanyise we first worked with a model text of an autobiographical recount (Mike Hart's). The purpose of this exercise was to introduce ourselves, the 'university teachers', to the students, get some idea of the students' language abilities and to introduce the idea of writing history in a genre (autobiography) that students were likely to be familiar with. In an adaptation of Rose's curriculum cycle, we paraphrased the text and then read it. In the detailed reading stage, we focused students on the purposes of the different stages and how tenses are used in the different stages. We also drew their attention to the use of material and mental processes and, especially, how time sequence is marked in the text. The follow-up activity, where the students drew their own timeline and then wrote a brief autobiography, was not formally assessed. We only commented on how they could improve the cohesion of the text through using language resources to signal the sequence of time. In retrospect, we feel we should have spent more time developing their writing in this genre as a basis for the less familiar genre of historical account to follow.

In the next phase of the process, we used the model text that we had developed earlier of the history of a school. In teaching this, we followed a similar process to the one we adopted with the autobiography, with paraphrase and detailed reading sentence by sentence. Although we identified key wordings in the text and elaborated on and explained them, we did not go to the following stages of preparing for writing and joint construction. We focused again on the stages of the text and issues of time and cause and effect relationships. This is illustrated in Table 9.2, an example of the materials we developed to guide our process, an extract from the record of events of the model text on the history of a school.

As a result of these processes, we were able to develop a set of criteria to guide students' writing of their school's history, as seen in Table 9.3. Particular attention was focused on time and cause and effect relationships. This served as preparation for the final phase of the process. Using the model text of the history of Khanyise school that

Table 9.2 Process of materials development

Stages	Linking and Language	Text
Record of Events: The purpose of this stage is to write about important things that happened in the time period signalled in the Introduction/Overview. Each paragraph is about one of the important events that were introduced in the Introduction. **First paragraph**: What caused the school to be opened.	**Words that show the order of time**: *Before Z school was opened in 1938; In 1928; in 1934; By 1935; in May 1935; In 1936; in January 1938* **Words which signal cause and effect**: *To cause it; because; and so; if the company...' ; as there was ...'; because In response to; as the rapid growth in student numbers; leading to; it was only when* **Action verbs** and **past tense** to record what people did: *was started; started; came; finished; had to travel; were not attending;* **Saying verbs**: *They asked; They said*	Before Z school was opened in 1938, many things had happened to cause it to be opened. In 1928 a primary school was started by the Catholic church because the community had grown. A sugar mill started in the area and so many people came to work in the area. The first group of students finished at the primary school in 1934. They had to travel to another high school in the H district. It was 20 kilometres away and there was no transport. By 1935 things had got worse. Many children were not attending school after they had finished primary school as there was no school and no transport. They could not get jobs because they did not have enough education. Protests from the church, parents and community were ignored by the government. They asked the company that owned the sugar mill to help them but they did nothing.

we had developed with Ms Ntombela, we broke it down into jumbled 'notes', as in Table 9.4. We then worked with the students in a number of ways to reconstruct the history of their school.

For the first exercise we did with the students, we used the model history of the school we had written and divided the *Introduction and Overview* and the first paragraph of the *Record of Events* into separate sentences each on a strip of paper. These were then put together in separate paragraph bundles. We explained the task to the students, explored the criteria we had developed for the genre, and revised the work that was done on time and cause and effect relationships. Each group of students was provided with the two bunches of sentences and they had to use their knowledge of the content and of text relationships

Table 9.3   Criteria for guiding student writing

Criteria

- *Introduction/Overview*: Has the writer introduced the reader to the history that is going to be described: where it took place; when it took place; and who were important people that were part of the history? Has it also given the reader a summary of the important things that are going to be described in the history (*Record of Events*)?

- *Record of Events*: Has the writer given the history of things that have happened in the order in which they happened? Has the writer also shown why some things happened and the results of these events?

- *Judgement (what the writer thinks about what the history of the school means for now and the future)*: Has the writer looked back over the events and said what s/he thinks about the past and how it affects the present and the future?

- Has the writer used words which show the order in which things happened; the causes of the things that happened and the results of things that happened?

- Has the writer used action verbs which show what people did in the history?

- Has the writer used past tense to describe the events that happened?

Table 9.4   History text in note form

Stages	History	Linking
Introduction and Overview:	From 1982 to the present. The beginning of the school and why it was started. The problems from 1997. The problems with fighting because of politics Improvements for 2000. The building of the school in 1983	Future tense to describe what the essay will do in the Record of Events e.g. *This history of Khanyise school will* ...
Record of Events: How and why the school began; what it	Nxamalala was full. Khanyise High School was established in 1982. Circuit inspector looked at all the schools in the area to see what was needed. The buildings at Sithunjwana were used until the building of Khanyise started. The circuit inspector decided that a secondary school was needed in the area. The government paid the teachers. Parents' money was used to start the building of the new school. It started with grade 8 to grade 10 and the grade 11s and 12s went to Nxamalala	Words which show the order of time: *Then, afterwards, before, first, until* Can you think of other words? These words can be put at the beginning of sentences and also in the sentences

Stages	History	Linking
	The circuit inspector was proud because he had helped many schools to be built in the area. The grade 11s and 12 s went to Nxamalala The first principal was Mr. N Maphanga from Sithunjwana.	

to organize the sentences in the appropriate order. When all the groups had successfully completed the exercise under the guidance of Ms Ntombela and the authors, we handed out copies of the two paragraphs from the original text. We paraphrased the text followed by a detailed reading, sentence by sentence, identifying, explaining and elaborating on key words, and particularly asking students to identify the time and cause and effect relationships exemplified in the text. Students were thus able to see how the 'notes' above had been used to create a coherent text and how the paragraphs related to the criteria. The success of the exercise was demonstrated by the students' ability to organize the bundles into coherent paragraphs and by the escalating levels of student participation in the lesson, especially when identifying time and cause and effect relationships in the text.

Table 9.5   From notes to final paragraph

Many students came to the school from the Gomane area. Mr N. Maphanga passed away in February 1983. There was a school bus from Gomane to Macksame. Mr R. Khumalo became the acting principal. Mr. R. Khumalo started the first building across the Sithunjwana river. Across the Sithunjwana river is where Khanyise school is today. Mr Gamora was appointed as principal. Mr Khumalo was transferred to head of a primary school.	*While* the construction of the new buildings were underway *in 1983* many things happened that affected the school. Mr. Maphanga passed away *in February that year* **and so** Mr Khumalo became the acting principal. **As a result**, Mr. Khumalo was in charge of the building of the new school *across* the Sithunjwana river *where* Khanyise school is *now* situated. *While* this was happening, many students came to school by bus from the Gomane area. **Consequently**, the numbers of children at the school increased. *When* the buildings were finished in 1983, Mr. Gamora was appointed principal of Khanyise school and Mr. Khumalo was transferred to the principalship of a primary school.

In the follow-up to this exercise, we gave the students the first sentence (controlling idea) of the next paragraph and asked them to use their 'notes' to write a coherent text. Again they worked in groups with the help of the teacher and then, in plenary with the teacher, jointly constructed a paragraph. This is illustrated in Table 9.5, with the notes on the left and the 'final' paragraph we worked towards on the right. This is how the rest of the text was developed, with gradually less support being provided by the teacher, although it still had to be significant given the literacy levels of the class.

5 Evaluation

There is little doubt in our minds as to the applicability of the genre approach and Rose's scaffolded *Learning to Read: Reading to Learn* methodologies. We feel they provide appropriate means to explicitly 'apprentice' students into the specialized, academic discourses of schooling. Our experience has also shown that, especially in schools like Khanyise, Rose's use of an everyday metalanguage (based on understandings developed by systemic functional linguistics) to scaffold literacy teaching is appropriate, at least in the earlier stages of reading and writing development, as is the case with the Year 8 students in Khanyise and many other secondary schools in South Africa. Teachers across the curriculum need three types of knowledge about grammar: knowledge of the grammar of discourses; knowledge of grammar to enable them to analyse the relation between text form and the social purposes of key school texts; and lastly knowledge of how language is best taught (Cope and Kalantzis 1993). As the majority of teachers and students in South Africa lack this sort of knowledge, the *Learning to Read: Reading to Learn* methodologies offer an appropriate means to intervene in this situation and provide students with access to the ability to read to learn, which is the foundation of success in schooling. Furthermore, it requires little in the way of resources, which is important in the straitened circumstances of much of South African schooling.

The appropriateness of the approaches adopted in the project were further demonstrated by the feedback we have had from Ms Ntombela, as well as from other teachers in the project. Teachers commented on the increased participation of students and improved writing as a result of the explicit focus on genre. For example, in Khanyise there was a particular group of girls who never participated at all in the early sessions we observed and were involved in. Ms Ntombela explained that they were older than the rest of the class due to repeated failure in their schooling and they thus felt 'ashamed' and alienated. Significantly, this group began to participate during the paragraph organization exercise and the subsequent detailed reading and identification of linking words that followed. Another teacher spoke of getting the 'best writing' she had received from a class as a result of taking them through a genre-approach process. This same teacher was given the task of extra one-on-one work with a student who was floundering in school through her inability to read and write in English. Using the *Reading to Learn* strategies, she brought about a transformation in the student's academic life, and other teachers, impressed by what they witnessed, have expressed interest in this approach.

However, constraints of the school system and on the authors' time have had negative effects on the programme. All the teachers in the project, although they experienced the value of the genre approach and Rose's strategies, felt unable to use them in a sustained and systematic manner as they took too much time from the demands of an already overcrowded curriculum dominated by continuous assessment. However, Rose argues that the initial time spent on reading development is compensated for by massive benefits later when students are able to read independently and learn from reading. The impasse created by this systemic barrier means that many students will be deprived of the most crucial skill required for success at school and illustrates Taylor's conclusion that C2005 is leading to widening inequality. Bourne (2003: 498) warns that this is a consequence of the development theories underpinning progressive curricula that require teachers to evaluate students against fixed norms of attainment. In these circumstances:

> *Evaluation replaces instruction* [our italics] and certain children are not given access to the academic discourses on which, Bernstein argues, the development of scientific concepts ultimately depends. Bernstein (1990) thus describes the 'nurturing' classroom which naturalizes development as providing a 'masked pedagogy' through forms of covert evaluation which construct students at different levels of competence.

The authors' time constraints also created problems for the development of the project. Changing and increasing work pressures severely restricted our ability to meet regularly with the teachers and to sustain the development of materials. On top of this, school demands often meant changes to appointments and thus the chances of our times coinciding diminished considerably and hampered the smooth development of the project. Our planned process of regular meetings with all teachers to run workshops and to share and evaluate materials and experiences, coupled with classroom observation, demonstration lessons and evaluation, while effective, became increasingly difficult to reconcile with work demands made on both the authors and the teachers.

6 Implications

There are number of implications of this evaluation. The experience of the project has demonstrated the appropriateness of the genre approach and the *Reading to Learn: Learning to Read* method, especially in the context of the progressivism of C2005. These approaches have little currency in South Africa at the moment and the challenge is to find ways of developing their use in the schools. We have alluded to the fragility of our project, and thus any further intervention needs to be properly funded and be officially supported and sanctioned by the Department of Education. This will create the space for innovation within the school system and aid 'buy in' to the project from teachers. We are thus looking to set up a more sustainable small pilot programme in a few schools that will involve teachers across the curriculum and will be systematically monitored and researched. If we are able to demonstrate success in these schools we will be able to develop the scope of this sort of intervention further.

The literacy crisis alluded to earlier by Macdonald (2002) and the problems created by C2005 in this regard are receiving increasing attention. At an education conference held in March 2005 by the Western Cape Education Department, evidence from Learner Assessment Studies of Year 3 and Year 6 indicated that achievements in teaching students to read and write were depressingly low. Morrow, an educationist commenting on this assessment, concluded that if the quality of schooling is understood in terms of giving students access to the modern world, and if such access depends on literacy and numeracy, then the schooling system is not providing this equally. He quotes Rose's argument that the basis of inequality in both the classroom and society is the way in which the school system provides unequal access to the capacity to learn from reading, which is the basic mode of learning in secondary and tertiary education. Calling for a '*learning*-centred education', Morrow argues that the one contribution that all teachers can make in overcoming inequality is to focus strongly and persistently on developing students' capacity to read and to learn from reading. He quotes another delegate who warns that South Africa 'will be torn apart unless we tackle the issue of growing inequality' (Morrow 2005: 5). The stakes are thus high and provide added impetus for the further development of projects based on the theory and practice that we have described in this chapter.

References

Bernstein, B. (1990), *The Structuring of Pedagogic Discourse*. London: Routledge and Kegan Paul.

Bourne, J. (2003), 'Vertical discourse: the role of the teacher in the transmission and acquisition of decontextualised language', *European Educational Research Journal*, 2, (4), 496–521.

Cope, B. and Kalantzis, M. (1993), *The Power of Literacy: A Genre Approach to Teaching Literacy*. London: Falmer Press.

ERA Initiative (1999), *Easy readers for adults in South Africa: an investigation into their usage.* (unpublished report).

Harley, K. and Wedekind, V. (2003), 'A time for discipline: disciplinary displacement and mythological truths', *Journal of Education*, 31, 25–46.

Jansen, J. D. (1999), 'Why outcomes-based education will fail: an elaboration', in J. Jansen and P. Christie (eds), *Changing Curriculum: Studies on Outcomes-based Education in South Africa*. Cape Town, Juta, pp. 145–56.

JET (2000), *Mahalahle Baseline Report*. Johannesburg: Joint Education Trust

Macdonald, C. A. (1990), *Swimming up the Waterfall: A Study of School-Based Learning Experiences. A Final Report of the Threshold Project*. Pretoria: HSRC

— (2002), 'Are children still swimming up the waterfall? A look at literacy development in the new curriculum', *Language Matters*, 33, 111–41.

Morrow, W. (2005), *Unpublished Summary on the Provincial Education Conference of the Western Cape Education Department*, 23–4 March.

Pretorius, E. J. (2002), 'Reading ability and academic performance in South Africa: Are we fiddling while Rome is burning?', *Language Matters*, 33, 169–96.

Rose, D. (2004), 'Democratising the classroom: a literacy pedagogy for the new generation'. Paper presented at the Kenton Khalamba Conference, Cathedral Peak, KwaZulu-Natal, November.

Sukhraj, P., Mkhize, T., and Govender, S. (2000), 'Untrained teachers let loose on our kids: thousands lack proper qualifications and some know no more than pupils', *Sunday Times*, 8 February: 1.

Taylor, N. (2001) ' "Anything but knowledge": the case of the undisciplined curriculum'. Paper presented at *Curriculum Dialogue Seminar: What counts as worthwhile knowledge for the 21st century South African citizen?*, GICD, Johannesburg, February.

Taylor, N. and Vinjevold, P. (eds) (1999), *Getting Learning Right: Report on the President's Education Initiative Project*. Johannesburg, Joint Educational Trust.

Vinjevold, P. (1999), 'Learning materials', in N. Taylor and P. Vinjevold (eds), pp. 163–84.

Webb, V. (1999), 'Language study and language use in South African schools: a view from the politics of language'. Paper delivered at the NAETE fifteenth Annual Conference, SACTE, Pretoria.

Part Three

SFL Approaches to Literacy across Disciplines

10 Reconstruing 'personal time' as 'collective time': learning the discourse of history

Caroline Coffin

1 Introduction

History is a subject area in which there has not been a strong research focus on student writing although there has been considerable work on 'reading' history (e.g. Wineberg 1991) and historical understanding (e.g. Lee and Ashby 2000; Van Sledright 2000). In particular, little attention has been paid to the role played by language. This is despite the growing recognition that developing control of subject specific forms of language and literacy is an important aspect of building disciplinary knowledge and understanding. The chapter focuses specifically on time and the different linguistic constructions of time which operate in school history, a focus motivated by the fact that time is a key concept in history but is not one that all students learn to handle effectively. Research suggests, for example, that the utilization of chronological order and the representation of the duration of historical periods can be difficult tasks even for adolescents (Carretero *et al* 1991: 35; Stow and Haydn 2000; Wood 1995). This difficulty is of general significance for successful learning of history since, as Lomas points out, 'without chronology there can be no real understanding of change, development, continuity, progression and regression' (Lomas 1993: 20).

As a way of providing insight into students' different degrees of competence in handling time and chronology, reproduced below are two texts which were written by Year 7 history students (aged approximately 11–12) enrolled at an Australian secondary school. Both were written in response to a set of photos depicting changes in Aboriginal history and the prompt *What has happened to the Aborigines since the time of white settlement?* The two responses are markedly different in their use and linguistic construction of time. In Text 1, for example, the writer makes little use of time resources, aside from the temporal circumstance *since* provided in the title and the conjunction *then*. In addition, his main tense choice is present tense. The writer of Text 2, in contrast, makes far greater use of time resources with the result that the reader is moved through a series of chronologically organized events tracing the historical development of Aboriginal people from 1788 onwards. Resources include circumstances of time: location and duration (e.g. *for a long, long time, till in the 1960s, in the 1970s*) as well as phasal processes for phasing in the different stages of an event (e.g. *started to get*).

Text 1

(Note: all original errors have been preserved and xxxx indicates illegible words)

Since the white settlement the white people have caught the Aboriginals and xxxx the Aboriginal up so then the white men kill them so they can have the land. The other picture with the man standing with he shield and like a stick has been painted to represent the colour of his colours what they wite use. The picture below is lots of people in the streets fighting for maybe they want the Aboriginals they walk on the Dark side of Life and the people have put writing on the walls that say things they are holding things that say things.

And just a bit more for the top one with the Aboriginals they are in a jail the white men may have caught them because they had a fight and caught some for slaves maybe.

The Aboriginal on the left he might have them colours on him as I mentioned before and for some thing else I just remembered he might put them colours on him because a death for xxxx and so on. he is in the bush leaning on a tree

Text 2

Aborigines arrived in Australia some 40 000 years ago, and were said to have mostly come from Asia. They were and still are very spiritual people who treat everyone as an equal and who treat and respect their land like their mother.

Aborigines lived in peace and harmony with their environment until the white settlers came to settle in Australia in 1788. This is when the Aborigines life changed. All of a sudden their land was being taken away from them, their women and children were being killed, and they were treated inhumanly by the white settlers. The white settlers did not acknowledge the aborigines as part of the Australian population. Aborigines were deprived of many of the rights that white people had such as voting, being allowed to own their own home, chance of employment, education and proper medical care.

This kind of treatment of Aborigines went on for a long, long time and it wasn't till in the 1960s that they too started to get some rights. In the 1960s they got the right to vote like other white Australians but the Aborigines wanted more rights so in the 1970s they set up an embassy (a tent) and had many protests and rallys demanding more rights and demanding for them to be treated as equals.

The texts above represent typical patterns that occur in school history writing. Whereas the writer of Text 2 has produced a narrative text in which the use of chronology contributes to a sense of historical development and change, the writer of Text 1 appears to have little control over, or understanding of, the role of time in history and writes a less valued 'picture observation'. This inability to handle and express temporal relations appropriate to the discipline area is not uncommon and is clearly of concern. For example, 'understanding chronology' is now a major attainment target in the British National History Curriculum for 2004. Perhaps even more significantly, there has been some acknowledgement within the educational literature that difficulty with chronology and time may be at least partly a linguistic problem, with Stow and Haydn (2000: 94) going so far as to claim 'the centrality of language development in the acquisition of an under-standing of time'.

The research reported on in this chapter is a response to the problems associated with students' development in understanding and representing time. Working within systemic functional linguistics (SFL), two key interconnected aims guided the shape of the project. The first aim was to use SFL to ground concepts such as chronology and narrative and to develop an empirical account of how time is typically – and successfully – configured and reconfigured at different points in the school curriculum. The second aim was to make such a description accessible and meaningful to teachers so that they could raise students' awareness of how to handle time effectively and thus produce successful texts.

In the chapter I first consider the wider context of culture in which general understandings of time have developed and circulate, and which play a role in shaping historical uses of time. I then examine the more specific context of situation of school history, focusing on the genres that students need to write at different stages of the curriculum and in particular the different temporal resources they need to deploy in order to be successful. It is at that point that I will show how the grammatical classifications applied within the broader SFL model (e.g. circumstances of location: time, temporal processes, etc.) can be semantically configured in ways that are particularly revealing of the way time operates in history.

2 Context of culture: time concepts and constructs

This section focuses on the 'grand' notions of time which are naturally absorbed within the western cultural tradition and which percolate down into historians' treatments of the past. First I consider the overarching concepts of linear and cyclical time and their inter-connection with historical notions of change and continuity, and then I look at the three main time 'constructs' which have been developed as a means of measuring and locating events in time. An examination of these 'macro concepts' and 'macro constructs' is important not only because they are fundamental to the way in which historians perceive and think about the past but because they can contribute to our understanding of how successful students anchor such notions in their writing.

2.1 Macro time concepts: linearity and cyclicality, change and continuity

Two key concepts which emerge as fundamental in framing general thinking about time are linear and cyclical time. In relation to historical thinking both these notions are linked to the core historical concepts of 'change' and 'continuity'.

Linear time can be described as:

> an abstract, spatial quantity that is divisible into single units; as a two dimensional linear, directional flow or succession of equal rate that extends from the past to the future (or vice versa).
>
> (Adam 1995: 33)

In its conceptualization of time as a successive movement through space, a linear model implies a 'process of increasing complexity, together with inevitability and irreversibility' (Stanford 1994: 19) as well as connoting progress and 'a grand plan' (Carr 1986: 29). Western Enlightenment philosophy and science of the nineteenth century, with their notions of evolutionary development and teleological schemes, were particularly influential in strengthening such a view of time.

Cyclical notions of time, in contrast, arise out of the observation of natural processes in which 'plants grow, produce seeds and die and people and animals are born, live and die' (Adam 1995: 22). Implicit in such cycles of return are notions of sameness and repetition which dominate (but do not necessarily exclude) concepts of forward movement and cumulative progress and change. Fernandez-Armesto (1999: 246) points out that in cyclically influenced societies 'historiography reflects the cyclical vision: you get cyclical history, or, in deference to the ultimate changelessness the cycles encompass, no history at all'. He argues (1999: 248) that such views on temporality operate not only in the histories of ancient and traditional cultures but in most history writing across the ages, with 'cyclical episodes' punctuating 'what are essentially teleological schemes'. In essence, it would appear that a cyclical concept of time is linked to the notion of continuity in that cycles of activity frequently involve recurrent patterns of human behaviour that appear to remain constant over time, for example, cycles of war, economic booms followed by depression, the rise and fall of particular empires and so on. Eggins *et al* (1993) in their analysis of history textbooks have noted cyclical patterns in the characterization of empires and civilizations which are typically born, reach a peak and then decline. In these cases the analogy with life cycles of birth, growth and death are even more marked.

The following extract from a student narrative (Text 3) illustrates a self-contained cycle of activity in which aboriginal guerrilla warfare begins, continues for a number of years and then ends. In my research, it emerged that such cyclical episodes of conflict and war are frequently integrated into forward moving linear narratives in which large stretches of history are patterned with cycles of repeated human activity.

Text 3

In 1790 the Eora people <u>began</u> a guerrilla war against the Europeans. The Aborigines <u>continued to resist</u> the European invaders by burning their crops and houses, taking food, destroying cattle and killing some settlers.
This period of black resistance in Sydney <u>finally ended</u> **in 1816**.

Key: <u>underline</u>: processes construing a self-enclosed cycle of activity
     bold: Circumstances of time construing forward linear movement

2.2   Macro time constructs: the calendar, chronology and narrative

Aside from the more general concepts of linear and cyclical time, the macro constructs of the *calendar*, *chronology* and *narrative* play a central role in shaping our temporal understanding and organization of past events. These constructs are related: the invention of calendar time makes it possible to develop timelines and chronologies, which in turn make it possible to record and provide accounts of past events in the form of historical narratives. In other words, these constructs provide the means of locating, referring to and recording events and, in so doing, provide a framework in which the past can be explained and discussed.

Perhaps the most visible and important time construct used by historians is the standard and communicable scale of reference manifest in calendar time. Calendar time is pivotal to historical study in that its three main features constitute the computation of, or division into, chronicle time, i.e. the use of a founding event such as the Birth of Christ (BC), the reference to an axis and the use of units of measurement designating the constant intervals between the recurrences of phenomena. Whilst such temporal measurement is generally ingrained in adult thinking, it is important to remember that such an approach to time reckoning may not be completely transparent to students. Indeed, the philosopher Ricoeur makes the point that although historians now use calendar refigurations of time unreflectively, calendar time was the main intellectual tool to give rise to a historical consciousness (Ricoeur 1988: 106). On this basis, it is likely that developing control over calendar time is an important gateway for students to pass through if they are to begin to see and think about the past from a historical perspective.

Likewise, whereas adults may accept chronology and its use of calendar time as a way of carving up the past, we need to think about problems students may have. They may, for example, need to be explicitly taught the specialized terms for creating chronology; for example, the use of *kings, queens, dynasties, empires, centuries, millennia, ages and epochs* as different ways of slicing up the past. As commented on earlier, an understanding and use of chronological divisions is fundamental for success in history, for, without the ability to sequence, 'the past is chaos' for students (Wood 1995: 11).

The third macro construct is the historical narrative, which, by providing elaboration of temporal sequences of events, can flesh out the bare bones of a timeline (as illustrated in Text 2) and, optionally, build in causal links. An important point in relation to narrative is that, although historians typically refer to narrative as if there were only one form, the linguistic analysis carried out as part of the study reported here revealed that there are in fact different types of narrative which students need to develop control of (discussed further in section 3).

In sum, this section has considered the context of culture in relation to both macro concepts and macro constructs of time. Since these grand notions of time permeate into historical writing and the texts produced by school students, they provide important background knowledge for understanding the relative success or failure of particular texts. In the following section we move to the context of situation – secondary school history – and examine the way in which such notions are linguistically realized in the different genres produced by students at different points in the curriculum. The aim is to show that linguistic analysis of temporal resources illuminates the way students need to learn how time functions differently as they move through the curriculum.

3 Context of situation: the genres of school history

Genre, within the SFL tradition, is designed to show how the overall purpose of a text influences its structure and lexicogrammatical patterning. Based on the genre analysis of a large corpus of history student writing which I conducted as part of a major Australian Literacy project, the *Write it Right* (WIR) project (Veel, this volume, see Chapter 3), it emerged that there are three overall purposes for writing school history (Coffin 2006a, 2006b):

1. Recording the past (e.g. *Aborigines arrived in Australia some 40 000 years ago ...* – See Text 2)
2. Explaining the past (e.g. *There were 3 reasons why World War II occurred ...*)
3. Arguing about the past (e.g. *It can be argued that the main cause of World War 2 was ...*)

It also emerged that, within the narrative or 'recording' genres, different types of recording genre can be distinguished. These sub-types proved to be important in terms of the temporal resources deployed and are therefore set out in Figure 10.1.

A third key finding was that, whereas the recording genres are organized around an *external* timeline with events unfolding in a temporal sequence, the explaining and arguing genres are organized as

	Autobiographical Recount	(AR)	(recording one's own life)
Recording	Biographical Recount	(BR)	(recording someone else's life)
genres	Historical Recount	(HR)	(recording events in the past)
	Historical Account	(HA)	(accounting for why events happened in a particular sequence)

Figure 10.1 The recording genres

a sequence of steps within an argument and thus *internal* time (discussed further in section 3.2) is the main organizing principle. Extracts A and B are from a recording and an explaining genre, respectively, and illustrate this difference. In extract A, calendar devices are used to order external events chronologically (*From 1790 onwards, in 1794*), whereas in extract B ordinatives (*one, second*) and conjunctive adjuncts (*finally*) order factors internally.

Extract A (recording genre)

The Eora people had lived in the Sydney area for at least 40,000 years before the Europeans arrived. They had lived by hunting, fishing and gathering and believed that they were the guardians of the land.

After the Europeans arrived in 1788 they occupied sacred land and destroyed Eora hunting and fishing grounds. From 1790 onwards the Eora people responded to this invasion by participating in a guerrila war against the Europeans.

In 1794 under the leadership of Pemulwuy the Eora organized an attack on Brickfield where thirty six British and fourteen Eora were killed.

Extract B (explaining genre)

During the First World War there was considerable opposition to conscription for the following reasons: opposition to the war among different groups, fear of increasing government power and economic factors.

One reason for so much opposition to the war was the number of different groups of people concerned ...

A second reason was fear of increasing government power ...

Finally, there were economic factors behind the opposition to conscription ...

Finally, in terms of the relationship between students' production of particular genres and the different stages of the history curriculum, research showed that, whereas in the earlier years students tend to write recording genres (though there may also be some practice in writing explaining and arguing genres), in the later years they produce complex explanation and argument genres (see Figure 10.2). Indeed by Year 12 (approximately 17–18 years), the expectation (reflected in assessment practices) is that successful students will primarily produce argument genres. However, it is important to note that, in these genres, as well as in explaining genres, there are often narrative elements embedded as evidence for the arguments put forward.

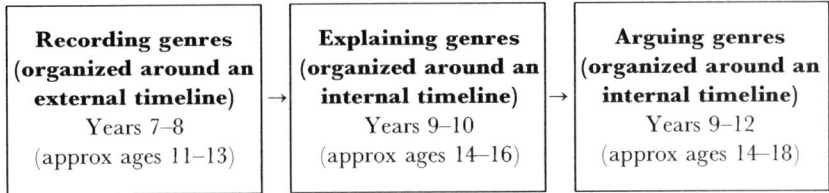

Recording genres (organized around an external timeline) Years 7–8 (approx ages 11–13)	→	Explaining genres (organized around an internal timeline) Years 9–10 (approx ages 14–16)	→	Arguing genres (organized around an internal timeline) Years 9–12 (approx ages 14–18)

Figure 10.2   The key history genres: social purposes and the changing role of time

4 Examining the lexicogrammar of time in school history

Having shown how a genre analysis provides a map of the major types of text which operate at different points in the history curriculum, the following section reports on the analysis of the lexical and grammatical construals of time in each of these genres and how they change over time as students move through secondary school. The data for the analysis consisted of 38 successful student texts representing the key genres outlined in section 3. These texts were gathered as part of the WIR project from a range of Sydney schools as well as published exam essays. They were considered successful based on assessment comments and marks, alongside discussions with history teachers.

In terms of lexical and grammatical resources for construing time, SFL offers a number of categories including those listed below:

- circumstances of time, e.g. *in the 1920s*
- temporal processes, e.g. *followed*
- systems of tense
- temporal conjunction + dependent clauses, e.g. ***when*** *the Romans came*
- cohesive adjuncts, e.g. *first*
- mood adjunct of temporality, e.g. *still, yet*.

For the purposes of the research reported on here I decided to reconfigure these resources along semantic lines in order to:

a) capture how time operates in the particular context of school history
b) make the categories accessible and useful to teachers and students.

A set of semantic categories which cut across grammatical classifications was devised and then trialled as part of a pilot analysis.

For reasons of economy, I decided to exclude tense and for reasons of infrequency I excluded mood adjuncts. The final set of temporal categories (which were modified as a result of the pilot analysis) is as follows:

Sequencing
Segmenting
Setting
Duration
Phasing
Organizing

In the remainder of the section I provide an overview of each category together with exemplification of key lexicogrammatical resources. Further discussion is given in the findings section (section 5). At this point, it should be noted that temporal realizations in the data did not always fit easily into a single category. In such cases, allocation to a category was based on the primary function of the realization in relation to its context.

Sequencing
This category references the linear unfolding of events in which temporal logic binds together previous and subsequent events, e.g.

> *When* we got on the plane I waved to them and started crying.
> *After* Macquarie had been sent back to England, Greenway received only limited work from the new Governor, Thomas Brisbane.

Sequencing includes simultaneous and successive relations. In simultaneous relations the two events overlap to some extent:

> **When we got on the plane** (event 1) I waved to them and started crying (event 2).

In successive relations, the first event does not continue beyond the beginning of the second event:

> **After Macquarie had been sent back to England** (event 1), Greenway received only limited work from the new Governor, Thomas Brisbane (event 2).

Table 10.1 Key sequencing resources

Key linguistic resources	Examples
temporal conjunction and dependent clause (simultaneous)	**When the Empire is at war**, Australia is at war
temporal conjunction and dependent clause (successive)	**After coming to power in 1959**, Castro used terror extensively …
external conjunctive adjunct	The Great Depression in 1929 <u>then</u> precipitated both policies of aggression and appeasement.
process	A bottomless deflationary whirlpool <u>ensued</u>.
ordinative	<u>Last</u> year was a highlight in my life

Segmenting

This category is concerned with the division of time whereby time loses its seamlessness and natural fluidity. Carved into segments, it becomes a central organizing principle for historical meaning-making. Segments can gather up relatively small lapses of time (e.g. *a week*) or, using specialized lexis, can encompass larger, historically significant stretches which span years, decades or centuries (e.g. *the Middle Ages, the Classical period*). Only specialized terms were quantified in the study.

Table 10.2 Key segmenting resources

Key linguistic resources	Examples
nominal group, nominalization, specialized (i.e. historically meaningful) lexis	the Gold Rushes, Word War II, the Cultural Revolution, the Locarno era, the Great Depression

Setting

Setting refers to the location of events at a particular point in time (e.g. *in 1928*). In contrast to sequencing, settings in time do not need to be interpreted as part of a sequential flow with reference to previous and subsequent events. Instead, events may be located within the framework of calendar conventions (i.e. dates, years and centuries) e.g. *in the nineteenth century*. Segments of time are frequently integrated into settings in time e.g. *after **the Middle Ages***.

Further angles on settings in time are construed through the use of definite or indefinite terms. That is, time is measurable in standard units (e.g. *on 26 July*) but may also be expressed in less precise terms (e.g. *a few days ago*) (see Halliday 1994: 152–3).

Table 10.3 Key setting resources

Key linguistic resources	Examples
circumstance of time: location	25 million were suffering malnutrition <u>in 1931</u> <u>Soon after World War I</u> people around the world realized just how much a disaster the war had really been.

Duration

Duration references how long an event lasts. Temporal extent may be measured in standard units e.g. *for 40,000 years* or in less definite terms e.g. *for a long time*.

Table 10.4 Key duration resources

Key linguistic resources	Examples
circumstance of extent: duration	The Eora people had lived in the Sydney area <u>for at least 40,000 years before the Europeans arrived</u>. It maintained this position <u>for nearly half a century</u>.

Phasing

Phasing is used as a general semantic term to capture the temporal resources which construe the beginning, continuation and end phases of an event or activity. These *stages of becoming*, i.e. *inception, duration* and *conclusion* are not limited to taxis relations between verbs (cf. Halliday 1994: 279–80). As discussed earlier (see Text 3), they may be used to stage and shape events as a self-contained cycle (i.e. with a beginning and end). Such construals of time have the potential to evoke recurrent, repeated patterns of activity and can therefore contribute to the notion of continuity. In addition they are a means of dividing up time into smaller segments, e.g. *the **onset** of the Wall Street Crash*.

Table 10.5 Key phasing resources

Key linguistic resources	Examples
process	For young women full skirted dresses, bows and bangles <u>ceased</u> to be fashionable
nominal group	<u>The onset of the Great Depression</u> diminished national economies . . .
circumstance	<u>By the end of the Great Terror</u>, Robespierre had stamped his personality firmly on the Revolution
conjunctive adjunct	<u>Finally</u>, in 1939, when Germany attacked Poland, Britain and France declared war on Germany.

Organizing

This semantic domain refers to the way in which time plays a role in the rhetorical organization of texts. As previously discussed (in section 3), time can be used to structure a text in tandem with the unfolding of an external activity sequence (*then, later*), resources that are included in the 'sequencing' category. In addition, time can be used to structure a text in relation to the internal steps of an argument, thus serving as a rhetorical device to order factors or arguments (*the first factor, secondly, finally*). The use of resources which realize *internal* time are placed in the 'organizing' category.

Table 10.6 Key organizing resources

Key linguistic resources	Examples
internal conjunctive adjunct	<u>Firstly</u>, from the perspective of the United States, it can be argued that this is reflected in their States, it participation in the peace settlements and in foreign affairs in the 1920s.
internal ordinative	The <u>first</u> reason was opposition to the war among different groups.

Table 10.7 provides a summary of the main linguistic sources which instantiate the six temporal categories as discussed above and which were quantified in the analysis reported on in the following section.

Table 10.7 Temporal categories and linguistic resources

Temporal category	Key linguistic resources
Sequencing	dependent clauses (simultaneous or successive) with temporal conjunction, external conjunctive adjunct
Segmenting	nominal group, nominalization, specialized terms
Setting	circumstance of time: location
Duration	circumstance of extent: duration
Phasing	process, nominal group, conjunctive adjunct, circumstance
Organizing	internal conjunctive adjunct, internal ordinative

5 Temporal analysis: key findings

The lexicogrammatical resources realizing each of the temporal categories were quantified in terms of their average frequency per 500 words for each genre family or, in the case of the recording genres, each sub-genre. In the case of the recording genres, the averages for each of the sub genres are presented because it emerged that within this group there are a number of key shifts in the use of temporal resources as students move from narrating events from a personal perspective (the *autobiographical recount*) to narrating events which take place over a longer period of time (the *biographical and historical recount* and the *historical account*).

The analysis thus provided empirical evidence of the different choices in semantic category and lexicogrammatical realization that students typically make at different points in the curriculum. The findings of the temporal analysis are presented in graph form throughout this section. In each of these graphs the average frequency of the temporal resources for the different genres is displayed. The following acronyms will be used:

AR = autobiographical recount	BR = biographical recount
HR = historical recount	HA = historical account
Exp = explaining genres	Arg = arguing genres
Sim = simultaneous	Suc = successive

Sequencing

The most striking finding in this domain of temporal meaning (see Figure 10.3) was the relatively high frequency of sequencing resources in the autobiographical, biographical and historical recount relative to

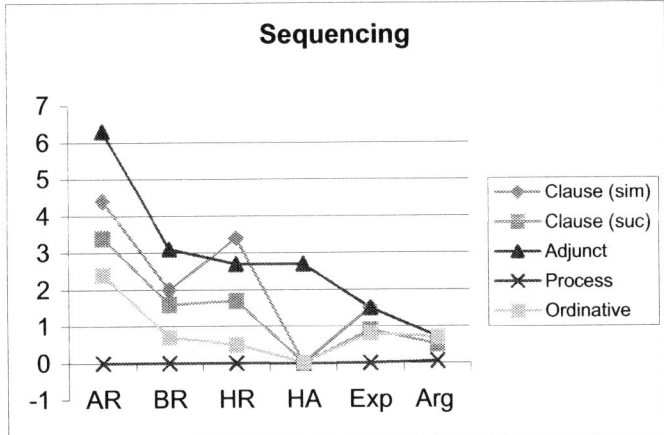

Figure 10.3   Sequencing: deployment of resources in successful texts

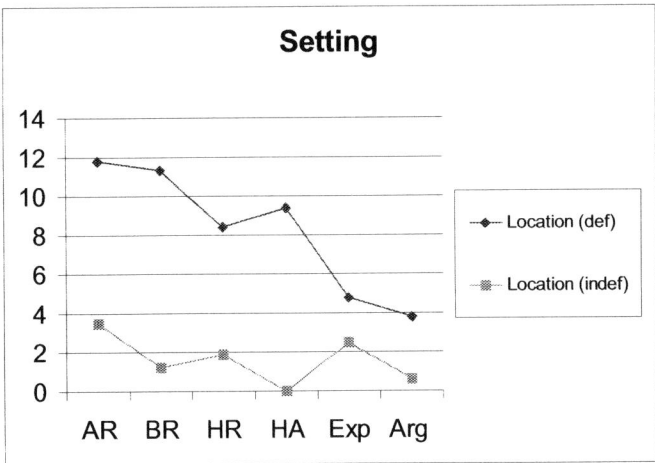

Figure 10.4   Setting in time: deployment in successful texts

all other genres. In particular, there was a high frequency of use in the autobiographical recount. In terms of linguistic realization, it emerged that the most common grammatical resource in the recording genres is the dependent clause, with simultaneous relations being more common than successive.

Setting
Figure 10.4 shows that resources for setting in time, like those for sequencing time, are most frequently used in the recording genres and particularly in the autobiographical recount. In the arguing and

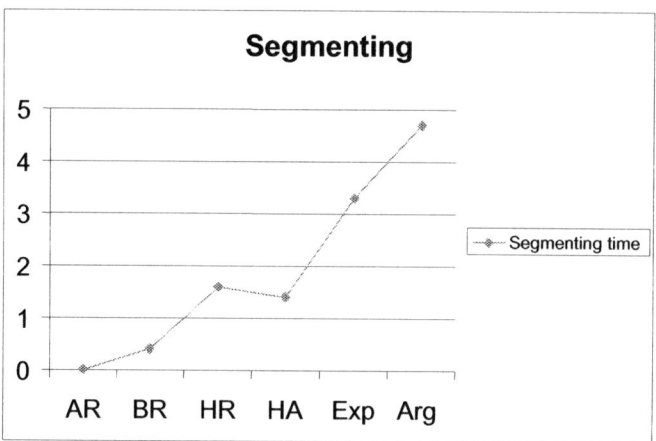

Figure 10.5 Segmenting time: deployment in successful texts

explaining genres, it emerged that resources for setting in time are more common than are sequencing resources. Finally, the figure shows that definite circumstances are far more common than indefinite ones.

Segmenting
As displayed in Figure 10.5, the noteworthy finding emerging in this category of analysis was the relatively high frequency of segmented time in the explaining and arguing genres compared to the recording genres.

Organizing
The key finding in this category was the use of time as a rhetorical organizer in the explaining and arguing genres. Thus, whereas external time is used to organize the recording genres, it is internal time which structures the genres that come later in the school curriculum (see Figure 10.6).

Duration
Perhaps rather surprisingly, Figure 10.7 shows that circumstances of extent: duration were relatively infrequent particularly when compared to circumstances of location (see Figure 10.4).

Phasing
Figure 10.8 serves as further confirmation that time resources are more common in the recording genres than the other genre 'families'. However, phasal resources – unlike sequencing and setting resources –

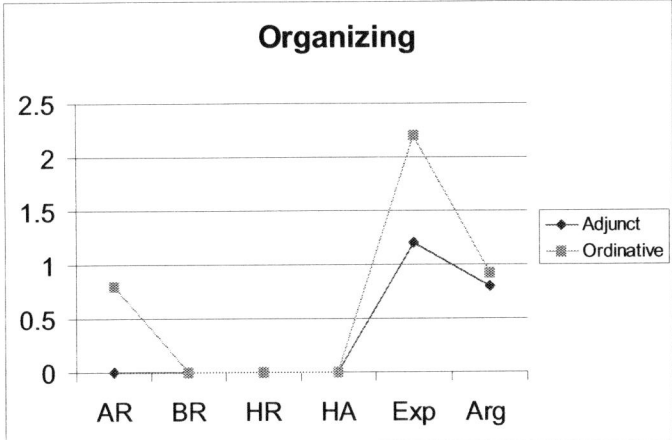

Figure 10.6 Time as organizer: deployment in successful texts

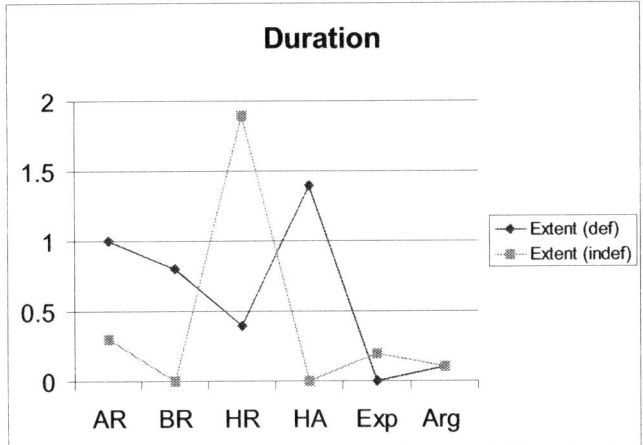

Figure 10.7 Duration: deployment in successful texts

are spread fairly evenly across the four types of recording genre. In terms of linguistic realization, it is striking that processes are the favoured choice in the recording genres whereas less congruent realizations are common in the explaining and arguing genres.

In summary, we can see that to write successful texts, different configurations of time are required at different points in the curriculum. One of the major trends that emerged is that there is a decrease in resources used for sequencing and setting in time and an increase in the use of resources for segmenting time. In the next section I discuss the pedagogic implications of these trends and patterns.

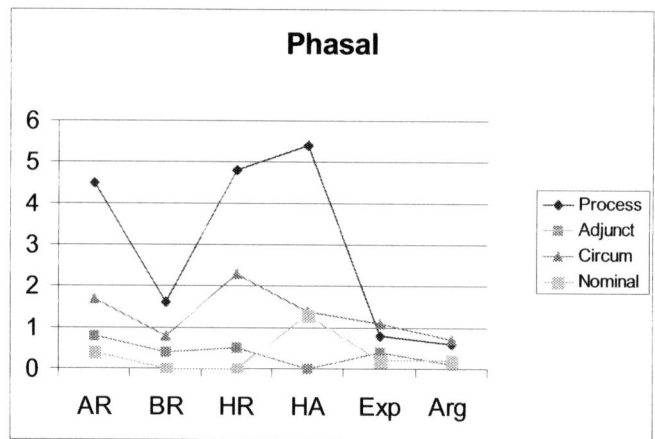

Figure 10.8   Phasing time: deployment in successful texts

6 Writing successful history texts: developing temporal resources

Based on the findings highlighted in the previous section it would seem that there are three major shifts in representing time that students need to make if they are to write successful history texts. That is, they need to:

i)   move from personal to historical time
ii)   develop different ways of representing historical time
iii) dismantle the timeline as an organizing device.

In this section I discuss each shift. In addition, in relation to the first shift, I show the results of a literacy intervention conducted as part of the WIR project. This provides an illustration of the way in which linguistic analysis can be applied in the classroom, particularly if linguistic analysis and categories are mediated in ways that are meaningful to teachers and students within a particular subject area.

6.1   *Learning to move from everyday notions of time to historical time*

Moving from recording past events in everyday terms towards framing past events in historically valued ways is the first important shift that history students need to make. This movement is illustrated in the first and final drafts (Texts 4 and 5) of an autobiographical recount written by a Year 7, 11-year-old girl, Virginia. These texts were collected as pre- and post-intervention data during a pilot literacy intervention program conducted as part of the WIR project. The first (pre-intervention) draft, Text 4 below, shows how Virginia makes very little use of segmenting or setting resources to organize events chronologically. Rather, she repeatedly uses memory, albeit mediated, to project from the present into the past. The main resource is *I remember* plus temporal conjunction and dependent clauses. Thus time and the past are experienced from the inside, from the standpoint of the writer, and consequently the reader is not positioned to have a strong sense of a linear movement through time.

Text 4

I was born in a hospital in Burma. I was born at 9.00 am on Wednesday. I remember when all of my relatives were all crowding around me when my parents brought me home. they were saying how cute I was. I remember when my sister was born I use to always fight with her. I also remember my first birthday. I remember when I was 5 and I had to come to Australia. I was crying because I didn't want to leave my relatives. I also remembered that I had a big brother and sister but they had both died. My brother died when he was 7 because he had a car crash and my sister died when she was just born. I also remember when I started kindergarten I was so excited I was jumping up and down.

Other texts written by Year 7 students and collected during the literacy intervention programme displayed similar patterns to those in Virginia's text, thus exemplifying how novice writers in history often begin producing written history texts with very little understanding of how to draw on the framing function of setting and segmenting resources. However, after a period of five weeks, in which the history teacher and I collaboratively developed materials to raise students' awareness of the typical features of an autobiographical recount, the final drafts showed a dramatic improvement in students' use of settings as a means of organizing events along a culturally shared chronology. This development is illustrated in Virginia's final draft (Text 5 below). This text shows how she is beginning to move from personal time towards a more socially and historically oriented construal of time. For example, the increase in the use of resources for setting in time and the location of these in hypertheme (paragraph initial) position give a strong sense of events unfolding along a timeline. Most significantly, this chronology exists outside the writer and is accessible through a socially shared set of calendar conventions (in bold).

Text 5
My Life by Virginia A.
My Name is Virginia A. I was born in Burma **at 9.00 am on Wednesday 9th April 1980**. The following recount is about the most important events that happened in my life.
My Earliest memory was the death of my brother and my older sister. My brother died when he was seven in an car accident. My sister died when she was just born.
In 1985 it was a sad time for me because I left my relatives behind and came to Australia. I remember when they were all crying when we were at the airport. When we got on the plane I waved to them and started crying.
One year later I started kindergarten at Glebe Primary school. I was excited and was jumping up and down.

6.2   Developing different ways of representing historical time

Virginia's final draft is clearly a more successful text than its earlier incarnation and this is primarily because she has learned to use temporal settings as a framing device to create a linear record of events in her life. The use of settings and in particular the use of the noun group to bundle together events is an area that Virginia and all Year 7 students need to develop further control of if they are to be successful in moving from recording events in their own relatively short lives to recording those in other people's lives (the biographical recount) and hence to recording events across decades and centuries (historical recounts and accounts). At the same time, they need to reduce the use of dependent clauses to sequence simultaneous and successive events.

The sample historical account, Text 6, illustrates both the increase in the use of setting in time and the use of the noun group in bundling together events which belong to longer spans of time (i.e. ones that extend beyond the span of a human life). These increased spans of time show how public rather than personal temporality becomes established as a 'norm' in this sub genre. That is, events are bound together in a culturally constructed and historically meaningful way with specialized terms (in bold) used to refer to them.

Text 6 also shows how, aside from learning to handle large segments of time, students at this point in the curriculum must also be able to handle the gaps in time – the increasingly stretched out 'stepping stone' dimension of 'historical time', whereby many events are 'edited out' and long gaps (unaccounted for) exist between one event and another. Again, I would argue that by drawing students' attention to such historically valued representations of time, teachers can help students to develop competence in handling time and chronology and so produce successful history texts.

Text 6
What has happened to the Aborigines since the time of white settlement?
In the late 18th century, when the English colonized Australia, there were small tribes, or colonies of Aboriginal natives who had lived harmoniously and in tune with their surroundings for 40 000 years ...

As a result of their belief in 'terra nullius', from 1788 onwards, the English began to occupy sacred land and use Aboriginal hunting and fishing grounds.

This abuse by the new British government soon led to Aboriginals becoming involved in a physical struggle for power. **The first main period of Aboriginal resistance** was from 1794 to 1816 when the Eora people, under the leadership of Pemulwuy, resisted the Europeans through guerrilla warfare.

This Aboriginal resistance resulted in the colonizers using different methods of control. **In the 19th century** Protection stations were set up where Aboriginals were encouraged to replace their traditional lifestyles with European ones. Many Aborigines resisted, however, and as a result were shot or poisoned.

In 1909, the continuation of Aboriginal resistance led to the NSW Aborigines Protection Act which gave the Aborigines Protection Board the power to remove Aboriginal children from their own families and place them into white families, often as cheap labour.

6.3   Dismantling the timeline as an organizing device

The third major shift in students' management of temporal resources occurs when they move from organizing the past in chronological terms to interpreting past events in the form of rhetorically organized explanations and arguments. This requires a shift from using external conjunctive adjuncts and ordinatives to internal ones and requires the ability to explain long term and simultaneous trends and developments rather than simply record a linear string of events. Text 7 below illustrates how conjunctive adjuncts and ordinatives are used to internally scaffold an explanation for why there was considerable opposition to conscription during World War I.

Text 7 (abridged explanation)
During the First World War there was considerable opposition to conscription ...

One reason for so much opposition to the war was the number of different groups of people concerned ...

A **second** **reason** was fear of increasing government power . . .
Finally, there were economic factors behind the opposition to
conscription . . .

The third major shift therefore requires that the chronological
timeline be dismantled. Not surprisingly, as revealed in the findings
section, the use of specialized terms to represent time in the explaining
and arguing genres is more than twice as frequent as in the recording
genres. Again, there is a role for SFL in the classroom in that such
shifts can be linguistically pinned down through language awareness
activities.

7 Conclusion: learning the discourse of history

This chapter has demonstrated how semantic categories can be used to
show what students need to do at different points in the school
curriculum. In particular, it has shown how successful secondary
school students move from retelling past events in the form of
chronologically organized historical narratives (in the earlier years) to
providing more complex analyses of events in which time plays a
rather different role (in the later years). Of particular interest, the
analysis revealed that, as part of this movement, successful students
need to learn at an early point how to conceptualize and use time in
ways that move beyond personal perception and lived experience. And
it may indeed be this initial shift that proves problematic for students
who have been identified in the educational literature as having
difficulty in understanding and representing chronological time and
historical duration.

The movement from the representation of more familiar and
directly experienced stretches of time to larger historically labelled
stretches suggests that successful learning of the discourse of history is
partly a process of shedding personally oriented construals of time and
expanding a more publicly oriented 'technology' of time. This means
that, as students develop their control of historical discourse,
perceptions of time that are internally influenced by the individual's
subjective sense of pace and movement through time are superseded by
a conventionally agreed upon objective public or social temporality.
As part of this process, the distance between past and present
intensifies. In other words, the interlocking temporal spaces (in
autobiographical recounts) of past and present, and personal and
public, are teased apart and a more detached sense of time appears to
develop.

Clearly, learning to use a wide repertoire of temporal resources represents significant development for secondary school students whose own personal experience of large stretches of time is limited. This chapter has given some insight into how the findings of SFL linguistic analysis can be presented in a form that can be educationally useful. That is, based on the success of literacy intervention programmes conducted as part of the WIR project, the argument can be made that awareness raising activities or explicit teaching of temporal semantic categories are likely to aid students' understanding and use of temporal resources (see Coffin (2006a) for a discussion of how linguistic findings can improve students' history writing, and Coffin and Derewianka, 2008 for a discussion of the visual representation of time and multimodality). In addition, close linguistic analysis of successful texts provides empirical evidence of how time or other domains of historical significance are represented (see Coffin, 2002, 2003, 2004 for discussions of how SFL analysis can provide important insights into how *cause* and *evaluation* operate in historical discourse). The findings of such analyses can be used by teachers to give students a clearer sense of what is required at different stages of the curriculum as they move along their own timelines and develop control of different genres.

References

Adam, B. (1995), *Timewatch: The Social Analysis of Time*. Cambridge, UK: Polity Press.

Carr, D. (1986), *Time, Narrative, and History*. Bloomington, USA: Indiana University Press.

Carretero, M., Asensio, M. and Pozo, J. (1991), 'Cognitive development, historical time representation and causal explanations in adolescence', in M. Carretero, M. Pope, R. J. Simons and J. I. Pozo (eds), *Learning and Instruction: European Research in an International Context*, Vol. 3. Oxford, UK: Pergamon Press, pp. 27–48.

Coffin, C. (1997), 'Constructing and giving value to the past', in F. Christie and J. R. Martin (eds), *Genres and Institutions: Social Processes in the Workplace and School*. London: Pinter, pp. 196–230.

— (2002), 'The voices of history: theorising the interpersonal semantics of historical discourses', *Text*, 22, (4), 503–28.

— (2003), 'Reconstruing the past: settlement or invasion?', in J. R. Martin and R. Wodak (eds), *Re/reading the Past: Critical and Functional Perspectives on Time and Value*. Amsterdam: Benjamins, pp. 219–46.

— (2004), 'Learning to write history: the role of causality', *Written Communication*, 21, (3), 261–89.

— (2006a), 'Learning the language of school history: the role of linguistics in mapping the writing demands of the secondary school curriculum', *The Journal of Curriculum Studies*.

— (2006b), *Historical Discourse: The Language of Time, Cause and Evaluation*. London: Continuum.

Coffin, C. and Derewianka, B. (2008) Time visuals in history text books: some pedagogic issues. In Unsworth, L. (ed.) *Multimodal semiotics: Functional analysis in contexts of education*. Continuum, London: UK.

Eggins, S., Wignell, P. and Martin, J. R. (1993), 'The discourse of history: distancing the recoverable past', in M. Ghadessy (ed.), *Register Analysis*. London: Pinter, pp. 75–109.

Fernandez-Armesto, F. (1999), 'Time and history', in K. Lippincott (ed.), *The Story of Time*. London: Merrell Holberton, pp. 246–9.

Halliday, M. A. K. (1994), *An Introduction to Functional Grammar* (second edition). London: Edward Arnold.

Lee, P. and Ashby, R. (2000), 'Progression in historical understanding among students ages 7–14', in P. N. Stearns, P. Seixas and S. Wineberg (eds), *Knowing, Teaching and Learning History*. New York: New York University Press, pp. 199–222.

Lomas, T. (1993), *Teaching and Assessing Historical Understanding*. London: Historical Association.

Martin, J. R. (1992), *English Text: System and Structure*. Amsterdam: Benjamins.

Ricoeur, P. (1988), *Time and Narrative, Vol. 3*. London: The University of Chicago Press.

Stanford, M. (1994), *A Companion to the Study of History*. Oxford, UK: Blackwell.

Stow, W. and Haydn, T. (2000), 'Issues in the teaching of chronology', in J. Arthur and R. Phillips (eds), *Issues in History Teaching*. London: Routledge, pp. 83–97.

Van Sledright, B. (2000), 'Concept- and strategic-knowledge development in historical study: A comparative exploration in two fourth-grade classrooms' , *Cognition and Instruction*, 18, (2), 239–83.

Wineburg, S. S. (1991), 'On the Reading of Historical Texts: Notes on the Breach between School and Academy', *American Educational Research Journal*, 28, (3), 495–519.

Wood, S. (1995), 'Developing an understanding of time-sequencing issues', *Teaching History*, 79, (April), 11–14.

11 Exploring a novel through engagement with its grammatical form: perspectives for a primary/ middle school classroom

Lorraine McDonald

1 Introduction

> ... our way into most of the meanings of most texts is obviously through their language: texts after all are linguistic objects, and a literature text is no exception to this rule ... in verbal art the role of language is central. Here language is not as clothing is to the body; it **is** the body.
>
> (Hasan 1985: 91, emphasis in original).

While many literature teachers would agree with Hasan that paying close attention to the language of literary texts is an important part of the study of literature, this approach is not always included in classroom practice in junior or middle schools. The analysis of literature texts for children and adolescents can offer insights into new ways of achieving teachers' understanding of 'how texts teach what readers learn' (Meek 1988). This chapter details a series of grammatical analyses of literary excerpts, based on systemic functional linguistics (SFL, Halliday 1994), including some transcript examples of classroom practice in order to show readers the 'distinctive contribution [a study of] the language of a literary text might make to children's reading experiences' (Williams 1986: 63). When, as literature teachers, we work with young people, we usually support them well in engaging with literary themes and characters, settings and imagery. What we do not always do, however, is explicitly draw attention to how the grammatical features – the 'verbal art' (Hasan 1985) – construct those literary signifiers we spend so much time discussing. However, when students recognize how an author has worked with the language – the lexicogrammar – they may more fully appreciate the role of the author's craft in developing these aspects of the novel. They may also gain critical awareness of how they have been positioned by the text.

The analyses presented here are offered as samples of ways meanings are revealed when we pay attention to the language of a novel. For example, attending to any disruption of narrative convention is always productive: when authors of young people's literature deliberately flout typical narrative principles I suggest they seek to interest their audience in the novel's construction and have them consider particular nuances of the story. Observing patterns of transitivity at significant points in a novel may alert readers to activity sequences where aspects of literary theme and characterization, discourses and ideologies may be displayed. Noting lexical strings and their meronymic (associated) relationships can be useful when highlighting how descriptions of setting and characters can create emotional moods in a novel. The novel excerpts presented in this chapter demonstrate the potential for such analyses. While the novel is written for young people in an age range between 10 and 15 years, the linguistic principles can be applied to any text.

The set of excerpts are from an Australian children's novel, *I Am Susannah* (IAS), by an award winning author, Libby Gleeson (Gleeson 1987). The novel is constructed within the literary genre of realism, where setting and characters simulate real world settings and human characters. In *IAS*, Gleeson narrates a story of a pre-adolescent girl's (the eponymous Susie/Susannah) induction into womanhood.

Linguistically, Gleeson deploys a number of strategies of text presentation and grammar to disrupt the typical narrative form. Italic font is inserted to highlight shifting points of view, while grammatical games are played with the mood and tense system to construct characterization. Thematically, Gleeson offers a challenge to traditional discourses on the roles of women in contemporary society. The SFL analyses offer a level of delicacy which highlights aspects of how these atypical narrative and discursive conventions are constructed.

2 Disrupting narrative convention: 'Playing' with the mood system, tense and Thematic patterns

Emphasis on the role of language in constructing different genres, including narratives, has been foregrounded in school curricula in a number of countries in recent times. Readers are usually familiar with the way that dialogue in western narratives normally draws on the full resources of the mood and tense systems. As characters are constructed to imitate human negotiation, they make statements (declarative mood), ask questions (interrogative mood) and give commands (imperative mood) as can be seen in the following scene, where one of Susie's teachers, Mrs. Chamberlain, talks with Susie after class:

'Give me a hand with these brushes.'   Imperative mood/command

'Have you heard from her yet?'   Interrogative mood/question

'She must be busy settling in.'   Declarative mood/statement
(Chapter 1: 5)

Readers also expect the narration to proceed as a series of statements (declarative mood) in past tense. This convention can be seen in the examples below, with the past tense highlighted:

> She **lay** on her back in the warm sun, her eyes half-closed. (p. 1)
> Susie **sat** at her desk, pen in hand and writing paper in front of her. (p. 39)
> Sonya **stood** at the end of the darkened hallway. (p. 92)

These expectations of the conventional narrative are thwarted, however, as Gleeson also employs a set of alternative constructions, as we shall see.

In *IAS*, conventional practice is consistently interrupted by other forms which cast their own pattern across the novel. One atypical pattern is evident in the use of the historical present tense to construct narration. While this narrative strategy has been utilized in adult writing for centuries (for example, Sterne's *Tristram Shandy* 1759/1965), *IAS* was one of the first novels for children and young adults, at least in Australia, to employ this device. Examples of Gleeson's use of the historical present can be seen below:

> Eyes **meet**. The woman **steps back**, mouth **open**. Susie **runs**. (p. 49)
> Susie and Kim **hide** behind the red hibiscus, **bury** their faces in the trumpet flowers. (p. 96)

The use of the historical present in literature makes stories more vivid primarily by bringing past actions into the immediate present. As the conventional arrangement of declarative past tense is taught as a feature of narratives to students in a number of education systems, it is significant to young writers and readers when such variations occur.

A second atypical narrative pattern is evident in the ellipsis or omission of the subject and/or finite element of the process. In the following examples, the ellipsed declarative is presented, with potential completed declaratives also displayed to highlight the distinction:

Ellipsed subject:
    Text: *Sneak up behind the tomb with the anchor on top.* (Chapter 2: 16)

Potential: (They) Sneak up behind the tomb with the anchor on
   top.
Text: *Laughing.*
Potential: (They are) Laughing.

Ellipsed process:
   Text: *Susie and Kim in the cemetery after school.* (Chapter 2: 16)
   Potential: Susie and Kim **(are)** in the cemetery after school.
   Potential: Susie and Kim **(play)** in the cemetery after school.

These atypical patterns in the narration combine to produce
particular dramatic effects of immediacy and involvement of the
reader, which cumulate through the novel. One clear example of this
patterning of historical present tense and ellipsed subject is at the start
of the novel, where the opening paragraph disrupts assumptions about
the construction of narrative, while simultaneously producing a
reading of intimacy and presence. The opening paragraph of *IAS* (p.
1) is reproduced below. Of particular grammatical interest here is how
the use of the historical present tense and ellipsed statements produce
significant Thematic patterns.

Susie and Kim start Kindergarten on the same day. Three years old, fight
over a one-wheeled scooter and a hairless doll. Friends. Sleep at each
other's houses. Lie on the upstairs balcony and blow peas through a straw
at kids going past. Sprawl on the bed in Susie's attic and stare at the
church spire and the tall golden tower over the city. Run home down King
Street, press noses against glass windows, dig up sixty cents from the
bottom of tunic pockets and share a sticky cake, sitting on the low brick
fence of the doctor's surgery. At four o'clock in the sundrenched cemetery,
play chasings over the roots of the Moreton Bay fig tree, lie on the warm
headstone of the boy who was lost at sea and talk. Friends.

The use of the simple/historical present tense in this opening
paragraph gives timelessness to the propositions being made – the
reader gets a strong image of the ongoing nature of these events.
There is a sense of currency as the present tense contemporizes these
past events into the 'here and now', for much of the paragraph is a
flashback, as indicated by 'Kindergarten' and 'Three years old'. As
well, this timeless quality lends authority to the account – this is the
way it *is* – and this certainty is reinforced by the lack of modality in
the text. The reader is thus positioned to accept the account of Susie
and Kim's activities as given and the text economically establishes
the history of this friendship as a highly active one, where the
characters have spent many years doing things together in a variety
of settings.

The ellipsed subject (which could be 'Susie and Kim' or 'They') also contributes to the construction of the intensity of the friendship between the characters. The coordinated noun group 'Susie and Kim' is thematized as the opening subject for the narrative. Conventionally, a reference chain such as 'They' would construct Susie and Kim as ongoing subject in the clauses which follow, for example, '(they) fight over a hairless doll ... ' or '(they) sleep at each other's houses'. By ellipsing the reference chain, the action verbs are in Theme position (for example, 'Sleep', 'Lie', 'Sprawl') and the girls' friendship as an activity-based relationship is foregrounded. This concept is reinforced when 'Friends' appears as a singular item: it acts as a kind of bracket around the list of material processes (action verbs) which construct the activities and, in its position as the final information, 'Friends' strengthens the effectiveness of the paragraph. Thus Gleeson disrupts traditional narrative convention in the opening paragraph of her first chapter and her readers are positioned to accept the powerful image of friendship which is necessary as motivation for the narrative which follows. They are also inducted into a text which will continue to 'play' with narrative convention.

3 Classroom work: observing tense and Thematic patterns

IAS was read and discussed with a fifth-grade class of 10- and 11-year-old students in Sydney, Australia, as part of a literature programme. The programme took place over a ten-week period and the teacher returned to the opening paragraph of *IAS* in the third lesson of the programme, after she had established the characters and the initial events with the students. The teacher wished to draw attention to the language of the novel in order to observe the constructed nature of the story. This kind of observation complemented her support of the students' response to the characterization and plot events through engaging their empathy and recording analogous experiences.

In the transcript excerpts following, the teacher invites the students to examine the tense (48T) and location (55T) of the material processes (processes are verbs in traditional grammar; in this class the students were using both terms) and to 'observe' a 'pattern' deliberately 'put' by the author (61T). While occurring as one long set of interactive turns in the classroom, it will be presented in sections here for clarity of discussion. (Transcript has been edited for clarity; turns numbered from original; T = Teacher, S = Student; T has text on overhead transparency; students' names have been changed; tonal emphasis indicated by capital letters.)

48T	... Ok, now, let's come back to all those words that you have just been identifying, come back to this first one and tell me girls and boys what is the word that we would give to identify all of these words that you have given me, words such as start, fight, sleep, lie, sprawl, et cetera. In terms of we have been working on, how would you identify those words. How would you categorize them?
49S	They are happening now.
50T	Happening now. Good, cause they are in the present tense. It's not like '*STARTED*' Kindergarten. If you '*STARTED*' Kindergarten, you know that the story is being told in yesterday time. What is another piece of information?
51S	Processes
52T	They are processes, aren't they? Talking about processes, they are?
53S	Verbs
54S	Doing words

In this excerpt, the teacher asked the students to name the grammatical qualities of the words under scrutiny, rather than be concerned with their semantic qualities. She refined the students' scrutiny of the material processes they had named 'OK, now, let's come back to all those words that you have just been identifying' (48T) through using and eliciting metalanguage 'they are in present tense' (50T), 'Processes' (51S), 'Verbs' (53S). This metalanguage precisely identified the pattern deployed by the writer and allowed the teacher to examine the text for the Thematic position of these 'actions' in turns 55T–66S below.

55T	Most of these words are actions. Just give them to me again, because I want you to see if you can actually notice something quite special about the placement of these processes. Just run through some of these with me again. You can all identify them. Tessa? Nicole?
56S	Fight
... (Students name processes from overhead transparency)	
61T	... 5T, put your thinking caps on and answer me this question. For the most part, there are a couple of exceptions, but for the most part, where are these words located in that paragraph? Where are most of the words POSITIONED in that paragraph? ... this is actually a bit of a pattern for you to observe here ... there is something interesting about where Libby Gleeson has put these words. Jamal?
62S	At the beginning of each sentence
63T	YES. Have a look. At the beginning of each sentence. Now

	see if there are some exceptions. Like '*start*', is it at the beginning of the sentence? And '*fight*' isn't, but look – (T marks them on projected screen)
64S	'*Run*'
65T	– and if they are not at the beginning of the sentence, if they are not at the beginning of the sentence they are in like a key position like '*press*' and like '*dig*', or '*dig up*'. There are a lot of those.
66S	It seems like they are moving from place to place (unclear)

In the excerpt above the teacher scaffolded the students' attention in several ways. She constructed 'message redundancy' (Gibbons 2002) when she verbally reviewed the processes the students had already named and she visually reviewed them by marking them on a projected overhead transparency. Then she linked the known information to the new idea when she highlighted their 'interesting' placement by the author, alerting the students to the 'pattern' they create. Sharpe (2001) calls this type of support 'contingent scaffolding': the teacher reviews in different ways and makes clear links between given and new information. In 66S one student appears to pre-empt the teacher's next step when she notes the meaning constructed by the pattern. The excerpt continues below.

67T	... So they are positioned at the beginning of most of the sentences, if they are not at the beginning of the sentence, then they follow a pattern in the sentence – look at '*RUN home down King Street, PRESS noses against glass windows, DIG UP sixty cents in the bottom drawer, SHARE a sticky cake*' and on and on it goes. They are positioned right at the front or at the beginning ... Now what impression, what image does that create for us about these two people? In terms of what you could learn about the characters in the story, what does this conjure up in your minds '*START Kindergarten, fight over a scooter, sleep, lie, blow, sprawl, stare, run, press, dig up, share, sitting, play, lie, talk*'? What does that tell you about these two people?
68S	They're active
(T responds to each answer with 'Yes'.)	
70S	They are normal friends. They act like normal friends.
72S	They are very good friends.
74S	They do all these things together.

In this interaction the teacher initially reiterated her emphasis on the patterning of the processes and then asked three questions which connected the grammatical knowledge accumulated in the lesson with its semantic effect in the novel. The essential point made here was that the students' understanding of, and knowledge about, the characters was constructed in the grammar of the novel:

> 'Now what impression, what image does that create for us about these two people?'
> ' ... what does this conjure up in your minds ... '
> 'What does that tell you about these two people?'

One reading of this set of questions suggests that the students were situated to attend to the dynamic quality of the solidary relationship between meaning and grammar: that is, it is in the accumulation of the process types that the quality of the characters' friendship is realized. The student responses in 68S–74S imply that they were able to connect the grammatical construction with the text's meaning. Their responses draw together the various activities named in the paragraph into a general principle for Susie's characterization.

It could be argued that the students' final realizations about the nature of the characters' relationship may have been 'discovered' through other methods. The focus on grammar, however, encouraged an understanding beyond an interpretative one. Not only had the students interpreted the characterization appropriately but the close study of the language also developed the students' awareness of how language constructs their relationship.

4 Mental projections of Susie and mood choices: constructing multiple perspectives

Throughout the novel Susie's mental projections are signalled by the changed text presentation of italic font. As the italicized text signals Susie's thoughts, it positions the reader interpersonally to take up Susie's point of view, without the need for any projecting clauses with mental processes such as 'she thought' or supporting quote marks. The italic font gives a textual signal to the young reader that a focalizing shift is occurring (Toolan 1988) through juxtaposition of Susie's public and private worlds. The three scenes presented below show how multiple perspectives are made available to young readers in this novel in the construction of characterization and theme.

Scene 1 Just after the opening paragraph studied above. Kim has just announced she is leaving for Melbourne

[Kim's] straight black hair fell below her shoulders.

Who will I sit with? Kim. Always Kim.
'Do you want to go?' (Chapter 1: 2)

In the first line above, the narrator describes Kim's hair (perhaps through Susie's eyes) for the reader to imagine. The second line presents Susie's projected thoughts as a rhetorical question using 'I', which she answers. In the third line, Susie is given a verbal projection, in the form of a question to Kim, using 'you' – a question which hides her concern for herself. Here the shift in the participant pronoun from 'I' to 'you' reveals how Susie is hiding her feelings from her friend, a familiar strategy to the students in the Australian classroom. Attention to these kinds of observations helps readers to recognize how Susie's introspection is constructed.

Scene 2 Sonya is giving instructions to Susie and her peers about playing spin the bottle at her elder sister's party. Susie is not given any verbal projections in this scene.

'What if you don't like him?'
Kiss him. Yuk.
'Yeah, what if he's got pimples and stinks like Geoffery Meaney?'
Susie bit into a bruised, bad part of her apple. She spat the brown mouthful onto the ground.
Kissing. Only with Mum and that's on the cheek. She always smells warm.
'You've all got to play.' Sonya waved her piece of paper.
'And if he's pimply and stinks, it doesn't matter. It'll be dark and you don't have to look at him'
... 'Put a peg on your nose' (Chapter 5: 34–5)

The theme of peer pressure is evident in Scene 2 after Sonya tells her friends what they 'have to' do. Gleeson presents a silent Susie (in the narration she's eating an apple), yet the italicized mental projections, interspersed between the spoken dialogue, indicate her hesitation to move into unfamiliar intimacy. Susie's silent resistance is heightened through contrast with her peers' apparent acceptance of the situation. The scene is constructed to contrast Susie's verbal silence, in the public world of the text, with her mental voice in her private internal world, enhancing the quality of introspection in her characterization.

The strategy of constructing mental projections as italicized clauses simplifies the complex textual world of *IAS*, as the italic font provides its own contextual boundary for another set of interactions. The third scene demonstrates shifting contexts and time frames in three consecutive paragraphs in the novel, which have been numbered for reference in the comments following.

Scene 3 Susie is hidden and watching the Blue Lady. They are in an historical cemetery, situated near both their houses

i) The woman looked up for a moment. She scratched the side of her head with the end of her pencil, turned the page of her drawing pad and started again.
ii) *What's she drawing? People don't just draw. Kids do at school, and art teachers. And me when I'm at home, in my room, by myself.*
iii) 'You draw so well,' Susie's mother says to her when she looks at her project book. 'You must get it from your father. I can't draw for nuts.' (Chapter 3: 20)

In (i), the context moves from situated 'story' time in the third person, with past tense narratorial voice, to (ii), a context of internal thought through mental projections involving interrogative, declarative and ellipsis, in present tense, and then to (iii) a context of pre-story time – a flashback scene constructed in the present tense, which returns to the narratorial voice yet constructs Susie's memory. The italic font then economically plays with interpersonal meaning, and with experiential meaning, to disrupt narrative convention. The use of present tense creates both a sense of immediacy and the intensity of her memory. In summary, the SFL analysis offers a delicate insight into how the traditional grammatical patterns in realist narrative fiction are disrupted in this novel and the effect of this disruption on characterization and point of view.

In *IAS*, Gleeson also challenges ways that females can be portrayed in literature. She foregrounds managing a household, but also has her women painting a boundary wall and holding professional jobs successfully. Some of the ways this feminist discourse is constructed are detailed in the following sections.

5 Constructing a feminist discourse: Foregrounding domestic events through transitivity and meronymy

In *IAS*, Gleeson presents her female characters as individuals involved in domestic and feminine activities. Feminist theorists have long argued that the spheres of private and public life are regarded differently. Private life is perceived as the world of the feminine while public life is masculine, and it is male interests, events and occupations that have traditionally provided the field for narrative concerns (Morris 1993). In *IAS*, Gleeson introduces domestic and personal female occupations as noteworthy events. These pursuits, such as shopping for clothes, washing the dishes and applying make-up, conventionally have been considered as mundane and not worthy of narrative attention. The domestic settings in which Martha, Susie's mother, is placed ground the novel in the world of the private, the domestic, the home. When counter-pointed with other scenes which construct Martha as employed and as parent, they offer a picture of ways of being a mature female which is paralleled in contemporary life.

The domestic world is constructed through the narration where Martha is found in the kitchen, the laundry, the backyard and the bathroom. Gleeson economically constructs the details of Martha's activities through transitivity and lexical strings, accumulating associations through the meronymic relationships, as can be seen in Table 11.1.

Table 11.1   Foregrounding domestic events through transitivity and lexical strings

Participant/Actor	**material process**	non-human/ meronymic participants/goal	*circumstance*
kitchen activity sequence excerpt			
Her mother	**filled**	the kettle	
She	**wiped**	her hands	*on a tea towel*
Her mother	**stood**		*in the middle of the kitchen (with) her hands full of plates*
	to be put away		
Her mother	**squirted in**	*the detergent*	
	slid	the plates and cups	*into the water*
Susie's mother	**let**	the water	*out*
food preparation activity sequence excerpt			
Her mother	**began to wash**	the lettuce	
She	**pulled**	the leaves	*from around the heart*
	Plunged	them	*into a sink of cold water*
She	**tore**	them	*into pieces*
	dropped	them	*into a metal colander*
She	**tipped**	the lettuce	*into a bowl*
	began to slice	tomatoes	*quickly*

Table 11.1 displays how transitivity constructs the domestic settings involving Martha in the narration. The material processes indicate the range of activities that Martha undertakes as she 'wiped' and 'began to slice'. The other participants are non-human, such as utensils ('the kettle', 'the plates and cups') and food ('the lettuce',

'tomatoes'). The circumstances locate the environment of the house ('in the middle of the kitchen') and the environment for the processes and participants ('into the water', 'into a metal colander'). Other circumstances imply accompaniment, with the preposition ellipsed as '(with) her hands full of plates', and manner 'quickly'. Clearly what is foregrounded here is the domestic environment. The scene is instantly recognizable to young readers but not often given narrative space in literature.

The accumulation of activity sequences creates a background rhythm of domesticity which is strengthened by the meronymic relationships in the lexical strings. One scene of special interest is the bathroom sequence (Chapter 11) where a discourse of beauty is developed as both Martha and Susie get ready for different parties. The narration focuses attention on their physical bodies and this attention constructs a view of a female body very different from conventional (male) inscriptions. The narration details the dressing and putting on of make-up, with the effect of a zoom camera focusing on Martha and, later, Susie. Table 11.2 sets out some examples of Martha's activity sequences.

Table 11.2   Foregrounding female activity in narration through transitivity and meronymy: Martha

Participant/Actor	**material process**	non-human/ meronymic participants/goal	*circumstance*
applying make-up activity sequence excerpt			
Her mother	**stood**		*in front of the bathroom mirror*
Her face	**filled**	the space	
Her mother	**smoothed on**	some liquid make-up	
	blending	it	*with long strokes of her fingers*
She	**raised**	her eyebrows	
	Brushed	white powder	*into the arch*
		Pale blue	*on the lids*
		mascara thick	*on her black lashes*
	stretched	her lips	*over her teeth*
She	**painted on**	the red lipstick	
	pressed	her lips	*together*
getting dressed for her party excerpt			
She	**stepped into**	a black jumpsuit	
	Pulled	it	*over her hips*
	drawing < >**in**	her breath	

she	**pulled up**	the zip	
	stood back		
	patting	her flat stomach	
Martha's celebration of self			
She	**grinned**		*in the mirror*
She	**grinned**		*at Susie*
She	**clicked**	her finger	
	swung	her hips	
She	**giggled**		
	twirled		*around*
She	**smiled**		*at her reflection*
	held < > out	< her arms >	*from her sides*

In Table 11.2 the narration creates a scene of intimacy, as 'Her face filled the space' asserts. The reader is positioned with Susie as she watches 'her mother' confidently attend to her body and face. Martha's physicality is asserted through the material processes such as 'stepped into, rubbed, smoothed on, pressed, pat(ted)', while her behaviours, 'grinnedx2-giggled-smiled', and related actions, 'clicked-swung-twirled-held out', show her pleasure in her physical body and her celebration of a commonplace female ritual.

When Susie attempts to copy her mother in her own preparation, however, the selection for material processes and circumstances constructs Susie's naivety in this discourse of beauty. The scenes parallel each other and when both sets of activity sequences are compared it is evident how Susie's inexperience in these matters is constructed. Table 11.3 presents Susie's activity sequences.

The contrast between her mother's assured routine and Susie's uncertainty is clearly indicated in the transitivity choices. While Martha 'smoothed on' and 'blend(ed) ... with long strokes of her fingers' (Table 11.2), Susie 'rubbed' (in three different verb forms) the make-up 'in'; the make-up 'streaked almost orange' and then, with a washer, 'started to come off'; Susie's 'glow(ing)' skin is not from the beauty routine but because it is 'red raw'. The make-up, placed in the role of Actor, performs malevolently. In a final direct reversal of Martha's final triumphant gesture, where 'She ... held her arms out from her sides' (p. 86), Susie's action is one of defeat, she 'let her arms fall to her sides' (p. 87).

In both sequences, intimacy is also presented through constructing personal items as participants, in such lexical strings as 'jumpsuit-zip', 'cream-make-up-powder-mascara-lipstick'. This portrait of female activity is effectively sustained through the details of Martha's body

Table 11.3   Foregrounding female activity in narration through transitivity and meronymy: Susie

Participant/Actor	Material process	non-human/ meronymic participants/Goal	circumstance
(Susie)	picked up	the make-up base	
(that her mother had just used)			
(Susie)	poured	some of (the make-up)	onto her hand
	started to rub	(the make-up)	over her face
(The make-up)	streaked		almost orange over her pale cheeks
(Susie)	rubbed < > in	(the make-up)	hard
(Susie)	splashed	water	on her cheeks
	took	a washer	
	rubbed		harder
(The make-up)	started to come off		
Her skin	glowed		red raw
(Susie)	dropped	the washer	into the hand basin
	let < > fall	her arms	to her sides

which are given prominence in both participant and circumstance roles. Table 11.4 indicates examples of the shifting levels of intimacy for both Martha and Susie that is achieved through meronymy.

Column 1 presents the larger body parts named – 'hair, face, stomach, arms' – called a 'macro-level' of intimate detail; Column 2 displays a middle level – 'curls, eyebrows, lips, armpit'; Column 3 shows the tiniest features named – 'breath, lashes, freckles' – at a micro-level of detail.

Both Martha's and Susie's human-meronymic strings construct close-ups of their faces. The reader's view is zoomed from Martha's 'face' into the 'arch' under her eyebrows, her lashes, her lips and teeth. The camera also tracks across Susie's face to the hairs of her eyebrows, those under her armpit ('the half-dozen pale hairs' (p. 86)), her freckles, her eyelids. Through these intimate constructions the novel privileges the young female face and body in a way which resists more dominant media depictions of young women. In doing so, I would suggest, *IAS* articulates a feminist discourse which celebrates the embodied woman.

Table 11.4 Lexical strings showing shifting levels of intimate detail

Martha's body			Susie's body		
Col 1	Col 2	Col 3	Col 1	Col 2	Col 3
macro		micro	macro		micro
hair	curls		face	eyebrows	hairs
face		breath		nose	
face	eyebrows	arch		cheeks	freckles
	lids	lashes		forehead	eyelids
	lips	teeth		crown	
face					bottom lip
stomach			arm	armpit	hairs

6 Classroom work: Interpreting domestic discourses and naming transitivity elements

The class of 10 and 11-year-old students recognized the scenes of domesticity in the kitchen and bathroom: both males and females had participated with their parents in the kitchen and watched their mothers' beauty routines, as Susie does. The teacher used the drama strategy of readers' theatre to highlight the domestic discourses that thread through the novel. The students closely read selected excerpts as preparation for interpreting the text. In order to allocate speech roles and develop dramatic movement, they had to notice who was participating in the scene, what actions were taking place and the circumstances of those actions. Then, in groups, they presented their rehearsed readers' theatre to each other. This strategy positioned the students to make pragmatic use of the transitivity elements on an informal level.

On one occasion only, the teacher drew formal attention to one set of transitivity patterns, presented in Table 11.1 above, to highlight how the novel's realism genre was constructed. The transcript excerpt following shows how the teacher used the drama work as an entry point to observing the transitive elements.

65T	... All right, so we are taking a look at how this book is different from other books we have read and one of ways is that it is so realistic ... how is it realistic – we did this last week
66S	In books normally you don't get people washing up and going shopping and things like that

67T	You mean ordinary family life?
68S	Yeah
69T	But isn't that REAL? Aren't those scenes which we worked on in drama last week very REAL?
70Ss	Yes (together)
71S	You don't usually get the details
72T	So let's have a look at how Libby wrote some of that. And I know you have read this before . . . I have a chart here for us to fill . . .

(T displays chart with four headings adapted from the analysis and explains the headings:

Participant (who) process (action) participant (what) circumstances (other details)

She also displays and explains relevant excerpts from the text on an overhead transparency)

	. . . OK so WHO is the main participant in this section? Who is doing all the actions?
73Ss	Martha, Susie's mother
75T	Yes and what words tell us that?
76Ss	She – Her mother – Susie's mother (T writes them vertically on chart in a blue texta pen)
80T	Excellent. Now think about this. What PROCESSES, what ACTIONS, what VERBS, do you see? You performed these last week

(Ss name different processes and T writes them in a red texta pen. This sequence recurs with different colour texta pens for the other headings)

89T	Now boys and girls, we have these lists which we have built up and they tell us how Libby made her book so real. What would you like to say about it?
90S	She repeats herself – all the 'shes' and 'her mothers'

(T comments positively on each answer and guides their responses across the headings)

92S	It's got lots of tiny details like 'into pieces'
94S	It names 'lettuce', 'tomatoes' . . . the things they are doing

In this excerpt, the teacher used a visual scaffold to emphasize the relationship between the transitive elements. While this excerpt was essentially a naming or labelling exercise, the chart allowed the students to note the repeated participant in subject position, which all referred to Martha. They also observed the details of the activity sequences in the context of how the author had constructed a realism text. This brief sequence served as another moment when the students' attention was drawn to the deployment of language in the novel, where the semantic significance of the scenes had been previously reinforced through the readers' theatre activity. As had occurred at other times in the programme, they were asked to focus on the grammatical qualities and relationships between the words under scrutiny, rather than be solely concerned with their meaning.

7 Conclusion

In this chapter I have attempted to demonstrate how attention to the language of a literary text can provide insights into the levels and range of meanings the text offers, and that young readers are capable of such analysis. As Hasan (1985: 97) states, 'An individual will understand a text only to the extent that she or he possesses a sensitivity to the lexicogrammatical patterns as the creator of meaning potential'. One straightforward way to commence this sensitivity is to be alert to the patterns the text foregrounds. In IAS, the selection for mood, the italicized text presentation and the discursive positioning of the characters through activity sequences and transitivity, all drew attention to themselves as potential areas for analysis. Such attention to the language takes account of 'the child as reader' (Chambers 1980; Stephens 1992) by adding value to their repertoire of reading strategies. When students are taught to look for grammatically-based evidence for the literary themes, discourses and ideologies discussed in class they learn to critically appraise and appreciate the verbal art of the text. They also learn how to recognize how they are being positioned by the discourses, that is, they move towards becoming critical readers.

The transcripts indicate the contribution the scaffold of metalanguage and an explicit pedagogy made to student understanding. The teacher's use of metalanguage, while not extensive, is important as the shared terminology enabled explicit talk about narrative strategies and grammatical construction. In the literature programme the teacher returned to specific scenes previously discussed. She introduced a grammatical knowledge base that was external to the students, rather than drawing only on their personal experiences. This recursive pedagogy ensured that the students developed a deep knowledge of the text, as they moved between analogy and analysis. It also ensured that the explicit attention to the grammar of the text enhanced the enjoyable experience of reading the novel.

References

Chambers, A. (1980), 'The reader in the book', in N. Chambers (ed.), *The Signal Approach to Children's Books*. London: Kestral, pp. 250–75.

Gibbons, P. (2002), *Scaffolding Language Scaffolding Learning. Teaching Second Language Learners in the Mainstream Classroom*. New Hampshire: Heinemann.

Gleeson, L. (1987), *I am Susannah*. North Ryde: Angus and Robertson.

Halliday, M. A. K. (1994), *An Introduction To Functional Grammar*, second edition. London: Edward Arnold.

Hasan, R. (1985), *Linguistics, Language And Verbal Art*. Victoria: Deakin University Press.

Meek, M. (1988), *How Texts Teach What Readers Learn*. Stroud: Thimble Press.

Morris, P. (1993), *Literature And Feminism*. Oxford: Blackwell.

Sharpe, T. (2001), 'Scaffolding in action; snapshots from the classroom', in J. Hammond (ed.), *Scaffolding Teaching and Learning in Language and Literacy Education*. Newtown: Primary English Teaching Association, pp. 31–48.

Sterne, L. (1759/1965), *The Life and Opinions of Tristram Shandy, Gentleman*. Boston: Houghton Mifflin.

Stephens, J. (1992), *Language and Ideology in Children's Fiction*. London and New York: Longman.

Toolan, M. (1988), *Narrative: A Critical Linguistic Introduction*. London and New York: Routledge.

Williams, G. (1986), 'Literary discourse and children's reading development', in J. Collerson and V. Nicoll (eds), *Proceedings of the 7th Macarthur Reading/ Language Symposium: Children, Books and Teachers*. Milperra: Macarthur Institute, pp. 62–73.

12 Guiding senior secondary students towards writing academically-valued responses to poetry

Susan Marshall

1 Introduction

Students begin their secondary school study of poetry having left junior secondary English classrooms where they have been encouraged to make subjective, emotive, even 'gut' responses to the texts they read. Teachers may devise a range of activities which invite students to engage with a poem at an affective level: a dramatic reading or re-enactment, a piece of imaginative writing with an accompanying illustration, a PowerPoint presentation of visuals or images and a selection of songs or music to match the tone, mood or atmosphere of the poem. Without doubt, the tasks designed for students at the junior secondary level are appropriate in terms of pedagogy and methodology. However, they are not designed to produce the sort of texts which are valued at senior secondary level. Here, students meet a whole new genre of written poetry appreciation and analysis for which they have not had sufficient preparation. The transition from their creative, emotive reactions to a more objective, reasoned and considered response, that is to an academic response, needs to be carefully guided.

This chapter, then, shows how students can be brought to a deeper understanding of what is expected of them as writer/responder to literature at the senior level, initiating them into this rather narrow field of poetry appreciation. It uses a case study of a secondary school student learning the genre of response. As in the other chapters of Part Three, readers will find that, while the approach to teaching written poetry analysis described here is underpinned by systemic functional linguistics (SFL), it is a practical application of the theory. It is hoped that this approach can be easily understood and implemented by teachers whose background in SFL may vary, including those who have had very little exposure to it.

2 Context of the case study

This case study centres around 17-year-old Sophia (pseudonym) who came from a non-English speaking background, and who attended local government schools in Adelaide, South Australia from Year 1 (aged 6) to Year 11 (aged 16). Very little English was spoken in the home, Greek being the family language. The family made the decision to enrol Sophia at Eynesbury College for her final year of senior secondary study, Year 12. This school, in which I was working at the time, is somewhat unique in South Australia, in that it is an independent, non-denominational, co-educational, pre-tertiary college for students completing their last two years of senior secondary education. There are no prerequisites for entry to this school, except perhaps a desire to achieve and a general goal to secure a tertiary education place. Enrolments are drawn from over fifty secondary schools in greater Adelaide and include some students who have been home-schooled. Students can choose to come to the college for either their final (Year 12) or their last two years of senior secondary education (Years 11 and 12). They enter the school, then, with diverse skills and from very mixed educational backgrounds and life experiences, so that it is often the case that a teacher will have, effectively, only nine months to prepare newly enrolled students for their final external exams. Sophia presented as bright, enthusiastic and highly motivated and indicated early on that she had invested a great deal in coming to the school and that her goal was to pursue her studies in art and economics at university.

It is probably safe to say that most students of Sophia's age in Australia know very little about the structure and function of the language they speak, read and write, and it seems that in many Adelaide secondary schools at least, little has changed since Martin (1986: 12) made his claim that 'most teachers and students share next to no knowledge about language'. Whilst this may no longer be true, there are many students of Sophia's age who are completing their secondary education without the benefit of the changes that have been made to teacher-training. These students would struggle to name and label basic grammatical items in a clause or sentence and, more importantly, would not be able to explain the reasons for making particular grammatical choices and patterns in their writing. Some may have been introduced to the term *genre*; fewer would have heard of a system for describing elements of their written responses.

To be judged as successful performers in the areas of written responses to texts at the senior secondary level, students are required to demonstrate considerable mastery over a range of skills. Very often, assessment criteria will centre on a student's ability to identify the ideas, values and interests represented by the texts. Students are also required to show that they can engage with the ideas presented at a personal, analytical and critical level. In addition, many curricula expect students to show a depth of understanding of the interplay between the text creator and their own values, beliefs and experiences. Moreover, students need to reveal their awareness of the constructed nature of texts and of the influence of the sociocultural contexts in generating both the text itself and the response of the reader. Besides all this, they must also respond to texts, in this case poetry, in writing that demonstrates clarity, a depth of engagement and an ability to use the appropriate form and register. A student confronted with these assessment criteria, and having had little preparation, must feel quite daunted. Hasan's (1985: 27) statement that 'perhaps where verbal art is extraordinary is precisely the multiplicity of standards that appear equally relevant to its evaluation' might resonate with many students, and teachers.

3 Use of metalanguage

Before focusing on the study itself, I will make clear my position on the question of explicit teaching and use of a SFL metalanguage. Many researchers and practitioners fully support teaching students a metalanguage that 'permits students to distance themselves from experiences or texts and discuss them with considerable objectivity' (Johns 1997: 128). I most certainly agree with this approach, aware that, as we see in the chapters in this book, we can often be guilty of underestimating our students' capacity to grasp what seems like a 'new' language, with fairly technical terminology. After all, they seem to have no difficulty using the metalanguages which have grown up around new technology like text messages and chat rooms. In the case I describe here, however, although I strongly advocate the teaching of SFL metalanguage as part of classroom methodology that derives naturally from the teaching/learning process, the very limited time-frame in which to prepare Sophia for the public examination prevailed. I made a conscious decision not to introduce any formal terminology, SFL or any other, while leading Sophia through the taxing process of questioning almost everything she had regarded as appropriate for writing academic responses to poetry. This was harder than it might sound and, rather than simplifying matters, it presented a number of challenges as I grappled with how best to describe, explain and categorize the choices that were being made and how to discuss the impact of these lexicogrammatical choices on Sophia's writing: paradoxically both limiting it, in terms of creating, defining and sustaining the genre, and at the same time enriching her responses through a new refinement and precision of expression, appreciation, discussion, analysis, critique and evaluation in a situation of shared meaning-making. It will be obvious that I had to resort to some 'easier' generic labels for grammatical items to minimize intimidation and confusion, but anyone familiar with the technical SFL terminology can recognize the theoretical basis. For example, I referred to nouns as *things* and used terms such as *actions, thoughts, feelings* to refer to verbs or processes, always aiming to elicit these from her and then reinforcing the *idea* or *concept* behind the grammatical function by careful and selective questioning, examples of which can be found later in the discussion.

Although no SFL terminology was used in the case that follows, it is worth pointing out that, following a whole staff initiative, it was decided to offer a compulsory course in academic writing, based exclusively on SFL, to all students enrolling in the college for the two-year programme. This semester course most certainly teaches the metalanguage of SFL and the programme is supported and reinforced by an online interactive CD-ROM course entitled *WRAP: Writing for Academic Purposes* (Marshall 2002), easily accessible to all students at any time throughout their time at the college, via the intranet.

4 Applying SFL: the case study

If students begin their engagement with poetry at an emotive level and have spent many years in the junior English classroom completing tasks that validate this response, they inevitably find themselves in conflict with the expectations of curriculum assessment in the senior secondary school which demands of them a more formal, distanced and objective analysis and a lucid, considered written discussion. It would certainly be the aim of all English teachers that students engage with literature in the deepest and most meaningful way, acknowledging that this verbal art form is unique in terms of the curriculum: requiring not a body of knowledge to be learned and regurgitated but rather inviting students to engage in, and make meaning of the range and variety of experiences that is our shared humanity. As lofty as this aim is, there comes a time, as Hasan (1985: 27) states, when 'appreciation must give way to appraisal; the private must be made public; the internalized must be overtly externalizable – it should be possible to talk coherently about the bases of one's preference and evaluation'. Clearly, students need to be given a framework for writing about their initial, very valid, emotive responses in an effective academic manner.

The poetry unit began the year's course in English with a study of a short and deceptively simple sonnet entitled *Pieta*, by the twentieth-century Australian poet, James McAuley (1917–1976). For several lessons the class discussed a range of features of the poem and wrote notes and brief draft responses to a number of questions. Rather than show the class examples of poetry responses at this initial stage, I wanted to see just what these new students could write, so that their responses to the first essay task would act as a diagnostic tool, directing the focus of my teaching for the poetry unit. However, good use was later made of model essays, as were examiners' comments on previous exam paper questions. Students' responses to the first essay question below varied, although none of them as clearly in need of attention as Sophia's.

How does James McAuley explore the idea of loss in his poem *Pieta*?

The first paragraph only of Sophia's essay appears in Text 1; the remainder of her essay appeared in very much the same style. No changes have been made to spelling or other unwise or inappropriate language choices:

Text 1 Sophia's first draft (February)
OK well what have we got to discuss today? Its pretty obvious that the guy in this poem can't get over the fact that his baby who was premature died at one day old. Lets face it it would be awful for anyone. You really feel for this new dad because he tries to work out why his son died but can't find any answers. Lots of people die for no reason and this can be pretty sad. He asks alot of questions to the mother and God and sort of blames both of them in away. When he says, 'with one hand touched you' and 'wounds made with the Cross'. So James speaks a lot about losing someone special and how it really gets to people and makes them stay sad and grieving.

4.1   Register: awareness of audience and purpose

Sophia has made a clear and spontaneous response to this poem but it is easy to sympathize with a teacher who receives this piece of writing, and realizes just how much work needs to be done to bring it to a barely passing standard in terms of the assessment criteria for such a task at this level. The task for teachers here is to make explicit to students like Sophia exactly what it is that makes a text 'academic'. Even if Sophia were to proofread her response for spelling and other 'mechanical' errors, this 'essay' would not be valued as an academic text. The fact that a written academic response, is 'intended to encode our considered reflections on a topic' (Eggins 1994: 58) and has a structure whose features are determined well before the text itself is executed, would be foreign concepts to Sophia and many of her peers.

So, when Sophia's essay was returned and she scored a low failing grade, she was naturally devastated. Along with the grade, however, were detailed comments about some 'language and structural problems' that had let down the effectiveness of her spontaneously genuine and otherwise 'correct' interpretation of the poem, as well as an invitation to work with me on her essay-writing skills, as Eynesbury offers students a unique opportunity to work with teachers on an individual basis. Outside of the 2-hour lecture per cycle, teachers are available to work with students at other nominated times. In addition to this, the college has a literacy support coordinator whose work supports that of the teaching staff, often reinforcing the academic writing skills taught in the *WRAP* programme.

For most students who face difficulties with their writing similar to those of Sophia's, there are problems such as essay structure, the logical sequencing of ideas, spelling and proofreading strategies to deal with first. There is also the more demanding task of raising students' awareness of the choices they have for making meaning in their responses, and which involve a certain textual 'shifting around', a manipulation of the structure and order of their text. There is also work to be done in the area of word choice, of lexis. These two generic terms of 'structure' and 'language' are useful starting points to begin work with a student such as Sophia, despite the fact that these do not exist separately in terms of how a text works. When students see the way that these elements of structure and language work together to create and shape a text, they can begin to have more control over the kind of academic writing they need to produce in order to be effective and successful.

In Sophia's case her response definitely fails to meet the assessment criterion that requires students to respond in writing using the appropriate register. This is the most obvious problem with her essay, evidenced by her opening line. Her essay is dominated by language features of spoken discourse. This shows the difficulties many students have in recognizing the very different language choices that are made when creating spoken or written texts. Despite our friendly and informal classroom environment, or perhaps because of it, Sophia has misread the social role relationship that should exist between the student/writer and the teacher/reader in this particular field of academic endeavour. This has had an effect on her choice of language and the resultant impact of her response. Her response is chatty and informal, and the everyday lexis, such as 'dad', 'guy' and 'pretty sad' reflects this. The essay opens in a dynamic way – 'OK well what have we got to discuss today?' almost as if she were actually speaking to her peers in a discussion group situation. The lexis is inappropriate for the field of poetry analysis, and the use of colloquial expressions such as 'it really gets to people' and the abbreviations 'can't' and 'its' (*sic*) have no place in an academic response. She continues in a personal manner, addressing her readers through the second person pronoun and even using the first name of the poet! Sophia has encountered what Schleppegrell (2004) highlights as one of the keys to academic success: the challenge to use language in new ways that are different from everyday use.

In one sense, the mechanical problems with Sophia's essay are quite easy to treat. She quickly understood the simple instruction that drafts needed to be proofread carefully, and that no contractions or abbreviations were permitted in an academic essay, something that had not previously been pointed out to her. With the understanding of the need for these more formal choices, Sophia also realized that some of her other language choices would also need to change. When it was explained to her that people take on different roles as producers or recipients of texts, she could see that the essay was a kind of 'staged' piece of writing. This indeed is one of the keys to students' understanding of written genres. They need to become aware of and explore the constructed nature of both literature texts and their own responses to them; how each follows a schematic patterning so that 'the common purposes of an academic culture are achieved with language' (Droga and Humphrey 2002: 2). This crucial awareness of how goal-oriented meaning-making determines lexicogrammatical choices is the starting point for academic writing. Sophia knew that I would be reading and marking her essay and she mistook the friendly rapport that we had developed in the classroom for the kind of text that she thought she needed to write. Once she realized that I was, in certain respects, shifting my role to one of 'expert' and she was writing as 'informed student', and that she needed a different language with which to communicate her insights and analysis, she set about writing a very different draft. It did not take her long to work out that invitations to include the reader such as 'what have we got to discuss today?' and personal commentary such as 'you really feel for this dad' had no place in acknowledging and maintaining the appropriate social role relationship.

4.2   Register: nominalization, a powerful grammatical resource

It was not simply a matter of Sophia deleting the inappropriate lines from her essay. Take, for example, her statement that 'you really feel for this dad' and consider the complex process of text manipulation that she was asked to undertake in order to redraft this. Sophia was asked to write a single word answer describing a thing, either concrete or abstract, to several prompt questions from me about the poem. This strategy was aimed at eliciting from Sophia a list of nouns and, given her very limited understanding of grammatical terminology, either traditional or systemic, I relied upon the generic word *thing* for this task. Referring to the first few sentences of her essay, she was asked the question: 'Exactly what feeling do you have for this father?'. After some thought, Sophia wrote 'pity'. She was then asked to write a sentence using the word 'pity'. She then produced: 'I feel pity for this father'. In response to two subsequent questions, 'What has made you feel this way?' and, in order to emphasize the wider audience and therefore universal readership, 'Who has managed to make *the readers of this poem* feel this way towards the father?'. Sophia responded '(his) grief' and 'McAuley'. She expanded these into: 'I feel pity for him because of his grief' and 'McAuley makes us feel sorry for the father'. This last response showed her appreciation of the subtle shift from the highly personal to the more distanced and objective stance needed in an academic response. She was then asked to write a sentence incorporating the three choices she had made. She found it relatively easy to write 'McAuley has made us feel pity for the father in his time of grief'.

This ability to condense an idea into one thing, or noun, is prevalent in academic writing (Halliday and Martin 1993). While Sophia's original essay was grammatically complex, it was at the same time lexically sparse, as usual in spoken language discourse (Halliday 1985). Spoken language is language as action, complete with the focus on people as participants, engaged in doing things, as in Sophia's response to the poem: 'feeling', 'dying', 'not finding answers', 'not getting over a baby's death'. A more academic response requires a move away from this to language that is rhetorically organized, and is an activity which, is 'rehearsed' (Eggins 1994: 74). It is the result of planning, consideration, drafting and polishing and, above all, uses the language not of action, but of reflection. The way academic writers effect this shift is by using nominalization, a form of what Halliday (1994: 82–3) refers to as 'grammatical metaphor'. It is a feature of academic writing especially suited to the field of literary analysis, which deals with ideas, concepts, themes and ideologies, what Hasan (1985: 98) calls 'second-order meanings'.

Using a similar guided questioning strategy, Sophia was asked to highlight sections of her essay where she had used 'action language'. She readily identified such examples as 'losing someone', 'he asks a lot of questions' and 'he can't get over the fact that his baby died'. She was then asked to replace each action with a single word. In response to the action of 'losing someone' she substituted the single word 'loss'. In a similar way she isolated the words 'questioning' and 'inability to accept this death'. Sophia had elevated her writing from the immediacy of action, and therefore the literal, to a greater abstraction and timelessness through her lexicogrammatical choices. Nominalization allows a writer to 'organize texts in terms of abstract ideas, reasons and causes etc ... that is, rhetorically' (Droga and Humphrey 2002: 133). By focusing on the theme and idea behind the poem rather than putting the emphasis on the actions of the participants who, in this case, are less important than the universal idea of loss being explored in the poem, she had found a rich resource in nominalization, capturing a new precision in her writing. In a very real sense Sophia has been empowered as a writer by using nominalization, a feature of academic writing that Halliday suggests has come to serve as a mark of prestige and power (Halliday 1994: 353). With time and practice, Sophia would learn the value of using nominalization in her academic responses, realizing that it allows for concise representations of processes and qualities (Lock 1996).

4.3   Register: building lexical density through the nominal group

In addition, once Sophia had grasped the technique of nominalization she was open to further building up the lexical density of her essay by condensing meaning through the use of complex nominal groups. Initially, Sophia did what many students do when writing about poetry, confusing the intimate and emotional subject matter of a sonnet such as *Pieta* with the type of language choices needed to discuss the poem, largely those of spoken texts centring on the interpersonal. Variations in spoken and written discourse types can be seen as a cline (Leckie-Tarry 1995: 64), where the most formal written texts, like the ones Sophia's essay was struggling to imitate, are characterized by abstraction, and by language choices that are formal, metaphorical and symbolic, and where the text packages meaning as product rather than as the action or mental processes of spoken texts. Sophia, like many adolescents, produced writing with a focus on the concrete and on her own life experiences, experiences realized through such language choices as personal pronouns and mental processes: dying, feeling, finding answers and blaming to cite just a few from her draft. She soon learned, however, that nouns are useful grammatical items for an academic writer, allowing for more to be said by creating room through expansion of the nominal group, for other items that can describe, enumerate, classify, qualify, quantify and intensify (Halliday 1994).

Sophia went back to her second draft and looked again at the examples of action language that she had nominalized with the aim of trying to be more precise about those 'things' she was now discussing. Thus, the initial sentence 'the guy in the poem can't get over the fact that his baby who was premature died at one day old', nominalized in her second draft as 'the father's inability to accept this death', finally expanded into 'the father's inability to accept this **innocent** and **untimely** death', thereby demonstrating her control over some important features that go to make up an academic text. In qualifying this premature baby's death as 'innocent and untimely', Sophia demonstrates that she has engaged with the poem at a personal level, aware of the impact of such a devastating event, but she has resisted writing about this in overly sentimental and cloying ways. She confessed that she enjoyed this part of her drafting the most as she could be, to quote her, 'her most emotional' and it is perhaps this textual resource of creating complex nominal groups that teachers could exploit to match the need students have for finding appropriate ways to write about affective aspects of a poem but at the same time in a way that is academically valued.

Overall, this increased awareness of the role of nominal groups to create academic register and to build up meaning in texts enabled Sophia to experience greater success with her writing (see Chapters 5 and 7 for more examples of this type of work). Martin extends this further by claiming that students need to 'write abstract discourse if they are to interpret their world in a critical way' (Martin 1993: 219) and cites the foregrounding of nominal groups instead of clause complexes as the grammatical realization of such abstraction in writing. Clearly, however, this method of changing and altering segments of a text will only go so far, as Sophia soon realized, and 'cutting and pasting' left her with 'bits that didn't fit together'. This discovery led her to consider another feature of academic writing.

4.4   Register: modality in literary response

When Sophia had reorganized her content into nominalization, she found that a gap had now been created which needed to be filled by a tensed verb in order for her sentences to be complete. After examining models of good poetry essays, she was full of questions regarding writers' use of expressions such as 'seems' and 'appears'; she was able to propose her own interpretation for these examples of modality, saying that the writer is 'not always absolutely positive' his or her interpretation is correct. This ability to position oneself as a responder to literature texts who acknowledges the myriad interpretations possible is crucial in a field where well supported judgement, appraisal and evaluation are encouraged and necessary for success. Modality allows writers to 'acknowledge the contentiousness of a particular position ... or the deference ... for those with alternative views' (White 1998: 22–5). Rather than using an unmodalized declarative clause, as in 'his inability to accept. . .and his need to assign blame **are** captured in his constant questioning', Sophia chose to move away from this monoglossic reading of the poem, recognizing that not all readers would necessarily agree with her interpretation. By selecting the modal adjunct, '**seemed** captured', Sophia demonstrated her ability to move her text towards heteroglossia and away from what Coffin describes as the assumption 'that the proposition is unproblematic and that it enjoys broad consensus' (Coffin 2002: 506). She also found that words such as 'explores', 'provokes', 'reflects' and 'evokes', which she termed 'power words', appeared quite frequently, and in the present tense, in exemplary poetry essays. It was not long before Sophia was back at her draft, adding her 'power' words: 'explores', 'captured', mirrored' and 'evokes'. In selecting these metaphors Sophia demonstrated a control over the shape of her text, the meanings she wanted to make and how she wanted her readers to perceive her analysis and interpretation of the poem. She was beginning to understand the interplay between, on the one hand, how to evaluate phenomenon, in this case the poem, and how to acknowledge other possible positions. By doing this Sophia set about constructing a particular relationship with her readers through her lexicogrammatical choices.

4.5   Towards textual coherence – Theme choices

Sophia could see that her draft now resembled more closely that of an academic essay although there was one other textual skill that would make it more academically valued. After she had grappled successfully with nominalization as 'a resource for compacting information' (Fries 2004: 35) she could now manipulate this further to achieve greater text coherence, an essential feature of academic texts. I explained to Sophia that readers need signposts on which to 'hang' meanings, thereby helping them find their way through a text. In our English language system, we tend to put the main part of the message to be communicated in first place in the sentence as a 'jumping-off point, or point of departure' (Lock 1996: 222). This textual device, known as Theme in SFL, had the ability to create some potential confusion for Sophia who related the term to the main idea in a literature text and, for this reason, I again steered clear of SFL terminology. However, I asked Sophia to look at her sentence and to consider the effect created by what she had selected to place at the beginning of each sentence. Text 2 shows the Theme choices Sophia had made in this particular draft:

Text 2   Sophia's Theme choices
> *Loss* is a universal human experience. *It is clear that James McAuley* explores the devastating effect of a premature baby's death on a bewildered father. *The quotes 'with one hand to touch you' and 'wounds made with the Cross'* seem to capture the father's inability to accept this untimely and innocent death and his need to assign blame. *McAuley's use of enjambement* which breaks the rhyme of this poignant sonnet mirrors the father's shattered emotions and the premature death of the baby. *McAuley* is able to evoke great pity, as the title implies, for the father in his time of loss.

Because Sophia had not realized the importance of thematic development, her text fails to 'hang together' or to offer enough signposts for the reader to follow her line of discussion. Her choice of topical Theme tends to distract the reader, shifting the focus from an initial foregrounding of the essay's subject, *loss*, to the poet's techniques, *quotes*, which have not been adequately contextualized, continuing the theme of poetic techniques, *the use of enjambement*, and concluding with a focus on the poet, *McAuley*.

I asked Sophia to keep in mind that by inverting the order of her two-clause sentences, a pattern which is very common in literature responses, one of cause and effect or complementary clause structure, she would find that she could achieve a much clearer and more cohesive text, and one that could be linked more closely to the question. We spent some time cutting her sentences into clauses and rearranging these, discussing the effect on meaning that each choice created.

Armed with this final addition to her array of tools with which to manipulate her initial draft, she went away to finalize her essay for resubmission, the first paragraph of which is reproduced as Text 3:

Text 3   Sophia's final submission

Loss is a universal human experience. James McAuley's Pieta explores the devastating effect of a premature baby's death on a bewildered father. His inability to accept this untimely and innocent death and his need to assign blame seem captured in his constant questioning of both the child's mother, who at least was able 'with one hand' to 'touch' the baby, and God, who has inflicted lasting 'wounds made with the Cross'. Both the father's shattered emotions and the premature death of the baby are mirrored in McAuley's use of enjambment which breaks the rhyme of this poignant sonnet. McAuley is able to evoke great pity, as the title implies, for this father in his time of loss.

If we compare this paragraph to Sophia's initial attempt in Text 1, the difference is quite staggering. She has demonstrated an emerging understanding of what it means to operate in an academic context, using a very narrow and patterned discourse type. Evidently, in such a limited time, Sophia grasped some features of academic writing more readily than others. Her choices for Theme and thereby thematic patterning in her text may have been more judiciously made to effect a greater text flow (Daneš 1974; Fries 1981; Schleppegrell 2000; Alonso and McCabe 2003); however, she has attempted to foreground and focus predominantly upon the concept of loss as experienced by a grieving father, thereby showing control over her interpretation of the poem's central idea.

5 Conclusion

It has been my experience that many students find the transition from the kind of responses they are invited to make to literature in the junior school to those they must produce in the senior secondary school a difficult process. Faced with a complex and demanding set of assessment criteria, and equipped with little instruction as to how to meet these, their responses remain at a personal, affective and informal level. By demonstrating how to craft responses that take advantage of a number of textual and lexicogrammatical resources students can begin to write in ways that reveal their ability to explore the ideas, concepts and themes of literature in deeply analytical ways, as formal, serious reflections of a distant, objective specialist; characteristics well suited to and highly valued in an academic context.

Postscript

Sophia passed her final external English Studies examination, with a creditable B. She also secured a university place. She continues to write her own poetry but has not written a poetry essay since leaving school! She claims she still remembers and uses the 'tricks' she learned in our workshops to complete her university assignments.

References

Alonso, I. and McCabe, A. (2003), 'Improving text flow in ESL learner compositions', *The Internet TESL Journal*, Vol. IX, No 2, February. Available: www.iteslj.org.

Coffin, C. (2002), 'The voices of history: theorizing the interpersonal semantics of historical discourses', *Text*, 22, (4), 503–28.

Daneš, F. (1974), 'Functional sentence perspective and the organization of the text', in F. Daneš (ed.), *Papers in Functional Sentence Perspective*. Prague: Academia, pp. 106–28.

Droga, L. and Humphrey, S. (2002), *Getting Started with Functional Grammar*. Sydney: Target Texts.

Eggins, S. (1994), *An Introduction to Systemic Functional Linguistics*. London: Pinter.

Fries, P. (1981), 'On the status of Theme in English: Arguments from discourse', *Forum Linguisticum*, 6, 1–38.

— (2004), 'What makes a text coherent?', in D. Banks (ed.), *Text and Texture*. L'Harmattan: Paris, pp. 9–50.

Halliday, M. A. K. (1985), *Spoken and Written Language*. Geelong: Deakin University Press.

— (1994), *An Introduction to Functional Grammar*. London: Edward Arnold.

Halliday, M. A. K. and Martin, J. R. (eds) (1993), *Writing Science: Literacy and Discursive Power*. London: Falmer Press.

Hasan, R. (1985), *Linguistics, Language and Verbal Art*. Geelong: Deakin University Press.

Johns, A. (1997), *Text, Role, and Context*. Cambridge: Cambridge University Press.

Leckie-Tarry, H. (1995). *Language and Context: A Functional Linguistic Theory of Register*. London: Pinter.

Lock, G. (1996), *Functional English Grammar: an Introduction for Second Language Teachers*. Cambridge: Cambridge University Press.

Marshall, S. A. (2002), *WRAP-Writing for Academic Purposes*, CD-ROM. Adelaide: Method Media.

Martin, J. R. (1986), 'Intervening in the process of writing development', in J. R. Martin and C. Painter (eds), *Writing to Mean: Teaching Genres across the Curriculum*. Sydney, Applied Linguistics Association of Australia Occasional Papers Number 9, pp. 11–43.

— (1993), 'Technicality and abstraction: language for the creation of specialized texts', in Halliday and Martin (eds), pp. 203–20.

Schleppegrell, M. (2000), 'How SFL can inform writing instruction: the grammar of expository essays', *Revista Canaria de Estudios Ingleses*, 40, 171–88.

— (2004), *The Language of Schooling: A Functional Linguistics Perspective*. New Jersey: Lawrence Erlbaum Assoc.

White, P. (1998), 'Towards a grammar of power and solidarity – developments in the linguistics of evaluation, inter-subjectivity, and ideological position'. Paper presented at the *Tenth Euro-international Systemic Functional Workshop*. The University of Liverpool, 22–25 July.

13 Emergent disciplinarity: a comparative study of Theme in undergraduate essays in geography and history of science

Ann Hewings and Sarah North

1 Introduction

Research into academic writing may take as its focus the professional academic or the student, both of whom have to produce texts which conform in their respective ways to the expectations of the discipline. While investigations of the disciplinary features of professional academic writing add to our understanding of the sociology of knowledge and the rhetorical and epistemological underpinnings of academic discourse, research into student writing may be used to understand and facilitate the process by which novices gradually learn to write in ways that are acceptable within their discipline. So far, however, there has been little comparison of student writing across different disciplines. This is an area which has significance for many of today's undergraduates, who often move between courses that represent different disciplinary expectations. This study focuses on the essays produced by students in two different disciplines – geography and history of science – to examine how far their writing may be affected by the nature of their previous disciplinary study. In particular, we consider the students' use of Theme, as a feature that is susceptible to discipline-specific variation.

Our comparison of emergent disciplinarity brings together two separate studies of undergraduate writing, one by Hewings (1999) involving full-time first and third year geography students and the other by North (2003) involving part-time students of history of science with contrasting academic backgrounds in science or arts. Both studies used linguistic analyses based on the notion of Theme (Halliday 1994) as a textual organizer and indicator of rhetorical shaping in text structure. The exact methods of analysis were not identical and reanalysis of the data has been undertaken to make comparisons possible. The studies also involved the collection of interview and questionnaire data, providing insights which are used to inform the discussion.

We begin by reviewing research on disciplinary discourse before describing our own studies and the methods of analysis used. After discussing comparative data and the effects of disciplinarity, we conclude with implications for developing disciplinary understandings drawing on the notions of an apprenticeship cline (MacDonald 1994) or a network of semiotic domains (Gee 2001).

2 Research into disciplinary discourse

There is considerable research evidence of the discipline-specific nature of professional academic writing. A corpus-analytic study by Biber (1988) across a range of genres found that, within academic prose, it was possible to identify distinct disciplinary areas based on differences in the use of particular linguistic features. Other research (e.g. Bazerman 1988; Myers 1990; Swales 1990) has demonstrated that such differences in academic writing reflect the social and epistemological characteristics of the discipline. Work by Halliday and Martin (1993), for example, isolated features of science writing such as the preponderance of long nominal groups acting as a shorthand reference to previous work. MacDonald (1994) focused on the types of item in subject position in journal articles in psychology, history and literature and identified disciplinary preferences for particular or abstract subjects. Other researchers have also compared writing across disciplines, finding differences in a variety of linguistic features (e.g. MacDonald 1994; Swales *et al* 1998; Hyland 2000; Groom 2005). The main text-type analysed has been the research article, perhaps because of its important role in disciplinary construction, although similar disciplinary differences have also been reported in masters and doctoral theses (Charles 2003; Samraj 2004). Work on undergraduate texts is also indicating that disciplinarity is a feature even in novice genres (Drury and Webb 1991; Lillis 1997; Lea and Street 1998; Walvoord and McCarthy 1990).

Research in educational psychology suggests that students' beliefs about the nature of knowledge and their approaches to study vary along disciplinary lines (see, for example, Entwistle and Tait 1995; Paulsen and Wells 1998). Work by Kolb has indicated how initial predispositions may lead to disciplinary socialization:

> For students, education in an academic field is a continuing process of
> selection and socialization to the pivotal norms of the field ... Over time,
> these selection and socialization pressures combine to produce an
> increasingly impermeable and homogenous disciplinary culture and
> correspondingly specialized student orientations to learning.
>
> (Kolb 1981: 233)

As students become socialized within a disciplinary culture, their
academic writing may be expected to begin exhibiting characteristic
features of that discipline. However, the process by which students
come to make sense of and participate in academic discourse is not
necessarily straightforward.

In the United States, the tradition of teaching college composition
has in recent times shifted focus from generic academic writing to more
disciplinary-based writing. Writing-across-the-curriculum (WAC) has
led researchers to examine both the writing activities and the social
and institutional contexts which students experience. Walvoord and
McCarthy (1990), for example, undertook a comprehensive study of
undergraduate writing in four disciplines, based on student writing,
peer responses to drafts, student interviews and classroom observations. MacDonald (1994) suggests that students move along a
continuum in engaging with academic discourse (see Figure 13.1).
She posed the question whether or not students should be given help in
negotiating their way along this continuum and concluded in favour of
initiation through immersion, picking up the necessary genre knowledge through entering the disciplinary conversation.

| non-academic writing | → | generalized academic writing | novice approximations | → | expert insider prose |

Figure 13.1   A continuum from novice to expert practice

In Australia and the UK, an 'academic literacies' approach has
grown in significance in recent years, offering an alternative to the
immersion strategy discussed by MacDonald. The focus is on enabling
all students, whatever their background, to succeed at university level.
There has been particular emphasis on essay writing, based on
observations that students often do not understand the conventions of
essayist literacy, do not share the premises of their teachers, and
therefore fail to understand the messages they are being given about
what is expected in essay writing (Drury and Webb 1991; Lillis 1997;
Lea and Street 1998). The difficulties that students may have in

making sense of academic discourse practices are illustrated by Wineburg's discussion of a high school history class, which highlighted a contrast between an expert view of history as 'a belief system in which texts [are] defined by their authors', and the students' tendency to view history as 'not a process of puzzling about authors' intentions or situating texts in a social world but of gathering information, with texts serving as the bearers of information' (Wineburg 1991: 510). While such understandings may emerge over time through immersion, academic literacy practitioners would aim to demystify the process – helping students to see the underlying purposes and values of disciplinary writing and their linguistic realizations.

Work in Australian universities has developed from attempts to provide this sort of scaffolding at school level, underpinned by arguments about the importance of teaching children 'the sort of control and ownership that comes with literacy' (Kalantzis and Cope 1993: 57). The emphasis has been on explicating curriculum genres and their lexicogrammatical features. In geography, Wignell et al (1989) have examined the need for pupils to construct taxonomies which distil the abstract knowledge of the discipline. In history, Coffin has traced the development of specific lexicogrammatical features in writing at different levels (Veel and Coffin 1996; Coffin 1997, 2000, this volume), outlining a movement from the sequential organization of 'chronicling genres' to the more abstract rhetorical organization of 'arguing genres'. This development, she suggests, is part of the 'apprenticeship process of learning how to mean like a historian' (Coffin 1997: 227). Like MacDonald's continuum (Figure 13.1), this 'cline of apprenticeship' (Martin 2002: 272) suggests movement along a trajectory from novice to expert.

Other studies suggest, however, that a linear model may over-simplify the nature of disciplinary learning. For example, Samraj's (1995) study revealed the interdisciplinary variation experienced by postgraduate students in three courses in environmental science, illustrating the complexity even within one discipline for students writing different text types with different epistemological bases for different audiences. A further complication at undergraduate level is that specialist courses may be studied for general educational purposes, rather than to qualify as expert insiders (Russell and Yañez 2002). An alternative model of the way that students learn disciplinary discourses may be that of a network rather than a cline (Gee 2001), where familiarization with one semiotic domain may be more or less difficult depending on which other semiotic domains the student has already mastered.

In order to investigate the way in which students learn to produce acceptable disciplinary writing, we need to understand the nature of the writing they undertake, including the ways in which it differs from writing in other disciplines. Although research has been carried out at tertiary level, looking at both undergraduate and postgraduate writing (see, for example, Jones *et al* 1999; Ravelli and Ellis 2004), relatively little comparative work has been done on student writing in different disciplines. In particular, there has been little study of disciplinary learning when students approach from different routes. Our study compares undergraduate writing in the disciplines of history of science and geography, investigating the way that the students' use of Theme may reflect disciplinary differences in knowledge construction. In discussing the results, we consider the way previous study background affects disciplinary learning and how such learning may relate to writing success.

3 The research projects

North's research looked at a course in history of science (HoS) at the Open University, UK, a distance teaching institution which by its nature attracts a diverse range of students. The course is at level two – equivalent to the second year of a traditional full-time undergraduate degree in England. HoS can form part of either a BA or a BSc programme and as a result attracts students from both arts and science backgrounds. In their previous study, students would have undertaken assessed writing in a variety of different courses. It is therefore possible that they had begun to acquire discipline-specific orientations towards academic writing which would be observable in differences between the writing of students from arts and science backgrounds. To investigate this, 61 student essays were analysed (3079 t-units), 33 from 'arts' students and 28 from 'science' students. The essays were taken from four different assignments, but for each assignment all students wrote on the same topic.

The study by Hewings examined writing by first and third year students studying for a single honours degree in geography, either BA or BSc. The students had all come more or less straight to university after taking final school examinations at the age of eighteen. Geography was chosen for this research as the subject area incorporates traditions of enquiry that span the sciences and the social sciences/humanities. Physical geography draws upon methods and theories from biology, physics and chemistry, while human geography has closer affinities to economics, sociology and history.

Sixteen essays (1,243 t-units) were analysed on topics in human geography and in physical geography from those who scored highly and from those who received relatively poor marks. Students in the first year were all doing the same courses, while third year courses were selected from a range of options.

4 The analytical methodology

Both studies used, among other methodologies, an analysis of Theme choices in student writing. Theme, within the systemic functional linguistic tradition (Fries 1983; Halliday 1994), is realized in English by the initial constituent of the clause, organizing meanings at local clause level and at discourse level. Theme is 'the point of departure for the message ... the element the speaker selects for 'grounding' what he is going to say' (Halliday 1994: 34). Martin (1992: 11) describes first position in the clause in terms of highlighting the 'speaker's angle on the experience being constructed'. Theme may also be viewed more dynamically in terms of shaping the interpretation of succeeding text by limiting the options available (Mauranen 1993; Ravelli 1995, 2004).

While agreeing on the significance of the beginning of a clause in organizing the message and creating a dynamic angle on the unfolding text, researchers have had greater difficulty in reaching consensus over what elements should be included within the Theme, that is, where the Theme ends and the rest of the clause, the Rheme, starts. In our original separate analyses, we delimited Theme differently, Hewings choosing a more conservative interpretation and North taking a more inclusive approach. In order to allow comparisons, we have reanalysed the data to harmonize as much as possible; and the method of identifying Theme set out in this chaper is the result of that harmonization.

Theme is identified at the level of the t-unit, defined as 'an independent clause together with all hypotactically related clauses which are dependent on it' (Fries 1994: 229). In order to resolve differences between the two studies in the treatment of coordination, coordinated clauses with ellipted subjects are treated as single t-units. Sentence fragments are not classified. Following the traditional Hallidayan definition (Halliday 1994), Theme is identified as everything up to and including the first ideational element. This ideational element, realized by subject, predicator, complement, or circumstantial adjunct, is known as the topical Theme. Elements preceding topical Theme are classified as either textual Theme or interpersonal Theme along the lines set out by Halliday (1994).

We do, however, deviate from a strictly Hallidayan classification of Theme by recognizing a wider range of non-congruent interpersonal Themes. Within the interpersonal metafunction, 'modality represents the speaker's angle, either on the validity of the assertion or on the rights and wrongs of the proposal; in its congruent form, it is an adjunct to a proposition rather than a proposition in its own right' (Halliday 1994: 340). In the following cases, however, the writer's comment is expressed non-congruently, using an extraposed clause (example 1) or projecting clause (example 2). (In examples, G = geography student, 1 = first year essay, 3 = third year essay, HoS = history of science student, A = student with an arts background, S = student with a science background):

1. *It is obvious* from the descriptions of the various processes that soil creep is a very slow form of movement (G/1)
2. *I believe that* the translation of scientific texts from Greek and Arabic into Latin provided the foundation for all that followed. (HoS/S)

Writers may metaphorically indicate their attitude towards a proposition in a great many ways. Hunston, for example, classes projecting clauses such as *Terneld suggests that* and modal constructions such as *It is possible that* as 'carriers of interpersonal metaphor' (1989: 139). Whittaker lists the following types of interpersonal Themes, all of which indicate the writer's opinion on the veracity of a following proposition (1995: 111):

- Preposition Phrase: e.g. *In my opinion*
- Extraposition: e.g. *It is clear that*
- Projecting clause: e.g. *We would argue that*
- Nominalization of mental/verbal process: e.g. *There is a strong possibility that*
- Impersonal projecting clause: e.g. *It is also contended by Robinson et al that*

In the analysis presented here, we regard all such expressions of modality as interpersonal metaphor, and therefore class them, when clause-initial, as interpersonal rather than topical Themes.

In declarative clauses, the topical Theme is usually the grammatical subject. This is the 'unmarked' case. When the topical element is something other than the subject of a declarative clause, the Theme is said to be 'marked'. In t-units with an initial dependent clause, the whole of the dependent clause is analysed as marked topical Theme. Marked Themes are mostly circumstantial adjuncts and clauses, complements and predicated Themes (clefts), for example:

3. *From here,* water would follow the stream (G/1)
4. *If water becomes sufficiently concentrated* it might begin to cut a channel (G/1)
5. *Of equal importance* was American silver mining (HoS/A)
6. *it was He* who set the matter in motion (HoS/S)

In the following discussion of results, we focus on comparing the students' use of marked Themes and of multiple Theme (that is, where a topical Theme is preceded by textual and/or interpersonal Themes).

5 Results

Comparison of marked Themes shows a clear disciplinary effect, with the history of science essays including 47 per cent more than the geography essays (see Figure 13.2).

The majority of marked Themes were circumstantial adjuncts and dependent clauses, which occurred in 15.5 per cent of t-units in the geography essays and 20.7 per cent in the history of science essays. The

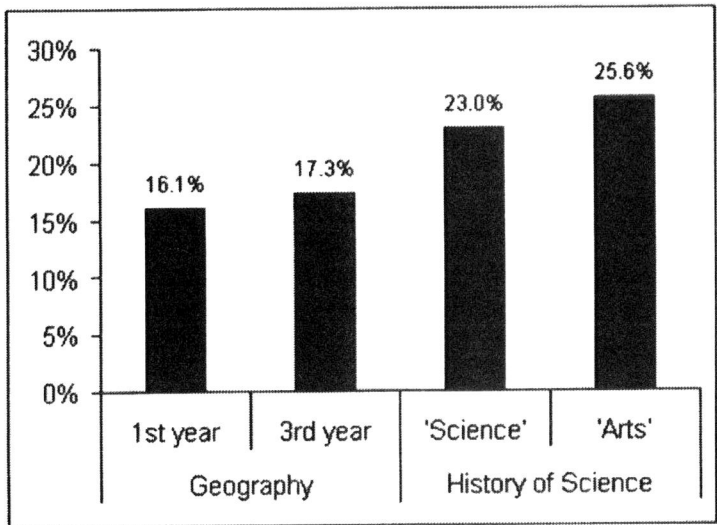

Figure 13.2   Incidence of marked Themes in geography and history of science essays

relatively high proportion in history of science is in line with other findings that have suggested a preference for circumstantial adjuncts in history (Taylor 1983; Lovejoy 1998; McCabe 1999). By its very nature, history tends to deal with particulars rather than generalities (Becher 1989; MacDonald 1994), and thematizing circumstantial adjuncts serves to foreground the location of particular events in time and space. Circumstantial adjuncts of manner were also frequent in the history of science essays, associated in particular with comparisons between theories:

7. but *like Gassendi*, Descartes points to God as the original creator of matter and also the preserver of its constant motion. (HoS/A)

In geography, circumstantial adjuncts foregrounding time and location were also common and occurred particularly within parts of the text which gave specific examples:

8. *In the Cumberland Basin, Australia*, changing climatic conditions have had considerable effects on river channel morphology (Pickup 1976). (G/3)

However, since geography tends to draw on detailed analysis of examples to generalize about processes, this led to many Themes giving reasons or causes for observed phenomena:

9. *For this reason*, women are said to experience a 'glass ceiling' when it comes to entering positions of power (Davidson and Cooper 1992). (G/3)

While circumstantial adjuncts and clauses formed the bulk of marked Themes, there was also occasional use of highly marked Themes – complements, predicated Themes and finites – as in examples 10 to 12:

10. *Fundamental to Decartes' philosophy* is the place of God as the architect of the laws of matter and motion. (HoS/A)
11. *It was this development* that differentiated the West from any other part of the world. (HoS/A)
12. Neither *is* cultural isolation credible. (HoS/S)

Highly marked Themes involve more overt writer intervention to persuade the reader towards a particular interpretation (Francis

1989), and suggest a conception of writing as a rhetorical performance, rather than as a transparent representation of reality. Such Themes accounted for 3.7 per cent of all topical Themes in the history of science essays, compared with only 1.1 per cent in the geography essays, and thus represent another point of difference between the two disciplines.

While the essays show evidence of disciplinary variation in the use of marked Themes, there is little evidence of differences relating to students' previous learning experience. In geography, third year students used only slightly more marked Themes than first year students, while in history of science, students with an arts background used only slightly more than those with a science background. When we turn to multiple Themes, however, a very different picture emerges. Here the disciplinary effect is slight, and variation is much more noticeable *within* each student group.

Multiple Themes occur when the topical Theme is preceded by textual or interpersonal elements; Figure 13.3 indicates the incidence of these types of Themes as a proportion of all t-units. The geography essays showed a substantial increase in the use of textual and interpersonal Themes from the first to the third year, while the history of science essays showed a similar effect according to student background.

The changing proportion of multiple Themes in the geography essays might be explained by a number of factors: it could arise from

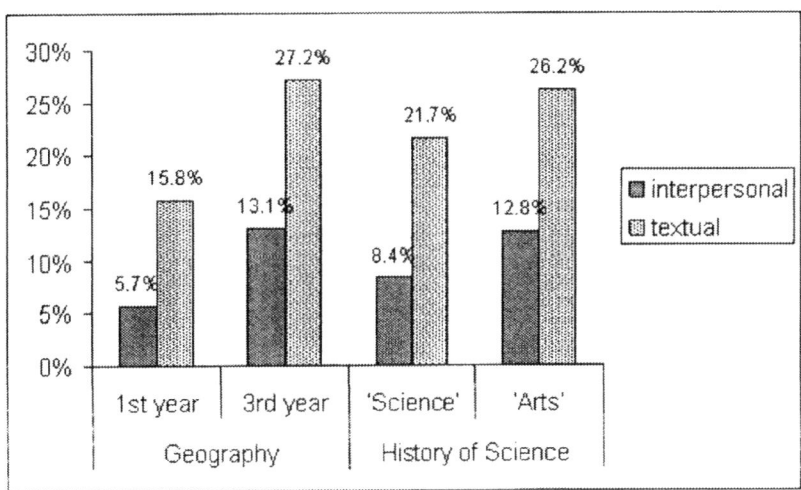

Figure 13.3 Incidence of multiple Themes in geography and history of science essays

the changing nature of the writing tasks at different levels of study, from the students' longer experience of academic study, or from their gradual mastery of the disciplinary conventions of writing within geography. Yet the history of science essays show similar variation in the use of multiple Themes as a function of the students' academic background, rather than their current academic level. In this case, the variation cannot relate to task differences, since the writing tasks were identical for all HoS students, nor to familiarity with academic study, since the students from a science background had previously taken more undergraduate courses than those from an arts background. The most likely explanation seems to be that experience of a particular type of academic writing may have encouraged increased use of multiple Themes in the student essays.

In both geography and history of science essays, the use of multiple Themes was associated with higher marks. Example 13, taken from the highest-scoring third year physical geography essay, illustrates the way textual and interpersonal Themes can be used to build a persuasive piece of writing:

13. *Unequivocally* hillslope erosion models have advanced since the first one in 1940, *but* these models are still not perfect.
    Currently it is fair to say that results from the models although representative of soil loss in an area are far from accurate.
    Perhaps the most promising advances in modelling are not the predictions made, but the theoretical advances in the model base.

The evaluative and persuasive nature of this paragraph permeates more than just the Themes, but is particularly indicated through the use of interpersonal Themes: *unequivocally, it is fair to say, perhaps*. It is the presence of these interpersonal Themes which helps distinguish essays that do more than just recount facts. The writer is prepared to intrude more openly into the text, albeit often in a disguised, objectivized format. That this engagement by the essay writer with the subject is valued is clear from the 'Guidelines' produced by the School of Geography. Its characterization of writing that will be awarded a first or upper second includes 'relevant criticism of topic – ideas – models, etc', 'textual argument', 'depth of interpretation' and 'imaginative discussion/analysis'.

Similar guidelines for the history of science course stress the need to construct a persuasive argument based on the critical use of evidence, pointing out that 'part of being a historian involves evaluating various interpretations of a given period, or episode, in the knowledge that there will be no one explanation that is definitive'. Once again it was found that the most successful essay writers were more likely to intervene overtly in the text through the use of textual Themes, and to use interpersonal Themes which framed their statements as a matter of interpretation rather than fact, as in example 14, from a high-scoring essay by an arts background student:

14. *Grant states that* it was the medieval natural philosophers within the long university tradition [...] who passed on the best legacy of developing science to the following generations of scientists. (Ref 3).
   However, historians have not all agreed about how and why science advanced during the period in question.
   Pierre Durhem, an historian of science, saw the 1270s as the period when modern science began because condemnation of Aristotle's work at that time catalysed scholars into thinking of alternative ideas like the possibility of a vacuum or the plurality of the worlds (Ref 4).
   Also, Frances Yates postulated that the magic factors in the neo-Platonism revived in Italy by the humanist Marsilio Ficino through his translations direct from the Greek texts, prompted the later scientific revolution in the 18th century.
   However, more importantly, it is said that Plato's philosophy inspired Renaissance natural philosophers to think about the world in a more mathematical way (Ref 5).

Despite the differences in the style of extracts 13 and 14, both exhibit greater use of multiple Themes than typically occurred in lower-scoring essays. The use of textual Themes indicates a piece of writing which has been formulated to show how ideas connect with each other – a means by which the writer creates 'relevance to context' (Halliday 1994: 36). Interpersonal Themes, on the other hand, are most strongly associated with presenting an 'angle' on the matter of the clause, and their use highlights the engagement of the writer in the persuasive dialogue that underlies academic writing.

6 Discussion

Several writers have pointed out that the need for rhetorical shaping in academic writing may differ according to discipline (Bazerman 1988; MacDonald 1994; Hyland 2000), and our results suggest some variation in this respect between undergraduate essays in geography and in history of science. Such variation can be related to epistemological differences between the two disciplines, with geography, particularly physical geography, having more in common with the hard sciences than does history. The framework of shared assumptions that underpins a 'hard' discipline allows writers to rely on a degree of consensus among their audience, while 'soft' disciplines deal with individual interpretations which are open to debate, and therefore demand more effort on the part of writers to persuade their audience (Hyland 2000). Such differences may perhaps help to explain why the history of science essays included more marked Themes, suggesting that the writers have had to do more work to shape their argument within a discipline where reality is seen as a matter of interpretation, rather than a matter of fact.

Evidence in support of this hypothesis comes from the students themselves. In interviews, the history of science students commented on the more 'factual' nature of science as compared to history, and those from a science background indicated some frustration with the lack of 'real answers', and what they regarded as 'waffle'. Similarly in geography, students with science A levels tended to characterize human geography in terms such as 'free-flowing' and 'not clear-cut', and to prefer what they saw as the more structured, less open-ended nature of writing in physical geography. Lecturers also commented that physical geography, particularly in the first year, was character-ized by a greater reliance on factual content, though it appeared that by the third year, qualities of thinking critically and developing an argument were highly valued by all lecturers.

Given these differing orientations to knowledge, it is perhaps surprising to note that the average frequency of interpersonal and textual Themes did not vary greatly between essays in geography and in history of science. As Figure 13.3 shows, the proportion of multiple Themes was similar in both disciplinary areas. The picture is complicated, however, by the fact that the geography essays were written in first and third year courses, while the history of science essays were at second year level. Moreover, as examples 13 and 14 demonstrate, essays may include a similar proportion of multiple Themes while nevertheless using them in rather different ways.

In this chapter, however, our interest lies less in the differences between the two disciplines than in those between students within the same discipline. In this respect, what is striking about the results is that textual and interpersonal Themes occurred more frequently in the writing of third year rather than first year geography students, and in the writing of HoS students with an arts rather than a science background. In both cases, the use of multiple Themes was associated with higher marks, suggesting that students who used them more frequently were more successful in meeting disciplinary expectations for academic writing. Interpersonal Themes represent ideas as open to interpretation, and the students' use of such Themes may signal higher levels of engagement with disciplinary debate. Textual Themes, on the other hand, guide the reader's interpretation of the text, and may reflect the students' growing ability to take a more authoritative stance in their writing. In both cases, of course, the students may also be exploiting these features in order to display to the marking tutor their ability to handle the discourse of the discipline.

A student's developing ability to produce written discourse that conforms to disciplinary expectations could be seen as arising from a process of disciplinary apprenticeship which involves development along a continuum from novice to expert (MacDonald 1994; Veel and Coffin 1996). This view is indeed consistent with what was observed in the geography course, but is less clear in relation to the history of science course, which students took not as part of a single-subject programme of study, but as an individual choice within a modular programme. As a result, they embarked on the course with differing previous experiences of academic study and academic writing. Our findings thus suggest that students' ability to produce disciplinary writing may be hindered or enhanced by the writing they have done in other disciplinary areas, which may have affected not only the particular skills they develop, but also the views and values they hold about the nature of writing. Disciplinary studies would appear to be networked (Gee 2001) in such a way that for any given course, some prior courses may provide a better grounding than others. In the case of the history of science course, it appeared that previous arts study prepared the students more effectively for their writing than previous science study.

Research into professional academic writing has demonstrated that the criteria for evaluating writing vary across disciplines, and it is likely that such variation is also reflected in undergraduate writing. Lea and Street (1998), for example, note the case of a student whose writing was seen as lacking 'structure and argument' in anthropology, though judged acceptable in history, while Stockton (1995) comments on the 'remarkably low' grades that literature majors received in history. Yet relatively little is known about disciplinary differences in undergraduate writing, and the way that these may affect students' success in negotiating the demands of courses as they cross disciplinary boundaries.

7 Conclusion

Our aim in this chaper has been to question a view of learning to write within a discipline as a simple unidirectional process. From the tutor's point of view, students may appear to progress along a continuum towards expert writing in a discipline. But from students' points of view, this may be merely one thread within a tangle of different writing experiences. Our research suggests, firstly, that student writing demonstrates at least some disciplinary variation, such that what is valued in one context cannot be assumed to be valued equally in another context, and secondly, that students' success in writing within one disciplinary area may be affected by what they may have learned about writing through previous academic study. The evidence we provide here is limited, involving a study of one particular feature – the use of Theme – across two disciplinary contexts. Yet the results are, we suggest, sufficient to highlight the need for further cross-disciplinary research into student writing, in order to disentangle both the features that characterize good student writing in different disciplines (which are not necessarily the same as in professional academic writing), and the way that different influences, from a range of previous experiences, combine to shape a student's writing in any particular context. Without such understandings, it would be difficult to design effective strategies for supporting student writing in the disciplines.

References

Bazerman, C. (1988), *Shaping Written Knowledge: The Genre and Activity of the Experimental Article in Science*. Madison: University of Wisconsin Press.

Becher, T. (1989), 'Historians on history', *Studies in Higher Education*, 14, (3), 263–78.

Biber, D. (1988), *Variation across Speech and Writing*. Cambridge: Cambridge University Press.

Charles, M. (2003), ' 'This mystery ...': a corpus-based study of the use of nouns to construct stance in theses from two contrasting disciplines', *Journal of English for Academic Purposes*, 2, (4), 313–27.

Coffin, C. (1997), 'Constructing and giving value to the past: an investigation into secondary school history', in F. Christie and J. R. Martin (eds), *Genre and Institutions: Social Processes in the Workplace and School*. London: Cassell, pp. 196–230.

— (2000), 'Defending and challenging interpretations of the past: the role of argument in school history', *Revista Canaria de Estudios Ingleses*, 40, 135–53.

Drury, H. and Webb, C. (1991), 'Literacy at tertiary level – making explicit the writing requirements of a new culture', in F. Christie (ed.), *Literacy in Social Processes: Papers from the Inaugural Australian Systemic Functional*

Linguistics Conference. Darwin: Centre for Studies of Language in Education, Northern Territory University, pp. 214–27.

Entwistle, N., and Tait, H. (1995), 'Approaches to studying and perceptions of the learning environment across disciplines', *New Directions for Teaching and Learning*, 64, 93–103.

Francis, G. (1989), 'Thematic selection and distribution in written discourse', *Word*, 40, (1–2), 201–23.

Fries, P. H. (1983), 'On the status of Theme in English: arguments from discourse', in J. Petöfi and E. Sözer (eds), *Micro and Macro Connexity of Discourse*. Hamburg: Buske, pp. 116–52.

— (1994), 'On Theme, Rheme and discourse goals', in M. Coulthard (ed.), *Advances in Written Text Analysis*. London: Routledge, pp. 229–49.

Gee, J. (2001), 'Learning in semiotic domains: a social and situated account'. Paper presented at the International Literacy Conference, University of Cape Town. Retrieved from www.ched.uct.ac.za/literacy/Papers/GeePaper.html

Groom, N. (2005), 'Pattern and meaning across genres and disciplines: An exploratory study', *Journal of English for Academic Purposes*, 4, (3), 257–77.

Halliday, M. A. K. (1994), *An Introduction to Functional Grammar* (second edition). London: Arnold.

Halliday, M. A. K. and Martin, J. R. (1993), *Writing Science: Literacy and Discursive Power*. London: Falmer.

Hewings, A. (1999), *Disciplinary Engagement in Undergraduate Writing: An Investigation of Clause-initial Elements in Geography Essays*. Ph.D. thesis, University of Birmingham.

Hunston, S. (1989), *Evaluation in Experimental Research Articles*. Ph.D. thesis, University of Birmingham.

Hyland, K. (2000), *Disciplinary Discourses: Social Interactions in Academic Writing*. Harlow, Essex: Pearson.

Jones, C., Turner, J. and Street, B. (eds) (1999), *Students Writing in Higher Education: Cultural and Epistemological Issues*. Amsterdam: John Benjamins.

Kalantzis, M. and Cope, B. (1993), 'Histories of pedagogy, cultures of schooling', in B. Cope and M. Kalantzis (eds), *The Power of Literacy*. London: The Falmer Press, pp. 38–62.

Kolb, D. A. (1981), 'Learning styles and disciplinary differences', in A. W. Chickering (ed.), *The Modern American College: Responding to the New Realities of Diverse Students and a Changing Society*. San Francisco: Jossey-Bass, pp. 232–55.

Lea, M. R. and Street, B. V. (1998), 'Student writing in higher education: an academic literacies approach', *Studies in Higher Education*, 23, (2), 157–72.

Lillis, T. (1997), 'New voices in academia? The regulative nature of academic writing conventions', *Language and Education*, 11, (3), 182–99.

Lovejoy, K. B. (1998), 'An analysis of sentential themes in academic writing: implications for teaching sentence style and revision'. Paper presented at the Conference on College Composition and Communication, Chicago.

MacDonald, S. P. (1994), *Professional Academic Writing in the Humanities and Social Sciences*. Carbondale and Edwardsville: Southern Illinois University Press.

Martin, J. R. (1992), *English Text*. Philadelphia/Amsterdam: John Benjamins.

— (2002), 'A universe of meaning – how many practices?', in A. M. Johns (ed.), *Genre in the Classroom: Multiple Perspectives*. Mahwah, NJ: Lawrence Erlbaum, pp. 269–78.

McCabe, A. M. (1999), *Theme and Thematic Patterns in Spanish and English History Texts*. Ph.D. thesis, Aston University.

Mauranen, A. (1993), 'Theme and prospection in written discourse', in M. Baker, G. Francis and E. Tognini-Bonelli (eds), *Text and Technology*. Philadelphia: John Benjamins, pp. 95–114.

Myers, G. (1990), *Writing Biology: Texts in the Social Construction of Scientific Knowledge*. Wisconsin: University of Wisconsin Press.

North, S. (2003), *Emergent Disciplinarity in an Interdisciplinary Course: Theme Use in Undergraduate Essays in the History of Science*. Ph.D. thesis, The Open University.

Paulsen, M. B. and Wells, C. T. (1998), 'Domain differences in the epistemological beliefs of college students', *Research in Higher Education*, 39, (4), 365–84.

Ravelli, L. J. (1995), 'A dynamic perspective: implications for metafunctional interaction and an understanding of Theme', in R. Hasan and P. H. Fries (eds), *On Subject and Theme: A Discourse Functional Perspective*. Amsterdam: John Benjamins, pp. 187–234.

— (2004), 'Signalling the organization of written texts: hyper-Themes in management and history essays', in L. J. Ravelli and R. A. Ellis (eds), pp. 104–30.

Ravelli, L. J. and Ellis, R. A. (eds) (2004), *Analysing Academic Writing: Contextualised Frameworks*. London: Continuum.

Russell, D. and Yañez, A. (2002), 'Big picture people rarely become historians', in D. Russell and C. Bazerman (eds), *Writing Selves/Writing Societies: Research from Activity Perspectives*. Fort Collins, Colorado: The WAC Clearinghouse/Mind, Culture, and Activity, pp. 331–62.

Samraj, B. (1995), *The Nature of Academic Writing in an Interdisciplinary Field*. Ph.D. thesis, University of Michigan.

— (2004), 'Discourse features of the student-produced academic research paper: variations across disciplinary courses', *Journal of English for Academic Purposes*, 3, (1), 5–22.

Stockton, S. (1995), 'Writing in history: narrating the subject of time', *Written Communication*, 12, (1), 47–73.

Swales, J. M. (1990), *Genre Analysis: English in Academic and Research Settings*. Cambridge: Cambridge University Press.

Swales, J. M., Ahmad, U. K., Chang, Y. Y., Chavez, D., Dressen, D. F. and Seymour, R. (1998), 'Consider this: the role of imperatives in scholarly writing', *Applied Linguistics*, 19, (1), 97–121.

Taylor, C. V. (1983), 'Structure and Theme in printed school text', *Text*, 3, (2), 197–228.

Veel, R. and Coffin, C. (1996), 'Learning to think like an historian: the language of secondary school History', in R. Hasan and G. Williams (eds), *Literacy in Society*. London: Addison Wesley Longman, pp. 191–231.

Walvoord, B. and McCarthy, L. (1990), *Thinking and Writing in College: A Naturalistic Study of Students in Four Disciplines*. Urbana, IL: National Council of Teachers of English.

Whittaker, R. (1995), 'Themes, processes and the realization of meanings in academic articles', in M. Ghadessy (ed.), *Thematic Development in English Texts*. London: Pinter, pp. 105–28.

Wignell, P., Martin, J. R. and Eggins, S. (1989), 'The discourse of Geography: ordering and explaining the experiential world', *Linguistics and Education*, 1, (4), 359–91.

Wineburg, S. (1991), 'On the reading of historical texts: notes on the breach between school and academy', *American Educational Research Journal*, 28, (3), 495–519.

Index of Terms

Index of Names